I was now on a mission

Into The Darkness Out Into The Light

"I could hear the cadence of a pastor-storyteller's voice in the rhythm of the sentences, the understated humor, and the absolute sincerity of the words. This book will be a beacon of hope to those lost on the sea of life. A changed life is simply the best apologetic we have, isn't it? A changed life— the come and see of Philip and the woman at the well—is worth all the finely crafted theological arguments in the world."
~Scott Stewart, Ph.D., Christian Author Services

Into The Darkness
Out Into The Light

One Man's Journey

Grant Cole

ISBN: 0692477012
ISBN 13: 9780692477014

Table Of Contents

Introduction

I F THERE IS one thing I know for sure, it is that the Lord wanted me to write this book. He made it painfully obvious.

A few years ago Bishop Tony Scott came to preach a revival at our church, Connection Pointe. During one of the services, as I was sitting with my wife on the front row, he called me out and began to prophesy.

He said, "There is something in you that needs to be released!"

I was caught off guard. I thought he might be referring to a spiritual gift that needed to be stirred up or to another ministry that I was to give birth to.

Pastor Scott continued: "And you said no one would be interested, but God wants me to tell you that *He* is interested." He started walking away but then turned around, pointed straight at me, and declared, "And you said no one would buy it!"

I had no clue what in the world he was talking about . . . until the next morning. For some reason, God often speaks to me in the shower. As the hot water flowed over my body, God brought to mind several times when people had told me that I should write a book to share my testimony. I would shrug and say, "No one would be interested in that. Why would anybody walk into a Christian bookstore with thousands of books written by high-profile pastors and buy a book written by Grant Cole? No one would buy it."

So there in the shower I spoke aloud and said, "Okay, Lord. If You are interested, then I'll write it."

I tried to start the book at that point in my life when I finally reached the end of my rope (which is now about chapter 23), but it was as though the Lord was resisting me. After much prayer, He made it clear in my heart that He wanted me to start at the beginning.

To be honest, I was concerned about what some of the people in my church and those I minister with would think about it, so I just put it off. Then one Wednesday night as I was opening the church service in prayer, my mouth went numb. In a matter of hours, I was admitted to the stroke wing at WellStar Cobb Hospital and eventually diagnosed with Bell's palsy.

But for the fact that I could no longer speak clearly, I felt fine. I had great fun entertaining all my visitors with jokes like, "How am I going to preath a thurmon when I can't thay any f's or s-th's?"

In the quiet of the night, though, a nurse entered my room and said, "Mr. Cole, your right eye has not blinked in three days. If you don't start keeping these drops in it, you will lose your sight."

After she left, I said, "Okay, Lord, what is going on here? You know my true passion is to study Your Word and teach it to the people I love. Why is it that the only two parts of my body affected by this are my eyes, which I need for study, and my mouth, which I need to teach?"

And as clearly as I am writing this to you now, the Lord said, "Either start writing or you will quit speaking."

I said, "Okay, Lord, the title of the first chapter will be 'In the Beginning.'"

The next day I was released from the hospital, and I am totally healed.

In the course of writing, the Lord flashed before me the faces of some of you reading this book. It is exciting to think that maybe one day the Lord will allow us to meet in person. Some of you were sitting in jail cells, and some of you seemed to be lying on bunks in a prison dorm or a drug program. But what really surprised me is how many of you are parents who seem to be looking for hope.

The only thing I can imagine is that some of you must have a child or a loved one who has been long bound by addiction and has wandered so far *Into the Darkness* that it seems it may never end. The Lord wants me to tell you that with Him, there is *always* hope, and it is my prayer that you will glean something from this book that will enable you to help them find their way *Out into the Light!*

The question is . . .

How does a straight-A student from a loving, upper-middle-class family with every social and economic advantage available to him end up serving time in six different prisons during three different stretches, go through five different drug programs, study psychology and Scientology and read every self-help book he can get his hands on, desperately looking for answers, *and wind up on his knees in a jail cell, facing a life sentence, void of any hope, and realize that all of those experiences were really just the end of the beginning?*

Well, it takes a journey, which is what I will share with you in this book, and they say hindsight gives us 20/20 vision. Looking back, we can see clearly the mistakes we made along the way, what situations and decisions led to those mistakes, and the impact those decisions had on our own life journey and on those around us—much like charting a map. That is what I pray this book will be for you—a map of sorts—that will not only help you avoid the dangers and pitfalls on the journey but point the way out if you or someone you know has wandered *"Into the Darkness."* Take heart! There is a way back *"Out Into the Light."*

1

In the Beginning

IFE STARTED OUT pretty well. I was born in 1957 in Toccoa, Georgia. A few large manufacturing companies helped support the little north Georgia town—Martin's Lumber Company, Trogdon Manufacturing Company (furniture), and Wright's Manufacturing Company (clothing). My dad was vice president of Wright's Manufacturing, which employed 1,100 people. I remember the other companies because the Martins and Trogdons were friends of ours.

My family lived comfortably. My earliest childhood memory is of waking up and pushing a button on the intercom in my bedroom wall to order breakfast from our maid, Lorraine. I loved her, and no, we were not like some of those pretentious people in the movie *The Help*, although we may have been surrounded by some in those days.

My dad was born in 1925 in Canada and grew up during the Depression. His father died when he was five, and his mother remarried and had four more children. Her husband lost both arms in an accident, so my dad worked in a mill as a teenager, sending home a dime a day to support his mother, his handicapped stepfather, and his younger siblings. My dad had a tremendous work ethic and a great respect for any man or woman willing to work for a living. If you were disadvantaged in any way, so much the better.

When men and women would come to the plant looking for work, if Dad didn't have an opening, he would let them work at our home until he could find them a job. Sometimes Lorraine would have two or three ladies helping her around the house, and we would have as many as seven men at a time doing yard work.

Dad lived well but never extravagantly. He might buy my mother a new car, or donate money to some cause she was involved in, but he never bought himself a new car in his life. If a man needed a job, though, he would pay him to paint our house . . . over, and over, and over again. Growing up, I never really noticed that some of the people my dad brought home were white and some were black until a new family built a house across the street.

One time my dad brought a black lady home to work with Lorraine until he had a job for her at the plant. She had a little boy about my age who would come with her. One day we were going on a walk with my little sister, who was in a stroller, so I was probably in the second grade at the time. As we walked out on the road, two little neighbor boys who had moved into that new house ran out and began yelling racial slurs. I had never heard such words before, but I knew they were vulgar. I never heard my mother or father utter a racial slur in their entire lives.

The look of hurt on that lady's face is forever etched in my memory, and so is the look of fear in her son's eyes. One of the boys was a little smaller than I and the other was a little bigger. I shoved the big one, and he fell into the culvert by his driveway. Then I picked up the little one and tossed him on top of the big one. I jumped down in there and started beating the devil out of those kids. It was new construction, so there were plenty of loose rocks lying around. I decided to give them a "Chinese haircut," but instead of using my knuckles, I used a piece of broken brick. After the lady pulled me off of those kids, and washed the blood off of me, I ran to my bedroom, shaking, crying, and finally falling into an exhausted sleep.

A startling *Bam! Bam! Bam!* on the front door jarred me awake. I heard my dad's voice and some man yelling and screaming the "*N*" word and "that blank-edy blank" kid of yours!" I knew I was in for it. I hightailed it into my closet and closed the door and sat on my toy box just a-crying. Life was over. I was as good as dead! Then finally the voices stopped, and I heard footsteps in the hallway. My bedroom door opened, and my dad's voice spoke: "Grant."

Oh, no, not my dad! Why couldn't it have been my mother? The closet door swung open, and I was ready to make a run for it. When I looked up with teary eyes, I saw my dad hovering above me with a smile on his face!

He asked, "So did you really beat up those two kids by yourself?"

"Uh huh," nodding my head and sniffling.

My dad reached into the closet, picked me up, and carried me into the kitchen for a meal. I don't recall the conversation, but I do remember going to sleep that night in my father's giant bed, snuggled under his arm, and thinking to myself, *beating the devil out of mean little kids is a good thing, and beating the devil out of a mean kid who's bigger than you is a great thing!*

I didn't see much of my mom or dad in my younger years. My father had never worked less than 90 hours a week, and my mother was always involved with building some hospital or doing some project with the Garden Club. Until summer, that is. Then it was party time. We spent every summer at our cabin on Lake Rabun. Other families spent their vacations there on a regular basis, so there were always plenty of new kids coming and going. There was a big marina and a restaurant. My dad was well-known, so I could go into the marina and buy food for all the kids to feed the fish or treat everyone in the restaurant to pizza. All I had to do was sign my name on the bill and Dad would take care of it.

Mom and I would stay there all summer, and every now and then, my dad would come rolling in with a whole bunch of businessmen and their families. There would be plenty of beer, liquor, steaks on the grill, and dancing to Nat King Cole at night, and boats and water skiing all day. One party we had in the pavilion by the lake I will never forget. In her work to get the schools in our county integrated, my mother met a man who had been a school janitor and had a band. The man's name was James Brown. Yes, *the* James Brown, the "godfather of soul"! I kid you not—I can remember being taken up into the pavilion with the band. They had scattered baby powder all over the cement floor so their feet would slide. They taught me how to do the twist. There was moonshine at that party. Not the cheap stuff, mind you. This was apple brandy, and all the men talked about how expensive it was because it took so many bushels of apples to make a single pint. To prove how potent it was, they poured some of it in the lake and flicked a lit match on it and we all watched wide-eyed as it flamed up like a bonfire. I was constantly going to the cooler to get the men beer, and I would pop the top and suck off the suds.

By the time I was eight or so, we would go out on our boat with a bunch of businessmen and their wives. All the women would be in the back chatting, and all the men would be up front talking about some big merger, or some great risk they took that proved everybody else was wrong. I ran the cooler, and when they wanted a beer, I would pop the top, take a big swig, and say, "Ehh." The men seemed genuinely impressed that I could drink beer, and sometimes I was the main attraction while my dad recounted the story of how I beat up those two kids.

Those days were good, and I had figured out two things that brought me close to this great man who was my father—beating the devil out of mean kids and drinking beer.

In 1968, when I was 12 and my parents were in their early forties, my dad decided to retire. We moved to the Atlanta area and bought a modest home. Dad opened a "One-Hour Martinizing" franchise, which later became known as Cole's Cleaners. We were open 12 hours a day, six days a week. Going from a 90-hour work week to a 72-hour work week was Dad's idea of retiring.

2

As Arrows in the Hand of a Warrior

"Children are a heritage from the Lord; the fruit of the womb is his reward. As arrows are in the hand of a mighty warrior, so are the children of one's youth." (Psalm 127:4)

THE LORD SAYS that children are *"as arrows in the hand of a mighty warrior."* So what does a warrior do with an arrow? He shoots it at a target and hits the mark. The fact that many well-meaning parents are not aware of this truth does not change the truth that their children are like arrows in their hands. They are pointing their children and shooting them in one direction or another by the words they speak and the things they do. Most parents don't realize the power of a pat on the back at a certain moment or that when they laugh at something their children interpret it as their approval.

My father never would have meant me any harm. He had no idea that I was like an arrow in his hand, but when we moved to Atlanta I still remembered the two things that brought me approval—drinking beer and beating the devil out of mean kids. I don't know whether it was because I started drinking as a child or if it just came naturally, but I could hold my alcohol way beyond my years. That's probably why I caught the attention of a group of older guys known as the West Oak Gang.

While I could shotgun a case of beer at the age of 12 as few grown men were able, I also came to realize that I was no fighter. I needed a cause. Not like these guys. They loved to fight. The summer after sixth grade, I caught a ride up to a local shopping center. All these guys had parked their cars and were hanging out in the parking lot, drinking beer and celebrating that school was out. Some rich kid drove up with his girlfriend in his brand-new hot rod that his parents had just bought him for graduation. One of the guys decided he didn't like this kid showing off his new car and pretty girlfriend. He went over, yanked the guy out of the car, and started beating the daylights out of him. Then several of the other guys politely removed the girl from the car and then rolled the vehicle over in the parking lot. Afterward, everyone took off.

That pretty much did it for me. I was in the back seat of the car, fleeing the scene with all these teenagers hooting and hollering with joy. All I could do was sit there and think about how rotten that kid must have felt with all of that happening in front of his girlfriend.

So I looked around. There was another group of kids who loved to drink beer, but instead of fighting they talked of love and peace. They called each other "brother" and shook hands when they met. There was only one problem: They were supposed to be the bad guys because they were the ones who took drugs. It was all very confusing to me. I had seen pictures on the news of these "bad" hippies out West with their signs saying "love" and "peace" while the police, who were the "good guys," beat them with billy clubs on some college campus.

This was the summer of 1969, and the hippie movement had come to the Atlanta area. Parents did not know what to do. While they didn't want their kids drinking alcohol or smoking cigarettes, that seemed the lesser evil than taking drugs. This was a time when teachers would bring newspaper clippings to school about how some child had found a sugar cube laced with LSD in some park and eaten it only to end up on some really bad permanent trip. They showed us a movie in the sixth grade called *Reefer Madness* in which a guy smoked pot, started hallucinating, and freaked out.

I kept asking myself why, if drugs were so bad, would people do them more than once? I decided there was only one sure way to find out. It just so happened that there was a group of middle school kids in the subdivision known to use drugs, and after all, I was about to start going to middle school with them, so I might as well get to know them. I can take you to the spot in the road where they sat around drinking Boone's Farm Apple Wine, smoking pot, and playing Spin the Bottle. It was quite a different scene from what I was used to. These kids were excited about who was going to kiss whom when the bottle pointed to them instead of who might get to beat the devil out of whom when the next chance came along.

I found that marijuana's effect on me was a lot like the high of alcohol. I remember standing there that night with a joint in one hand and a bottle of wine in the other, and saying, "You know, Jesus turned the water into wine, so we know it's good to get high, and this reefer is just like it!"

To that, one of the kids spoke up and said, "Not only that, brother, but the Bible says that God created the herbs of the field and saw that it was good," as he took another toke. Everyone laughed.

It amazes me how people love to find a verse of scripture to justify what they do and completely ignore all the rest, as if those verses have no value. Either the Bible is the Word of God or it is not. If it is, then you can't just pick out the parts you like. I have a friend named Stan who used to be called "Zig Zag" before he was saved. He has been clean several years now, after more than 40 years of addiction. Stan leads the drug program at our church and loves to pray with anything that moves. Not long after he came to know the Lord and started coming to Bible studies, he said, "You know, I always thought I knew what the Bible said until I read it!"

Let me say this: My father did not lead me astray intentionally. I know there are some of you reading this book who have experienced tremendous pain while growing up. You may have been abandoned or abused or maybe your parents were so lost that they led you astray on purpose. I want to make this one point about Psalm 127:4, which says, *"As arrows in the hand of a warrior, so are the children of one's youth."* Notice that it is only the *"children"* who are like an arrow in their parents' hand. In other words, no matter what has happened to you in your past, there comes a time when you are no longer a child and have to let that go.

When you are an adult, you are not an arrow in anybody's hand. You are a man or a woman with a free will, and there comes a time when you have to stand up, look the devil in the eye, and say, "Enough is enough! My father may have done this, and my mother may have been that, but I'm giving my life to God, and the buck stops right here!"

I promise you that, by the grace of God, you can turn your life around. God will be right there to help you every step of the way.

3

The Trip Begins

DURING THAT SUMMER after the sixth grade, my newfound group of friends talked continually about a guy named Greg. He was the main drug dealer at the local middle school. They talked about what a great guy he was and how he had the best of all the drugs you could ever imagine.

It wasn't long before I had the opportunity to meet Greg. A guy in my subdivision, Donnie, promised to introduce us and vouch for me. Not just anyone could do business with Greg. You had to be recommended. When I met him, it was everything I expected. He had the long hair, the gentle spirit, and everything else that epitomized all that the hippie movement "seemed" to offer. Among his wares, he had something called "four-way orange sunshine, which I knew meant a hit of LSD potent enough for four people. I placed my order, which came wrapped in a small piece of aluminum foil, and could hardly wait to get off the school bus and run home to try it before my parents got home from work. I went into the kitchen and unwrapped the foil and found this little bitty orange pill, so small I couldn't even pick it up with my fingers. It was so tiny that it did not seem possible to cut it into four pieces. I concluded therefore that it must be one fourth of a four-way hit. No way could anything so small really do anything to anyone! I pressed my finger down on the tiny pill, which stuck to my fingertip, so I licked it off (little did I know it was enough for 4 people).

I walked downstairs to the den and turned on the TV. They were showing one of the Apollo flights as the United States at the time was preparing to go to the moon. As the rocket blasted off, so did I—feeling as though I was pulling about 10 G's.

Immediately, I jumped up, and when I did, it was as though I was swimming through patterns and colors. My first thought was, *How do I get this stuff out of me?* I took off running to Donnie's house for help, not knowing that running is the worst thing you can do when you have taken too much LSD. By the time I reached the top of the hill, I bent over and threw up. There is no way to explain the experience when I stood back up, but to this day I remember my thought: *This is God. There is no way anything this wonderful can be wrong, and I am going to devote the rest of my life to make sure that everyone can experience what I am experiencing!*

Jesus warned us that Satan is the father of lies and the Apostle Paul told us that he can take on the appearance of an angel of light (2 Corinthians 11:14), and that is pretty much what happened to me. It has been said that sin can bring pleasure for a season and then brings forth death. As I am writing this, we are just coming to the end of summer. For quite a while now, I have pretty well known what to expect each day of this season. Each morning I would put on a short sleeve shirt knowing the day would be nice and warm. Pretty soon, though, we will wake up to a cool morning that becomes hot as the day wears on. We really won't know what to expect each day. After a while, it will just be plain cold outside. So it is with sin. You know what to expect for a while—you get used to the routine—and then, to your surprise, it's just not like it was. Then it's good again, and then bad; good, bad, good, bad; and then it's just plain cold outside. The pleasurable season has come to an end. But now it's too late. You're hooked, and chasing that illusive first high.

Before long I came to realize that you can't do LSD every day. You get burnt out, and the effect is not the same. So I would try another drug. In those days, we would hitchhike down to 14th Street in Atlanta, which people called "the strip." The police would patrol up and down the street while groups of people casually walked up and down the sidewalk. While it looked innocent from a distance, as you strolled through, people in the crowd would say the name of the drug they had. You may walk through a crowd and hear, "Columbian Gold," "Columbian Red," "Purple Haze," "Mescaline," "MDA," "THC," "RJS," "Quaalude." When you heard the drug you wanted, you would say, "Hey!" as if the dealer was an old friend you happened to run across and decided to talk to. You would step into a "head shop," do your deal, and then buy something as a gesture of appreciation to the proprietor.

The local high school got out at about 3:00 p.m., and the middle school I attended got out around 4:00. So when the last bell rang at middle school and Greg and I walked out, the street was lined with cars of high schoolers waiting to buy drugs. I always wondered why they just didn't drive down to the strip, but they seemed content to buy from Greg and me, which was fine with us. After we sold drugs all day in middle school, our host of waiting customers gladly drove us around the rest of the evening to wherever we wanted to go and then took us home. I felt on top of the world. Then the season began to change.

For Reflection . . .

You may be wondering where my parents were during all of this. Actually, my parents were more engaged in my life than most of my other friends' parents. My mom and dad came home each night about 7:00, and my father demanded I be home by 8:00 for dinner. I would take a break from selling drugs, come in and eat, and then tell them I was going to Donnie's house for a couple of hours. Of course, they didn't know my customers would be waiting. I kept my hair a decent length, as I was serious about the drug business and certainly didn't want to appear as a drug addict. I had a straight A average and even held down a job at 15 years old. In my father's eyes, I was an all-American boy.

Then you may ask, "Where were Donnie's parents? Well, they were right there in their living room while we hung out in the yard. I'm sure they were very pleased that their teenage son chose to stay home at night. From where they sat, they couldn't see us on the side of the house getting high and customers' cars coming and going.

4

A Death, A Murder, My First Arrest

N 1973, I was 16 years old and driving a brand new SS Chevelle, bought with money I had made selling drugs out of the back door of a restaurant where I worked as a dishwasher after school. Greg, who was two years older than I, was so fried by then that as far as I know he never even tried to get a driver's license. One night while I was selling drugs at work, Greg and a friend of ours named Randy went to pick up a few pounds of marijuana.

As I went out to meet them, I came upon a scene that looked like something out of a movie. Their car sat sideways on the highway, with the front smashed in and steam blowing out. Randy's door was open, and Randy's body was draped over the window with his feet touching the pavement on one side and his hands touching the pavement on the other. Blood poured from his face. The windshield was busted out, and when I looked into the car, there was no Greg.

It was obvious the wreck had just taken place; I was the first on the scene. When I looked up to see the headlights of an oncoming vehicle approaching, I saw the silhouette of Greg's body lying in the road. So I stood there on the highway at age 16 with an awful decision to make. *Should I run over and pull Randy through the window and lay him on the pavement?* Maybe it would slow the blood streaming from his head. *Or should I run to my best friend, Greg, and stop the oncoming vehicle in case they did not see him lying there and run him over? Or should I save the drugs, as I knew the police would be there soon?*

After a moment of deliberation, I chose to save the drugs. I knew Greg would have wanted it that way. As a matter of fact, any of us would have.

Looking back on it, I wonder: How could I not see that something was terribly wrong when we had begun to value drugs more than our own lives?

As it turned out, the car did not run over Greg, but he did die lying on the highway that night. Randy ended up in intensive care and eventually recovered.

A Murder Most Foul

After that tragedy, Randy and I became close friends and continued deeper into the drug scene. Soon, though, Randy began to act strange. When I talked to him, it was as though he heard different words, so he would answer me as though there was a different conversation going on. Then one day he told me how he had tortured some puppies and killed a neighbor's pet rabbit. I said, "That's it! You have to quit using drugs." I told other people not to sell him any. This infuriated Randy, and he called me one night and said he wanted to meet me at the Dairy Queen at 10:00 p.m. so we could fight it out. That made me angry, so I headed up there. He never showed up. After a while, I calmed down and felt bad about the whole thing. I called the next morning to apologize to my old friend.

He told me that as he was leaving the house the night before to meet me at DQ, he saw police cars heading down to his ex-girlfriend's house. So he went down to check on her instead of coming to fight me. She had come home that night and found her mother murdered. The news labeled it the most gruesome murder in our county's history, and as far as I know 40 years later it still holds that title.

After she and Randy broke up, she had started dating a biker, so at first everyone thought some bikers had attacked her mother. One day after school I drove by her house with my girlfriend. She looked at me and said, "I think Randy did it."

I said, "No way." Based on the reports of the massive damage to the home and ghastly mutilation of the body, I figured it had to be the work of a gang hopped up into some kind of mad frenzy.

It soon came out that it *was* Randy. I was called as a character witness to testify about the changes Randy had gone through as a result of his addictions. The defense attorney argued that while Randy committed the murder, the drugs had actually *caused* him to do so. The jury didn't buy it, and Randy was sentenced to the death penalty. His infamous story was printed in several crime magazines and was labeled as the *Barnaby Jones* murder.

Barnaby Jones was a murder mystery show starring Buddy Ebsen that came on TV at 10:00 each night. It would start with a murder, and the rest of the program was Barnaby Jones's figuring out whodunit. Apparently Randy was high when he saw the beginning of the program that night, which started off with a shooting. He then walked out of his house and went one block over to his ex-girlfriend's house. Finding her mother there alone, he acted it out—with a shooting followed by a savage beating and some 22 stab wounds. Of course, what was shown on *Barnaby Jones* did not hold a candle to what Randy did. Today's youth would consider the minimal violence of *Barnaby Jones* a joke given what they are subjected to day in and day out.

It seems that something disturbing as this would have gotten my attention, but instead I thought, *Well, I guess Randy just couldn't handle it,* as though all of this was merely an unfortunate "accident."

Death became part of life during my *high* school days—emphasis on "high." The saying "death comes in threes' was common, and it seemed to be true. There were a few murders, but most were overdoses. And there were so many who died in car accidents that I couldn't begin to give you a number.

My First Arrest

My first arrest was at high school. A close friend, Richard, was dating a girl, Joanne, who wanted him to settle down and get married. Joanne couldn't stand me because when I went to their house, Richard and I stayed up all night getting high. She eventually talked Richard into marrying her, and she told me that when they got married Richard was going to have to change his ways. I asked Richard if he really wanted to get married and settle down. If so, I would respect that and stay away as he started his new life.

Richard said, "I never even proposed. She just started planning the wedding and inviting her family, and now it has gone so far that I don't want to hurt her feelings!" Richard was one of the nicest guys I've ever met, and that seemed wrong to me. Then Richard asked me to be his best man.

Well, Joanne let me know real quick that I would never be best man at her wedding. I told her real quick that not only was I going to be Richard's best man but after the wedding we were going off to party. I said, "If you make Richard go through with this, I will see to it that you spend your honeymoon at home alone washing dishes!"

They were to be married on a Friday evening. When I pulled into the school parking lot that morning, the police were waiting for me. One of the officers said they had been informed that I would be carrying a large quantity of drugs. I knew right then that Joanne had called the police and tipped them off. And she was right: I was loaded down with drugs. After all, it was Friday, the busiest day of the week for drug dealers.

All I could think about was keeping the police away from the mother lode of drugs under my back seat, which was bolted in. I knew if I could just keep them from doing a serious search, it wouldn't be too bad. I began telling them the story of Richard and Joanne, and I could tell it rang true with the police that a disgruntled bride-to-be had called them and might have just exaggerated about *all the drugs* I would be carrying. I confessed I smoked a little pot (if a drug addict ever confesses anything, it's just the tip of the iceberg), and when they found my personal bag in the console, that seemed to satisfy them.

Then I looked over toward the school and saw an even bigger problem: The police with my girlfriend who had on her person quite a bit of drugs that she was carrying for me. I was scheduled to sell them that day after first period. Karen and I had been sweethearts since we were in the seventh grade. She did not use drugs, so how in the world she put up with me I'll never know. The fact that she didn't use was one of the main things that attracted me to her. By this time, she seemed to be the only clean, pure, and decent thing left in my life, and right then the reality of the danger I had put her in carrying my drugs for me started sinking in.

I readily admitted to the police that the drugs she had were mine in an attempt to get her out of trouble, but it did no good. When a person is arrested for drugs, the charges are not "ownership of drugs" but "possession of drugs." It does not matter whom they belong to. All that matters is who has "possession" of them. So now they had me for "possession" of what was in my console because the car belonged to me. They had my confession that what Karen had was mine, and they had her for possession of it.

So Joanne was right. I was not the best man at her wedding because I was in jail. Not surprising, though, was that their marriage didn't last.

It did not take long for the police to realize that my girlfriend was just a nice girl mixed up with the wrong guy. Let's just say one of the police officers took a special interest in her case and set out to rescue her from me. This fellow was not just any police officer. He was very passionate about his job, and had an older brother on the police force who was somewhat of a legend. I don't know if it's true or not, but there were stories of this guy's heroics. For instance, while pursuing a robbery suspect, he is reputed to have leapt into the back of a pickup truck, smashed his fist through the back window, and choked the guy until he pulled over and surrendered—Dirty Harry-type stuff.

Things changed after that between Karen and I, and our relationship eventually came to an end. Karen was just an innocent girl caught in the middle, but after this I was no longer just some kid dealing drugs and trying to avoid the police. Things had gotten personal between the police and me.

From this point on, I will change the names of the police, not to protect the innocent but to protect me because I don't want to make them mad again. For example, we will call the radical older brother "Officer Eastwood."

5

Graduation

GRADUATED FROM high school in 1976, and so much happened over the next 12 months that it just doesn't seem possible. My friend Tommy and I referred to each other as "blood brothers" because we had mixed so much blood sharing syringes shooting dope. It was obvious that his parents were into something illegal. After I graduated, Tommy's father came to me and said he knew the things Tommy and I had been doing and had a man he wanted me to meet. It turns out Tommy's father knew the man who was bringing in the cocaine and Columbian Gold marijuana I had been selling for quite some time. They had been watching me grow up in the business and were ready to help me make all my dreams come true.

Big Things Start Happening

Another friend I dealt drugs with was named Stanley. His older brother, Steve, wanted to meet me now that I had graduated. At the time, Steve lived with an older man. The age difference was so great that Steve and the older man actually portrayed themselves as father and son so no one would become suspicious of their relationship. They had a house out on a huge piece of property. As Stanley and I drove through the security gate to this house, I knew something big was about to happen.

It turned out that Steve and the man were bringing in marijuana from Mexico by the ton. The older guy seemed to have the resources for drug runners to swim the marijuana across the Rio Grande where trucks would pick it up and bring it to Atlanta. Steve was in charge of distribution. I had been buying this marijuana on a lower level from Stanley, but now I would be moving up. I was trusted totally, so money was not an issue. I could pick up 100 pounds at a time for $100 a pound, which was 50% less than I had been paying for it, and there was the prospect that if we could work together and meet certain quotas, the price could come down even more.

Soon I moved to a house on Shallowford Road. One day, a complete stranger came to my door. He walked right in and started talking to me as though he had known me all my life. He informed me that he was the distributor for the lab that manufactured all of the MDA I had been selling. He said they had been watching me and were interested in buying large quantities of the methamphetamine I had been selling. In those days, meth was a rare thing. Ever since my first hit of speed at 12 years old, it had become my drug of choice, so I was always known as being on top of that game. Of course, now I could buy all of the MDA my heart desired at a half-price discount.

All of this took place within the first 30 days after I graduated high school.

One night my girlfriend and I had gone to pick up a few ounces of that MDA. Of course, we had done some, and unless you have experienced it, there is really no way to explain the high. Some chemist from Georgia Tech had figured out how to combine a hallucinogenic like LSD, a stimulant like methamphetamine, and a narcotic like heroin into one drug called methylenedioxymethamphetamine, or MDA. The stimulant was so strong that your eyes would vibrate back and forth at tremendous speed. You would have to see it to believe it. It was referred to as strobing, and strobing while hallucinating was an incredible sight. The effect of the narcotic kept you calm the whole time so you didn't freak out.

Here we were, driving along high as kites on this stuff, when a big Lincoln in front of us slowed to a crawl. I decided to pass it, and as I got alongside the car, a rifle barrel came out the window. A flash of fire burst from the barrel with a deafening bang. I watched my windshield explode into a fireworks show, and I hit the gas. When the sparks cleared, my windshield was still there. At first I wondered if it had all been a hallucination until I saw my girlfriend ducking down and screaming, so I knew she had seen it, too!

We were in my SS Chevelle with big wide tires that sat so low to the ground you had to go over a speed bump at an angle to keep from bottoming out. The rear end was higher than the front, and the faster you went in that thing, the tighter it would hug the road. If I was flying down a curvy road, you had to put a seatbelt on or be slammed against the passenger window because it held the road so tight. I knew if I could get to a curvy road, there was no way that big Lincoln could stay close to me, and fortunately I knew all the back roads in this area. I made it to one such road, and when I looked in my rearview mirror, the Lincoln's headlights were jumping up and down. Instead of following the curves, it just plowed through people's yards in a straight line in an attempt to catch us. Then the Lincoln came to an abrupt stop, as though it had hit something.

We rode around for a while, trying to calm down and make sense of what had happened. I concluded that we had run up on some rednecks looking for trouble and that instead of a rifle barrel maybe that was a Roman candle (a firework) they had shot at my windshield. That would explain why there were so many sparks, and the reason it seemed so loud was because we were so high. I started to feel better about it. I dropped my girlfriend off at her parents' house and headed home. As I approached my house, I noticed a black Lincoln parked one block up, perfectly positioned to watch my house. Or was it?

Now, I'm just being paranoid and starting to imagine things! It's probably just a car parked there.

I passed by my house to get a closer look, and sure enough, two men were inside. This Lincoln did not have a scratch on it, and I knew the earlier pursuers had torn up their Lincoln. As I drove slowly by, we looked right at each other. On came the headlights, and yet again the chase was on. This time when I hit the curvy roads, however, the Lincoln backed off and didn't even try to catch up.

A little shaken up, I went and spent the night at a friend's house. The next day, I learned that some of my customers were looking for me. This was unexpected because they had just bought five pounds of marijuana, and it usually took them several days to move it. Bear in mind that in June 1976 there were not only no cell phones; but the beeper had not even come out yet. When I called the customers they were really upset. The afternoon before, in broad daylight, some armed men had kicked in their door. At first they thought they were being busted, and then they thought they were being robbed, until the intruders pulled out a bag of marijuana of their own, compared it to what I had sold them, and declared it was the same.

They stood my customer's wife and child before him and threatened their lives if he did not tell them who he got the marijuana from and everything he knew about him—*me*—and so he did. As they left, they held up and pointed to the bags of marijuana they were taking from him and said he needed to warn every person he knew that they had better not buy any more of "that" pot.

Now I understood that they weren't after me personally but after the marijuana. The next level above me was Steve and his partner, so I called and told them what was going on. They assured me they would find out what was happening. I said, "Well, I'm the missing link they are after, so I'm about to go missing!"

On my way out of town, I drove by my parents' dry cleaners to let them know I would be gone a while and not to worry. As I was talking to my dad, one of the ladies who worked up front interrupted us, obviously frightened. She said a car had come down the drive, but instead of coming to the window it had pulled behind my car and just sat there. She said when she walked over to ask if she could help them, they drove off. She said, "Mr. Cole, there was something scary about those men. I think they were about to rob us!"

I walked up front and looked out the window. Sure enough, there was the Lincoln, parked at the Texaco next door. I had no idea what these guys might be capable of. Now I had put my poor old nice-as-can-be, straight-as-an-arrow, honest-as-the-day-is-long parents in danger, so I began to tell my dad what was going on.

I told them about how my girlfriend and I had been harassed by some maniacs the night before, and now they wouldn't leave me alone. My dad was no dummy. He knew I was into the drug scene and was not telling him the whole story. About that time, a customer came in who was a World War II veteran like my dad. He had also been an ATF (Alcohol, Tobacco & Firearms) agent, and his son was now on the police force. My dad told him what was going on and pointed out the car.

The next thing I knew, the man walked over to the phone and said, "Well, we will just find out exactly who these men are and what they want!" In a matter of minutes, a police car pulled up and the officer, the customer's son, got out.

He came in and starting asking me a bunch of questions. Of course by then the car was gone from the Texaco. I told him how we had passed these guys and how they had hit my windshield with something. He walked out and took a look at my car.

"Son," he said, "they didn't just hit your windshield with something. They shot your windshield!" There was a groove in my windshield and a blue streak following it that looked like someone had seared it with a welding torch.

He said, "Do you see how the glass is powdered inside that groove? That's from the extreme heat as a bullet glazed off your windshield."

By this time, everybody was freaking out. This cop was on the radio telling everyone to be on the lookout for two men in a black Lincoln with out-of-state tags in the area, and so on. We waited for a while, and every now and then another cop car would pull in the cleaners and talk to this man and his son.

When it was obvious that the Lincoln was probably long gone, I said, "Well, I was about to go to Virginia to see an old friend anyway, so I'll be safe, and maybe you guys will catch them while I'm gone." Of course, I was really going to Philadelphia, but remember, that's what drug addicts do—lie.

For Reflection

So why does lying come natural to an addict? Proverbs 25:28 says, *"Whoever has no rule over his own spirit is like a city broken down, without walls."* A person addicted to drugs *"has no rule over his own spirit."* They will have every intention of picking up their paycheck and paying bills, but instead they spend it all on drugs. An addict will truly want to go home and spend time with their family, but will wind up on the other side of town getting high. As a result they are *"like a city broken down, without walls"* The enemy is free to move in and out at will. Spirits of lying, lust, and greed can move right in so an addict will lie, commit adultery and steal when beforehand they would have never done such.

My dad said he did not want me driving by myself anywhere, and then he asked the cop if he would like to make some extra money. When he got off duty, would he be willing to escort me to the state line? Not only did the cop agree, but he said he had another friend on the force who sometimes worked security off duty, and my dad agreed to hire him, too.

They got off at 6:00 p.m. and the cleaners closed at 7:00 p.m., so it was perfect timing. The cops, along with the old ATF agent, showed up just as we were closing. Off we went, me in my Chevelle with one cop riding shotgun and another in the back seat keeping their rifles in plain view in case anyone was watching. Then my dad and the ATF agent brought up the rear in my dad's station wagon.

In the commotion, I had never made it home to unload my car. I still had ounces of MDA, a trunkful of the 100 pounds of marijuana I had picked up the day before, and I always had some speed on me. As I drove down the road, I made the statement that I couldn't believe this was happening. To that, the cop in the front seat said, "Yeah, I can't believe this is happening, either. I'm riding shotgun and providing security for a car that smells like a bag of marijuana."

The cop in the back seat said, "Yeah, not just like someone has been smoking pot in here. I feel like I've got my head stuck in a big bag of it!"

To that, I looked straight ahead, rolled my window down, and went a little faster. We made it across the state line and pulled into a rest stop. One cop walked down to the highway to make sure no car had stopped in the emergency lane after seeing us pull over. Convinced the coast was clear, I said my goodbyes and headed for Philadelphia.

6

Back in the Saddle Again

HOOKED UP with an old childhood friend named David, who had moved
to Philadelphia. It turned out that he still loved to get high. He rented
an apartment from an Italian man, Al, whose family was in the Syndicate.
They had never heard of MDA, and as soon as Al tried it, there was no
turning back. By the time of the Bicentennial fireworks show, he had done
so much MDA that he ended up in the hospital and his family threatened
to kill me and throw my body in the river.

Now you'd think that when a bunch of gangsters decide that you're
too out of control to stay in their town, you'd realize you had a problem,
but I just thought they were a bunch of old men who didn't understand.
Of course, they were still dangerous, so I headed to see family in Canada.

A Bad Case of the "Canadian Flu"

While I was up there, I ran out of drugs for the first time since I was 12
years old. I was sick, felt horrible, and wanted to cuss everyone out, but it
never crossed my mind that it was because of the drugs. I blamed my sickness on some strange Canadian Flu, or the change in the climate, or that
horrible Canadian north wind. What north wind? It was July!

For Reflection . . .

You may think no one could be that blind or that I'm exaggerating, but I am not. If you are a parent and your child is on drugs or you have a spouse who is addicted and you're hoping this is simply some phase they're going through, you are about to find out just how powerless one human being is over another. You are not wrestling against flesh and blood, but against principalities, powers, and rulers of darkness (Ephesians 6:12). You can't sweep this thing under the rug and hope it goes away. You need to get around people who have gone through this before and learn about tough love.

In the parable of the prodigal son Jesus tells the story of a young man that blows all of his inheritance on prodigal living. Then when all the money is gone Luke 15:15-16 says "Then he went and joined himself to a citizen of that country, and he sent him into his fields to feed swine. And he would gladly have filled his stomach with the pods that the swine ate." It is amazing how low someone will go in prodigal living. This boy would "gladly" eat pig's food, and if your loved one is addicted they will "gladly" live their life in your basement or garage eating leftovers until the day they die. Then it goes on to say, "and no one gave him anything." And then "he came to himself," or you could say "came to his senses." If there are any parents who have ears to hear, let them hear.

Back Home Again

Well, back to Canada. All I could think about was getting out of there because obviously I had caught some strange disease. I called Steve, and he told me the coast was clear to come back to Atlanta.

When I first thought of writing this book, I checked with Steve to make sure I had the story straight, but he and I had a hard time recalling everything because 37 years had elapsed and everything had happened so fast. This is what I believe happened:

If you remember, the marijuana was coming from Mexico in waterproof containers. Smugglers swam it across the Rio Grande, and runners picked it up and brought it to Atlanta. One of the runners came upon a load of marijuana that someone else had brought across and decided to steal it. His plan was to sell it to us as if it were from our connection and keep the money. The dealers it belonged to found out it had come to Atlanta, located it on the street, and worked their way up. All the while, they warned people not to buy any more to stop the flow of it so there would be some left when they found out who had it. Everything was worked out, and the runner who stole it was dealt with. All was well. I headed home.

I could hardly wait to make my rounds and get back in the saddle again. My first stop was to see Steve and his partner so I could pay them and pick up a load. The atmosphere had changed at their property. The Mexicans they had been dealing with had brought them M-16s to protect the compound, so to speak, and Steve and the old man presented me with a gift—a brand new Colt Python .357 Magnum. It was a Bicentennial edition that had been given to a police officer as an award. Steve's brother had stolen it somehow.

The atmosphere had changed around my house as well. I had rifles beside every door and pistols sitting around all over the place. If someone came to rob us, everyone could grab a gun if needed. It never crossed my mind that any one of the many people at my house could have flipped out and started shooting everybody. I practiced shooting at street signs while flying up and down curvy roads so I'd be prepared for the next chase that might ensue.

It amazes me that while all of this was going on, I never stopped to ask myself, "What happened to the peace and love?" I had wanted to get away from the beer drinkers because I didn't have the heart to beat up people for no reason, but now I was preparing for the next shootout! In the beginning, I had just wanted to smoke a little, joke a little, and have a good time.

"I'm Pregnant"

I can't remember what day it was, but I could take you to the very spot in the road where I was driving when my girlfriend dropped the bomb: "I'm pregnant."

It was the heyday of the "sexual revolution." Abortion had been legalized three years earlier, and I could not even begin to count how many kids I knew who'd had one. Very often, someone who was dealing for me would come and tell me that so-and-so was pregnant. I would say, "No problem," and hand him a few hundred dollars. The guy would then run the girl downtown to "get it fixed." I considered myself a great guy for helping my customers with their personal problems—for having an "after all, we're in this together" kind of attitude.

I'm afraid that sometimes people hear a testimony and think all is well with that person—and now that they know the Lord, there are no consequences. *Don't believe it for a minute; it is not true.* The Bible tells the story of a man named Esau who made a bad decision and later regretted it. Hebrews 12:17 says, *"For you know that afterward, when he wanted to inherit the blessing, he was rejected, for he found **no place for repentance**, though he sought it diligently with tears"* (emphasis added). In other words, there are times that we can't take it back or ever make up for it. Of course, forgiveness is available to all, but the truth is that the weight of these children's deaths did not come upon me until I had been forgiven and my eyes were opened to the gravity of what I had done.

Think about this. Those two men who shot at my girlfriend and me that night wanted something from us. As far as they knew, we had stolen drugs from their people and were out selling it. We look at those men and say, "Now, those are some bad guys." Yet, at that time, I would gladly give some guy money to abort a child so none of us would be inconvenienced! Mother Teresa got it right when she said: "It is a travesty that a child must die, so you may live as you wish."

My wife, Dani, whom we will get to later, has taken this issue on as her ministry and serves as a pro-life counselor at Cobb Pregnancy Center. On

Thursday mornings, we pray for divine appointments to be set and thank God in advance for the lives that will be saved. I am very proud of her for this. I often wonder what I'm going to say to those children who were aborted on my dime when I get to Heaven.

In our environment in those days, I totally expected that my girlfriend would have an abortion. I was taken aback when she announced to me that she was going to have the baby. She was the first one I recall who had made that decision, and I thought she had lost her mind. Thank God she did. Today our son is a full-time missionary! I wonder what all those other aborted children would be doing with their lives by now. This we will never know, for there is *"no place for repentance."*

It may have taken me by surprise, but I respected my girlfriend for her decision, and it inspired me to do the right thing. She chose not to use alcohol or drugs while she was pregnant (and she didn't), and of course, I had every intention of cleaning up my act.

Then the battle began. Up until this time, I hadn't even known there was one.

7

The Battle Is On

"The thief does not come except to steal, and to kill, and to destroy . . ."
(John 10:10)

Addicts are always going to quit on "this day" or when "this happens." In all my years, I don't think I have ever seen one do it. The Bible says, *"The time of salvation is now."* If you're not willing to do it *"now,"* then you're just playing games with yourself. As for me, we would get married and I would change my ways.

Since there were only a few months before I was going to quit dealing, I needed to work extra hard to make as much money as possible so we could start a new life together. And since I would also have to quit everything but smoking pot, I needed to really enjoy all the chemicals while I still had the chance. After all, I deserved to party because I was such a great guy who was going to give up all this great stuff for my wife and child!

"Midnight Special" and "Blue Light Special"

Remember Tommy, my "blood brother," whose father introduced me to the Columbian connection? He was right by my side the whole time, except when I went to sleep, which was rare. We dealt drugs all day out of the house, and then about 2:00 a.m. when things would slow down, we would load up the car and hit the streets. I drove a Grand Prix by then with a big 455 engine. Again, I souped it up, put on wide tires, and dropped it low to the ground. I was prepared to outrun anything now—straight road or not.

We called those runs a "midnight special." We would knock on doors and wake people up, telling them if they had cash, we would give them a discount to buy now. One night a cop pulled me over when I knew I wasn't speeding. I rolled down my window and asked what the problem was. He said, "Oh, I'm just curious. What are you doing, son?"

I said, "What do you mean?"

He said, "While I'm out patrolling at night, I see this car all over the place. It's obvious you're not going back and forth to work."

I said, "We're just out riding around."

He looked at my license and said, "Grant Cole. I'm going to remember that name," and then he let me go. We will call him "Officer Mannix."

I was going with no sleep and was forgetting things, so Tommy carried a notebook to write stuff down for me. I said, "Tommy, make a note: We need to stay away from this area from 11:00 p.m. until daylight." We changed the name of those runs from the "midnight special" to the "blue light special" after that.

A Velvet Satan

In 1976, velvet paintings were very popular. They were painted in fluorescent colors like the old black light posters, but they were actually oil paintings. You would often see some hippie-looking guy on the side of the road or in some shopping center parking lot with a big selection of those paintings for sale. One such display caught my eye. When I pulled over to take a look, something strange happened.

The man was talking to a customer who was looking at the paintings. When I got out of the car, the man pointed his finger at me and said, "I have just the painting for you!" It was as though he knew me and had been waiting for me to get there.

He walked over to his van, pulled out a painting, and said, "Be careful. The paint is still wet. I just finished it." The only way I can describe the feeling I got is to say that the painting immediately grabbed a hold of me. It was beautiful!

It was a portrait of Satan. It was not like any portrayal of him I had ever seen. He was very handsome, sophisticated, intelligent, and sinister all at the same time. He had two small horns on his head, but they were barely noticeable. He was looking to the side, gazing at several items. There was a pair of dice rolled to "snake eyes," a hand of five cards, all aces, an array of pills, a glass of wine, a joint already lit with the smoke gracefully swirling into the atmosphere, and a syringe with a needle that seemed to glisten with a holy light promising some type of celestial high.

I had to have it. I would have paid any amount he asked for it, but he told me it was a gift. I couldn't believe it! The favor made me feel as though I must be special in some way. I bought a couple of other paintings as a gesture of my appreciation and went home and proudly hung them up. Of course, I gave Satan the prominent place in my living room where everyone gathered to get high.

It elicited a reaction from everyone who saw it. Some would fall in love with it immediately, as I had. Others would become uneasy and step back out of the room. I remember guys walking in with a girlfriend who would take one look at that painting and say, "Let's go." Then the guy would have to make a decision: What was more important—their girlfriend or the drugs they wanted? The drugs and Satan's portrait always seemed to win.

Strange things began to happen. One night as I was driving my girlfriend home I kept falling asleep. Every minute or so she would shake me awake. By the time I pulled into her parents' driveway, she was the one who was shaken! She asked me to stay there because she couldn't understand how I expected to drive home when I kept falling asleep. What she didn't know was that I had become comfortable going to sleep while driving.

It had actually started when I was on my way to Philadelphia. I would be driving up the expressway and see a bridge in the distance. I would nod off, and when I opened my eyes, I would be at the bridge. I thought to myself, *This car must be perfectly balanced to go that far without running off the road.* I never remember asking myself, "But who is keeping my foot on the gas?"

By this time, the fall of 1976, I essentially had begun to trust in my unseen co-pilot. I would go down a straight road, place my eyes on a spot in the distance, go to sleep, and wake up to turn the wheel. Then I would place my eyes on another spot in the distance and go back to sleep. Pretty soon, I would wake up, watch the steering wheel turn by itself, and then go back to sleep. Whether I was going to Peachtree Industrial to see the Columbian connection, or to Cedartown to see the MDA guy, or to Acworth to see Steve and his partner and buy marijuana, it had gotten to the point when the only time that I had to sleep was going to and from buying drugs.

For Reflection- Who's Driving Your Life?

Let me ask you a question: Who do you think was driving the car? In John 10:10, Jesus says, *"The thief does not come except to steal, and to kill, and to destroy. I have come that they may have life, and that they may have it more abundantly."* We need to come to a place where we recognize who is at work in our lives. When I took that first hit of LSD, I thought, *This is God.* But look whose picture ended up hanging on my living room wall.

I've shared this story with people who have been Christians all their lives, and they say, "Praise God! The Lord gave His angels charge over you, Pastor Grant, because He knew what you would do some-day!" Really? So you genuinely believe that God's angels are in the drug-running business? There is no way that God wanted me to get home safely with plenty of drugs so young people would have MDA to trip on while they sat in my living room staring at a portrait of Satan.

James 1:13 says, *"Let no man say when he is tempted, 'I am tempted of God'; for God cannot be tempted with evil, nor does He Himself tempt any man."* When you're living in sin and things go right in your eyes, that is a temptation to remain in that sin. God is in the repentance business, and very few people repent (change their minds) while everything is going their way, so to speak. It is amazing how many people will prosper in sin and thank God for their "blessing."

The only saying that I remember from the 1960s that had any truth in it was a quote of the great Christian missionary Albert Schweitzer that was put on posters and T-shirts: "If you love something so much let it go. If it comes back it was meant to be; if it doesn't it never was." That is what the Lord does with us. The Bible tells us that God is love, and love loves to be loved in return, so God gave you a free will. Without a free will, you cannot love. It has to be your choice. God will woo you and even miraculously intervene in your life to remind you that He is there, but He will not tempt you by helping you prosper in your sin.

For example, the Lord will let (or allow) a drug runner to crash his car and yet be there to miraculously save his life, thereby accomplishing a few things—stopping the flow of drugs, making the dealer's sin uncomfortable, and revealing the fact that there are forces greater than himself at work in his life so that he starts thinking beyond the natural.

Like one night years later I had picked up a load of meth. Fat Bears sister had a boyfriend with a lab up around Lake Lanier, and they were able to keep a steady flow of production like no lab I had ever seen. I had been staying up for weeks at a time so I kept nodding out on my way back as I was driving down Highway 400. By the mid 1980's I was driving a 1969 Chevelle with a big 454 engine, and the vibrations from that motor were so relaxing. I could tell that my unseen co-pilot was driving faster than usual so I said, "You need to slow down!" Immediately I felt my body pushed back into the seat from the acceleration of that car and I asked, "What are you so angry about?"

The only analogy I can give is if you have ever been walking in complete darkness, and although you can't see anything you can "feel" that you are about to bump into something. Well magnify that about a thousand times. I knew I was about to hit something, and when I opened my eyes WHAM! I hit the back of a big red Thunderbird so hard that it shot so far down the road it looked like a little speck off in the distance.

As I'm spinning around on Hwy 400 I'm just looking up in the sky amazed because it is broad daylight and it seemed like just a few minutes ago it was the middle of the night. I ended up perfectly parked in the emergency lane facing north bound in the south bound lane. Now granted The Lord's angels may have parked me safely in that emergency lane, and protected the people in the other car because miraculously no one was injured, but I promise you that was not one of The Lord's driving me that night! And it did get my attention, but I'm getting ahead of myself.

Here's the point. God will take everything the devil meant for evil and turn it into good. The Lord is so incredible at doing just that. When you experience it you may think your whole life was some elaborate plan of God, when in fact His Word clearly states that He had *nothing* to do with tempting you into sin.

Mistakes and the Master Weaver

Several years ago, our church went to minister on an Indian reservation in Arizona. At the airport, Indian blankets were on sale in the gift shops for about $50. When we got to Show Low, Arizona, there were places where you could buy the "real" Indian blankets. They were a fraction of the size of the ones in the airport, yet people would line up to pay $250 for one. This caught my attention, so I began to ask questions.

Real Indian blankets are still made by hand on an old-fashioned weaving loom. The weaver will begin a pattern of a color going in one direction and then make a mistake. At that point, they weave that color in the other direction until they make another mistake. That's how they end up with the back-and-forth pattern that we so easily identify as unique to Indian blankets. What makes those blankets so unique, beautiful, and valuable is the mistakes woven into the pattern. Each one is "one of a kind."

Can I tell you today that you are also "one of a kind." There are scriptures that describe God as the Potter and us as the clay in His hands. I've got news for you: He is also the Master Weaver, and you are His blanket. If you will just place your life in His hands, the Lord will weave every mistake you have made into something beautiful and unique. What will give your life and ministry the most value will be the mistakes you have made, placed in the hands of the Master Weaver.

The flip side of that coin is this: If you refuse to submit your life to the Master Weaver, then when you come to the end of your life and look back, all you will see is a mess of mistakes and a past life of no "real" value. And if the devil has his way, that is exactly how you will end up. My little sister Elaine told me the other day that she had come to realize that it didn't matter if you are miles away from God, as I was, or inches away from God, as she was. If you're away from God, then you are not with Him.

The Master Deceiver

The devil also knows that God has given you a free will, and he has no power over it unless you give it to him. The devil did not have the power to make Adam and Eve do anything, but what he could do was lie to them and tempt them to disobey God out of their own free will. When they did, they gave their God-given authority over to the devil.

In Luke 4:5-6, the devil came to tempt Jesus. He took Him up onto a high mountain and *"showed Him all the kingdoms of the world in a moment of time. And the devil said to Him, 'All this authority I will give You, and their glory; for this has been delivered to me, and I give it to whomever I wish.'"*

When was all this authority *"delivered"* unto the devil? In the Garden of Eden, when Adam and Eve chose to submit themselves to the devil's temptation and disobey God.

The good news is that Jesus did not make the same mistake. He resisted the devil, lived a sinless life, and submitted Himself to God, even to His death on the cross to pay for our sins. Now He has authority over the devil, and you can, too, if you will submit your life to God by accepting Jesus Christ as your Lord and Savior.

James 4:7 says, "*Submit yourself to God; resist the devil, and he will flee from you.*"

If you do not submit to God and open the door one inch to let the devil in, he will come to steal, kill, and destroy. All you have to do is give the devil a "toe hold" in your life. All I wanted to do was smoke a little, joke a little, and have a good time, but the devil does not come to party a little. His goal is to completely dominate and destroy your life, and he is good at hiding that goal from you.

At age 18, I had no knowledge of this or of the authority that I had given to the devil in my life when I began using drugs. I truly believed that I could just quit using when I got married, but it was too late for me. I was gone.

I started thinking, *You know, just because we are married there's really no reason I have to quit doing drugs right now. When I really need to quit is when the baby is born. Yeah, that's what I'll do. I'll quit when the baby is born!*

8

You're Kidding Me, Right?

A LONG CAME NEW Year's Eve, and the party was raging full force. One of my guys, Sonny, said he needed to make a delivery to another New Year's party in town. The customer was a new guy he had just started supplying, and I was always nervous any time a new person came onto the scene. The run should have taken less than two hours. When Sonny hadn't returned in three, I was worried. By then, he should have called the house to let me know what was going on. This was not like him.

I decided to take a couple of guys with me to the apartment where the party was supposed to be to make sure Sonny hadn't been robbed, beaten, or worse. I took Tommy, of course, and another guy, Butch, an up-and-coming professional wrestler who had become somewhat of an enforcer for me. He was a big guy who didn't use much drugs (yet), so usually he had his wits about him. He also had a legal permit to carry a gun. We were going to have to drive right through the territory of Officer Mannix, who I was trying to avoid during our midnight runs. I borrowed a car that belonged to a friend of mine's mother that was as inconspicuous as a car gets—that is, until you put three geeked up, wide-eyed dope fiends in it at 3:00 in the morning on New Year's.

Doing 36 in a 35: "You're kidding me, right?"

All three of us crammed into the front seat of this "little old lady car" because I needed Butch up front with his firearm at the ready, and Tommy was giving directions. He was tripping so bad he could barely see anything from the front seat much less the back. I was so high that I was literally looking at the speedometer to tell how fast we were going. MDA would make things look like they were going in slow motion, so you could easily be going 85 miles an hour but feel like you were doing 45.

Sure enough, on come the blue lights flashing behind us. I knew I was going the speed limit, so I expected to pull over and let the cop go past on his way to catch some real bad guy. To my surprise, he pulled in behind us. He came to the window, shined his light in my face, and said, "I know you," all the while looking in bewilderment at this different car. I asked what the problem was. He said I was going 36 in a 35-mile-per-hour zone.

I looked at him and said, "You're kidding me, right?"

I had just turned 19 a couple of weeks earlier and had never misplaced my wallet. But to my surprise, when I reached back to retrieve my license: no wallet. Immediately, I thought it must have fallen out of my pocket, but I didn't feel it in the seat either. I decided I needed to get out of the car to feel around for it. Of course, I wasn't thinking too clearly at that point. When I opened the car door, it seemed to startle the officer. He placed his hand on the door and stepped back. I explained that I couldn't find my wallet and asked him to shine his flashlight in the car so I could see. I had forgotten that I had put my trusty Colt Python .357 Magnum Bicentennial Edition, given to a police officer as an award and stolen from God-only-knows-whom, under the driver's seat.

While the officer stood behind me, shining his light in the front seat as I leaned into the car and felt around for my wallet, he caught a glimpse of that pistol. The next thing I knew, I was face down on the pavement with the cop's knee in my back and the barrel of his gun in my ear. He was calling for back-up, and police cars were swarming in from every direction.

I found myself cuffed and in the back seat of a police car. Cops were asking me where I got that gun that was given to police officers as an award. Had I killed a cop and taken it from him earlier that night?

I asked the same question for the second time: "You're kidding me, right?"

Officer Mannix demanded to know where I had gotten the car I was driving. He had run a check on it and knew it belonged to a nurse at a local hospital whom he knew personally. Had I done something to her?

For the third time I asked, "You're kidding me, right?

In short order, I was sitting in a room in the hospital ER. Officer Mannix said that he was going to charge me with aggravated assault with a lethal weapon with intent to kill a police officer.

For the fourth time I said, "You're kidding me, right?" Then he demanded a urine test to see what kind of drugs I was on. When I refused, he closed the exam room door so it was just him and me.

He looked me in the eye and said, "Boy, I will strap you down to this table and operate on you myself to get blood out of you to run a drug test if I have to. Now ask me if I'm kidding!"

To that I said, "No, sir. I'll pee."

By the time I finally got to the jail, Tommy was already waiting with a bondsman to get me out. He and Butch had been questioned and released with no charges. The cops had even given Butch his gun back since he had a permit for it. I had a lot of charges, though. When I got a copy of the police report, I saw that Officer Mannix said that he had pulled me over for going 36 in a 35-mile-an-hour zone, and that when he had approached the car, I had "slammed" the door into him, "jumped" out of the car, and "dove" under the seat for a gun. I was charged with aggravated assault on a police officer, possession of a firearm as a felon, possession of stolen property (the gun), two felony drug charges, DUI, and driving without a license. They even charged me with car theft because the friend of mine's mother did not know I had her car when the cop first contacted her.

Of course, when I got a lawyer, many of the charges were dropped, such as car theft and driving without a license, as well as aggravated assault, as I had two witnesses who both had clean records. When I went before the judge, he said it was the only case he had seen that took two pages to list all the drugs a person was under the influence of while driving a car.

The only question he asked was, "What in the world is methylenedioxymethamphetamine?" For all of the other charges, I was sentenced to seven years to be served on probation and to attend a drug program, which ironically was in downtown Atlanta on 14th Street where it all began.

As for Sonny? He hadn't been robbed or hurt. He was just partying and so high he forgot to call.

9

Time for a New Plan

FIGURED IT WAS time to make some changes because things were changing anyway. I needed to get out of that house. Sometimes at night I would look out the front window and the traffic was so heavy it looked like shift-change time at Lockheed AFB. I knew that couldn't go on. My wife wasn't even living with me because my environment certainly wasn't conducive for a young pregnant girl who had chosen to abstain from drugs. Steve's partner had now been busted, unrelated to my own business, but all of that pot from Mexico had come to an end. Yes, things were changing.

Everyone seemed to believe that I was going to change after this arrest. After all, since this was my second arrest I really should have done time. Surely I would go to prison if I got arrested again. Not to mention that Officer Mannix easily could have killed me in the confusion when he pulled me over.

For Reflection . . .

Addiction: A Family Affair

I see families go through this all the time. Someone is addicted, and the whole family suffers. Then something happens, and in their sober minds and broken hearts, they just know this will be it—the turning point. *He's hit rock bottom*, they think. No one in his right mind would keep using after all these things have happened. And they're absolutely right: No one in their "right mind" would keep using, but addicts are not in their right mind.

I always tell families who are dealing with a loved one who is addicted to drugs to prepare themselves. Not only can you not change them, but there is no way to tell when an addict truly has hit bottom. One disaster after another will happen, and the family will finally give up all hope. Then one day the addict will be walking down the road, fall into a ditch, and say, "That's it." The problem for the addict is that when he climbs out of the ditch, no one any longer believes a word that comes out of his mouth.

Cocaine: A Hellish Experience

When I say it seemed everyone believed I would change, I'm only talking about the people who loved me. I don't think it ever crossed the addicts' minds that I would change, and the dealers sure weren't ready to stop.

I moved into an apartment that was close to the hospital where my wife was to give birth. Then here they came, money in hand, wanting drugs. The MDA guy came up with a great idea. Since the heat was on and it wasn't safe for me to be out driving, he decided to move in right down the street. He would deliver to me at the slowest time of day, about 4:00 a.m.

And the Columbian guy? He was excited because now that Steve's partner was out of the business, that left a huge opportunity for me to sell his marijuana instead. His cocaine business was taking off. You may have seen the movie *Blow*, a biopic about the explosion of the cocaine smuggling industry in the 1970s. Well, he was connected to those people. Almost overnight, the price of cocaine dropped dramatically, and the potency went through the roof.

Then the MDA guy announced that the people who made the MDA now had a dedicated lab for making methamphetamine. So, if there was ever a time to quit, it certainly wasn't now. The plan was to quit when the baby was born anyway, and I still had a few months!

I had set a goal that I wanted to reach before the baby was born, and then I would quit. The goal was to have 100 pounds of marijuana, 10 ounces of MDA, 10 ounces of methamphetamine, and 10 ounces of cocaine—all paid for, and $10,000 in my pocket (On the street that was an easy $100,000.00 which was a lot of money in 1977). *Then* I would quit. See, I would have the $10,000 to give myself a financial cushion, and I would have all those drugs to consume at my leisure since I would no longer be in the business.

I still remember the moment I reached my goal like it was yesterday. I was sitting on my couch in front of the scales on my coffee table, as I always was. I was going over all the figures and, lo and behold, I had done it. I remember slamming down the ink pen and walking over to the stereo, which was blasting the song *More Than a Feeling* by Boston. I turned down the music, which got everyone's attention, and I planned to turn around and announce my great victory to everyone there. But something strange happened.

As I turned down the knob on the stereo, it was as though everything in me was turning down with it. The music was low, and so was I. When I turned around, everyone was looking at me to see what was going on, but I was speechless. How could a person work so hard, for so long, finally reach his goal, and at that very moment of victory be so utterly empty and depressed? I was in shock! *How can this be? Something is wrong!*

Bound and determined to fight off this horrible feeling, I walked back over to the couch, sat down, and decided to do a big old shot of cocaine. I put a huge yellow rock in the spoon—way more than I could do. I knew it because I had already overdosed twice, as many of us had done. The cocaine was so potent that it was not uncommon for people to fall out on the floor and start flopping like fish out of water, foaming at the mouth, having convulsions. We tried not to let this happen because when you came to after such an episode you wouldn't remember anything and had therefore just wasted a perfectly good shot of cocaine. The fact that you almost wasted *yourself* was not the issue. The only person who did not push the limit when shooting cocaine was the MDA guy. He would always do little bitty shots, and I never understood why. I was about to find out.

Before that shot was halfway in me, I knew I was about to go out, so I just plunged it the rest of the way in. For the first time, I felt myself flopping on the floor, but this time I knew why. There was a huge hand reaching for me, and a powerful and absolutely terrifying voice commanded: *"COME WITH ME, ME, ME! COME WITH ME, ME, ME! COME WITH ME, ME, ME!"* as I was convulsing, trying to resist and go in the opposite direction!

The next thing I knew I was in the bathroom, having water poured on me while everyone else crowded around the door. I remember looking in the mirror to make sure I was still alive, and then I told everyone what was happening to me while I was convulsing on the floor. They all looked at me in disbelief, all except for the MDA guy, who turned white as a sheet and took off running out the door.

I went looking for him because it was obvious he knew something about this experience that I'd had. It took me two days to find him. He explained that he'd had the *exact* same experience but everyone convinced him it was just a hallucination. Deep down, he'd known there was more to it than that. That's why he was so cautious when doing cocaine. And what happened to me just confirmed his suspicions.

Any person into hallucinogens such as LSD or MDA knows that no two people have the exact same hallucination. As a matter of fact, it was a common practice for people who were sitting around tripping to compare what each person was experiencing from the same drug. We came to the conclusion that our experience was very real—and there was no doubt in our minds that if we had overdosed and died on cocaine we would have gone to hell. Now I, too, would be very careful. And since he and I were such good guys and cared so much about everyone, we would do our best to encourage everyone else to be careful also. We were rejecting the old adage "Don't play with fire" on a whole new level.

10

"Did You See the Size of that Chicken?"

I N THE MOVIE *Young Guns* there is a scene in which Billy the Kid and his gang have taken an Indian potion of Peyote to seek guidance from the spirit world. It is actually a very realistic portrayal of a group of people all using the same hallucinogen. One guy is waving his hands and enjoying the patterns he sees, while Doc is trying to create a new poem. Billy is practicing using his gun because he's the leader and is thus trying to maintain some type of control in case something goes wrong. Then there's "Steve the Regulator," who is hiding in a cave shooting his gun, obviously terrified, and screaming, "Did you see the size of that chicken?"

So it was with all of us growing up. Slowly but surely, one by one, I began watching people turn into "Steve the Regulator." It started back at the house on Shallowford Road. One guy, Bill, would get high and sit for hours staring out the window with a gun by his side. He had been in the Marine Corps, so I thought, *What a great guy to have around. He's watching out for all of us!*

Then I noticed I had two lookouts. Then three. By the time we were in the apartment, flopping around on the floor, I had lookouts at every window! Some even began to station themselves in the bushes around the apartment. When I saw that, I knew I had to get control of the situation somehow. Then it began happening to me.

Mustached Narcs Were Everywhere

One bright sunny Saturday morning, I pulled into a grocery store about a mile from the apartment. I had just copped from the MDA guy who moved in right down the street, and I decided to do one of my now "little-bitty" shots of cocaine before grocery shopping. As I was pushing the cart down the aisle, I could "feel" the police surrounding me. When I turned the cart onto the next aisle, a man with a mustache was walking my way. He looked suspicious, so I turned to go back the way I came. Sure enough, coming into the other end of the aisle was another man with a mustache! I backed up, and as I turned to try the next aisle, I spotted a man "acting" like he was getting a gallon of milk. He looked right at me, and (you guessed it) he had a mustache, too!

I have to think quick now! It's obvious these are plain-clothes narcotics officers who know I just copped from the MDA guy, and they're going to take me down in the grocery store because they know I'm unarmed!

I looked down the next aisle, and the coast was clear. I tried to walk slowly so they wouldn't realize that I was on to their plan, but the faster my mind went, the faster my feet went. *They're probably out searching my car right now! And what's up with the mustaches? I know! Since there are so many of them, all in plain clothes, they all grow mustaches so they can recognize each other when the shooting starts!*

By that time, I was running wide open. The end of the aisle was still clear, so I flew out the end, shoving my buggy to the left into a display. I figured all the police would run to the noise on the left, while I turned to the right and headed toward the door. As I came flying around the cash registers, a lady with a cart full of groceries was stopped square in front of the door, checking her receipt. For a brief second, I considered plowing her over like they do in movies, but I could tell she was an innocent bystander and I didn't want to see her get hurt.

Along the front of the store was a built-in bench where people could sit right inside the huge plate-glass windows that formed the front side of the store. So in full stride, I propelled myself off that bench, straight up, full force into that window with my right shoulder. Now this was an old shopping center built in the 1940s so it didn't have the big, thick safety glass like today. When I hit that window, it was as if I had been struck by a bolt of lightning! There was a flash of white light and a huge explosion!

I looked down at my hands on the sidewalk as I pushed myself back up onto my feet and saw that they were covered with blood. A loud ringing reverberated in my ears. I just knew one of those policemen had caught me with a round from a shotgun just as I was jumping through the window, so I took off. Running across the parking lot, I spotted my Grand Prix. No one was around it, but I sure wasn't going to take time to stop there. I just kept running.

When I got up to the main street, I glanced back at the shopping center. A crowd was forming, and people were pointing at me. As I was running down the road I was stung by all the slivers of glass in my T-shirt digging into my skin. In one motion, I pulled the shirt off, but as it went over my head, I could feel tiny shards of glass in my face. I looked down at my legs below my shorts and saw blood streaming down them from a myriad of little cuts. Or was it buckshot?

By the time I got to the apartment complex, I was so hot that I knew I had to cool my body down or die. The swimming pool in the middle of the complex was decidedly closer than my apartment in the back. It was full of water, though yet not open for the season, and people lolled around the area, walking, playing with their children, enjoying the gorgeous day.

The gate to the pool area was locked, but I was so keyed up that I catapulted myself over the fence and ran into the shallow end of the pool. I was so hot that I didn't even feel the chilliness of the water at first. I stood in waist-deep water and washed the blood from my body. A lady standing nearby looked at me, snatched up her child, and took off. Two other ladies walked up to the fence and asked, "What happened to you?" They seemed friendly, so I began telling them about how I was up at the shopping center when the police had started coming from everywhere and one of them shot me with buckshot just as I was diving through a window. Then I looked up the hill. "Uh oh!"

A guy dressed like a maintenance man was running down the hill from the office straight toward me . . . *with a mustache!* I should have known they would have officers in disguise staking out my apartment in case I got away at the grocery store! I jumped the fence and took off in the other direction. I came around a building, and there was a man with one arm around a woman and the other walking a poodle on a leash. *Oh, man, these guys are good. If it wasn't for that mustache, no one would ever suspect this guy was an undercover cop with that woman and dog as a disguise!*

I turned and saw the guy disguised as a maintenance man taking a statement from the two lady witnesses at the pool. I just knew that information would be used against me in a court of law! *Why in the world did I trust those two? How could I have been so stupid?*

I came around the next building, about to make a dash for the surrounding woods, when, I kid you not, just as plain as day, a police car stopped right at the end of the parking lot, blocking my way between the two buildings. I even saw the front end of the car tilt down as they slammed on their brakes, heading me off at the pass.

Oh, man! All covert operations were over now! I was at the wrong end of a full-fledged, world-wide manhunt! I rounded another building. Lo and behold, the coast was clear. I ran wide open between the length of the buildings, across the road, and into the woods. I kept running. I came upon a creek and jumped down into it. Cautiously, I peeked back at the way I came . . . and saw no one in the woods.

It occurred to me that while most of my drugs were in the car, I had a personal bag of cocaine in my pocket. I thought, *Man, I need to hide this dope!* Then I thought, *No, I'm never going to be able to come back to this part of the country again. I'm going to have to keep running, and there's a good chance I'll be caught. This may be the last chance I ever have to do another shot as long as I live!* I pulled the bag from my pocket, and the cocaine was already liquefied. Maybe pool water had managed to get in it or the heat from my body had melted it. Either way, there was no way to measure out a shot from the liquid, so I simply rammed in the barrel of my syringe and got a big scoop. It was thick and pasty, so I sucked a little creek water up into the syringe, shook it up, and plunged it into my arm.

Instantly, the woods became alive with activity. I could hear hundreds of police officers tramping through the leaves, combing the woods. I could hear loud speakers with police officers giving commands and search dogs barking off in the distance like in the movies. I couldn't see through the tree tops above me, but I could hear helicopters overhead. I took off running again.

Before long I came to the eight-foot fence separating the neighboring country club and golf course from my apartment complex. Once again, my body temperature was overwhelmingly hot. Across the golf course, I saw a sprinkler watering the grass. I knew if I could get to that cool water, I could survive. I climbed the fence, ran to the sprinkler, and splashed around, finally getting some relief. Then I realized I was out in the open. From the direction of the country club, two golf carts headed my way. *There's no way this country club would let police drive their cars on this beautiful grass, so they're after me in golf carts!* I took off running again, and the next thing I remember is that I was up in a tree, looking at my apartment door in the very back of the building. I didn't see any police, but I could still hear them.

When darkness fell, everything seemed to quiet down. I slid down the tree and darted to my apartment. Everyone had been flipping out wondering what had happened to me. When I told them the story, they all said I was just paranoid. They determined that I had not been shot, and said there was no way I could have jumped through the front window of that grocery store.

I said, "Well, how do you explain these cuts?"

They said, "Running through the woods all day and climbing trees in shorts with no shirt on!"

Naturally, I argued with them. They wanted the MDA and meth that was in my car, but no way was I going back down there!

Finally one guy said, "I'm going to see the grocery store for myself." When he came back, he confirmed that, sure enough, the front window of the grocery store had been busted out and was covered with plywood. A couple of construction cones sat in front of it. My car was still in the parking lot.

This set off quite an uproar with some of the already-paranoid night watchmen, who had been peeking out of my windows before this ever happened! Now they were seeing police in the trees and trying to convince everybody we all needed to make a run for it. The level-headed ones tried to calm everyone down and convince me that we needed to retrieve my car from the parking lot before something really *did* happen to the drugs. I relented and gave them my keys, but I warned them, "When you guys get busted, don't call this number because I'm not coming down there to get you out! They'll get me, too!"

They did make it back safely. The next day, as I drove out of the apartments, I had to slow down for a speed breaker. I looked to my left and studied the two buildings I had been about to run between when the police car had blocked my way. Unbelievable! What are the odds that at the precise moment of my insanity, the police would drive through those apartments, hit their brakes for that speed breaker, and look just like they were heading me off at the pass?!

My wife later told me that when all of this was going on, she realized something really bad was happening with me. It was right about that time that she went into labor.

For Reflection . . .

Second Timothy 1:7 says, *"For God has not given us a spirit of fear, but of power and of love and of a sound mind."* So if there is a spirit of fear, and it does not come from God, then where does it come from? It is demonic. And if you are experiencing it to any degree, the good news is you can be set free. Proverbs 28:1 says, *"The wicked flee when no one pursues, but the righteous are bold as a lion."*

11

What are the Odds?

ONE DAY I walked out of my apartment and smelled cocaine. Cocaine puts off an ether smell, but you certainly would not expect to smell it in the wide open outdoors. It would take a tremendous amount of cocaine to put off that smell, so I started sniffing. I realized it was coming from the breezeway, so I followed my nose until I located the spot in the wall where it was coming from—my next door neighbor's apartment. I had caught a glimpse of the guy a couple of times. He was around 30 years old, and I could tell he was straight (drug-free, that is).

A Neighbor In Need

I paced the floor until he came home from work and met him as he was about to go in. I said, "I've seen you around a few times, and I figured you were a straight, hardworking guy."

He said, "Yeah? So?"

I said, "Well, what's a straight, hardworking guy doing with so much cocaine in his apartment right behind this wall?" I pointed to the spot. "You know, there are people who come to my apartment, and if they ever smelled that cocaine, they would be coming right through that wall. And to be honest with you, the thought has crossed my mind a time or two in the last few hours."

He scanned the parking lot and said, "Come on in." It turned out that he had married a girl whose brother was heavy into the cocaine business. They had divorced, but the brother paid him big bucks to hold cocaine for him from time to time.

I said, "How much cocaine are we talking about?"

He said, "Different amounts. Sometimes 50, 60, 75 kilos."

Now, I mean, really. What are the odds? He opened up the kitchen cabinets. It looked like they were full of cans, but there was actually only one row in front. Behind it were huge freezer bags packed full of cocaine. Every cabinet was full. Even under the kitchen sink!

I said, "Oh, no! Don't put it under the sink! What if you have a water leak? You should have seen what swimming pool water did to my cocaine the other day!" Just kidding. I didn't really say that, but I do remember sincerely telling him from the bottom of my heart, "I can tell you right now that I'm going to have to help you." I mean, I really did love helping people, and this was one straight guy who obviously needed my help.

I said, "How in the world do you even get this in and out of here?" Of course, I was thinking, *especially with all my night watchmen peeking out the window*. He wouldn't divulge any more information, and I really didn't care. I had just one question: "How much is it a key?" Or better yet, "How about being neighborly and fronting me a couple?"

He said, "No, no, no! I'm not allowed to sell it! And you can't tell any-body about this!"

I said, "Your secret is safe with me, but I definitely want to buy some. We have the perfect set-up here."

He said, "I'm telling you, these people are very strict. I only get paid to hold it."

"How much do you get paid?"

"They pay my rent, bought my car, and gave me a thousand dollars."

I said, "A thousand dollars! You have got to be kidding me. You call that big money? You really do need my help! Do you realize that wholesale a kilo is twenty grand? Fifty kilos, that's a million dollars! I wouldn't even know where to begin adding up the street value! No! No! No! This can't be! No one is going to treat a good friend of mine like that!"

I paused. "By the way, what's your name?"

"Jimmy."

"Well, Jimmy, this is your lucky day."

To make a long story short, I was disgusted with these drug smugglers (whoever they were) for taking advantage of this nice, straight guy. Now I was on a mission to help open his eyes, to correct this travesty of justice. Once I got him to try a little of my cocaine, it wasn't hard to convince him that we should try a little of his. It was on then. We were wide open.

"Son, Everybody Knows You're Holding"

There were always many people at my apartment. Some would come and stay for weeks. There was one girl Jane. Her story was that her father had kicked her out of the house. One day there was a knock at the door. Jane yelled, "It's my dad!" She ran and hid in the closet. Of course in my mind I'm thinking this must be some abusive father who had come to do his daughter harm.

I got my gun and held it to the right side of the door where it could not be seen just in case I had to shoot the old man to protect this girl. When I opened the door, there stood a man in a suit holding an I.D. in my face.

He said, "I'm *so-and-so* with the I.R.S., and I need to talk to you for a moment."

I laid my gun on the kitchen counter and stepped out the door, thinking, *This is some mistake.*

The first thing I noticed was this I.R.S. agent was wearing a Glock at his side. I said, "So you're an I.R.S. agent?"

He went on to explain that he was not *just* an I.R.S. agent. "I work on a special task force with the D.E.A. It's my job to figure out the taxes drug dealers owe when they are arrested, and I have heard that my daughter has been staying in your apartment." Now, I mean, really! What are the odds?

Of course, I told him I hadn't seen her lately. He informed me that her car was parked on the other side of the complex, and that she had run away from home.

I said, "Oh, wow! If I see her, I'll tell her to come home," while thinking, *if I don't kill her first.*

Then he said something that I recall as clearly as if it was yesterday. He said, "Son, everybody knows you're holding." With that, he drove away.

I walked back into the apartment, slung open the closet door, and let Jane have it. "So your dad kicked you out of the house, huh? He said you have run away, and you better get yourself home right now!"

She said, "No, I won't go home!" Then started going on about how mean he was to her, and how she would rather sleep in her car.

I said, "Well, you can forget that! He knows where your car is, and he's probably having it towed off as we speak."

She said, "No, he always leaves me my car." At that point, I realized this was an ongoing thing between Jane and her father, and it certainly didn't sound to me like he was some mean abusive dad. She even had a softness in her voice when she said it, but then she said something that really caught my attention. She said, "And besides, my car can't be towed anyway"

"What do you mean, your car can't be towed?"

She said that because of her father's line of work, the whole family had confidential status.

I said, "What does that mean?"

She went on to explain that when her tag was run, it was flagged so it could not be towed or pulled over by the police.

I said, "Your kidding me!"

She said she even had paperwork in her glove box that would let the officer know that her car could not be ticketed, no I.D. requested, no address run, no nothing.

Now, I mean, really? What are the odds? I thought about it for a second and asked, "So how big is your trunk?"

So here we went. I was flying around I-285, loaded down in an I.R.S./D.E.A. confidential, untouchable, drug-running machine. The only problem was that I was wasting away. I was just as insane as the decision to run drugs in that car. Everything was out of control, and I had nothing left in me to pull it all together. Anyone in his right mind would have quit, run, or moved as soon as that man came to see me. I remembered the words: "Son, everybody knows your holding."

May Day

I've heard people say of some criminal or sick person, "Deep down, he wants to be caught; he's making some subconscious cry for help." And that is exactly what I was doing. I just kept dealing drugs right out of that apartment while deep down I was waiting for it all to come to an end.

And it did.

One of my night watchmen said, "The police are out there!"

Then the one in the back said, "Yep, here they come." And then another confirmation that they were running between the buildings.

Now we had a plan. When you opened my back door, there was a stairway that went straight down. You could see my back door only if you were literally coming up the stairway. Just outside my door was a landing, and right above it, an attic door. It was just a simple 3-foot-square cut in the ceiling with a board you pushed up, presumably to give access to maintenance workers. There was a tall guy in the apartment, and he opened that door and started throwing bags of drugs up in there. Sure enough, when he was done, the board fell back into place as pretty as you please. When the police entered the stairway, looked up, and saw him, they just thought he was about to try and run down the stairs. They ordered him back into the apartment.

The police burst through the front door, yelling, "Jane! Jane! Where is Jane?" I'm pretty sure she was back in the closet again. They whisked her right out of there.

A big cop came right to me and announced who he was, while others were lining everybody else up against the wall. As soon as he told me his name, I thought, *Oh, no. It's Eastwood.*

He backed me against the wall and used the barrel of his pistol under my chin to push me up the wall until I was almost eye level with him.

He said, "Where is your car?"

I said, "I don't know."

About that time, I heard a cop yell, "I know that car! I'll find it!"

Eastwood asked me, "Do you know who he is?"

Of course I did. It was Mannix who thought I had tried to kill him.

Eastwood added, "You know, he was off tonight, so he is here on his own time."

"Well, aren't I special?" I could tell it was all he could do not to blow my head off.

He let me slide back down the wall and then started asking me questions. It was obvious that someone had been talking, for he knew every time I lied. I had furniture that was made with secret compartments in it, and they were busting it all open. I never realized I had so many guns in the apartment until they started laying them all out.

One particular dresser had a false bottom that was very well-constructed, and I noticed that the cops were rolling it over and beating on the bottom of it with billy clubs. Not everyone knew about that one. It was so well-made that they never got it open, so they must have thought they had been given some bad information or they would have just busted the thing to pieces. But their information was good. Somebody close to me had been talking. They had an informant.

The police walked me out the back door. Blue lights were slicing through the darkness everywhere. As they put me in the back seat of the car, Jane's father walked up and said, "I warned you!"

I spoke without thinking and the words surprised even me. I said, "What took you so long?"

It was May 9, 1977, less than a year since I had graduated high school believing that all my dreams were going to come true. It was strange because my first arrest on that Friday morning at high school was also on May 9. Now I mean, really. What are the odds?

For Reflection . . .

So often parents panic because their child has been "arrested," when in reality he or she has just been "rescued." An addict's loved ones are upset because the addict is "in" jail, when they should be rejoicing because the Lord just got him or her "out" of what they were "in."

12

Is There a Doctor in the House?

'M NOT SURE how many days I was asleep in jail, but when I woke up, I was sick and wanted a shot of something! I didn't really care what. I just needed out. The cell house I was in consisted of three cells with eight bunks in each, a dayroom at the end with three solid steel tables where we ate, a shower, and three toilets right along the wall beside the tables. I don't mean stalls. I mean toilets right out in the open, with a sign above them that advised: "Don't Worry About These Toilet Seats, Our Crabs Jump 20 Feet."

I started throwing up, and I kept throwing up. I thought maybe I had ulcers from going so long without physical food and from the stress of being so keyed up the last seven years of my life. Then I used the bathroom, and my urine was as black as tar. One guy looked at my eyes and said, "Oh, man! You're jaundiced!" I was getting so sick that the desire to get high was gone.

The inmates frantically rang the buzzer, hollering to the guards, "Get this guy out of here, or we're all going to die!" The guards seemed skeptical that I was really that sick. They simply told me to ring the buzzer the next time I threw up so they could come back and see for themselves. But every time I threw up, the inmates would ring the buzzer, and a guard would saunter in 10 minutes later. By that time, I'd be back in my bunk or lying on the floor.

"Dad, I'm sick . . . really sick"

One guard brought in an 8-ounce Styrofoam cup, passed it through the bars, and said, "The next time he throws up, have him throw up in this so we can see it for ourselves."

One guy piped up, "If you want to see what this guy is throwing up, you need to roll a mop bucket in here!"

At last it was time for our cell house to have some phone time. They had a pay phone on wheels that they would roll up to the catwalk every so often, and you would have to call collect. Men literally fought to get on that phone at times, but not on this day. The other inmates handed me the phone, offering to dial it for me to call for help—that is, the ones who weren't too afraid to get close to me.

Now my father and I had an understanding. He loved me, but he did not approve of the whole drug thing. So If I chose to go down that path, then I would have to accept the consequences of my actions. I was a 19-year-old man and a father myself. It was time to grow up. But as soon as I got that phone, I knew whom I needed to call. I could barely talk. I said, "Dad, I'm sick. I mean, really sick."

That was all it took. Within a few hours, the guards were calling me out. A lawyer was there to see me. It was all I could do to stand. I was so dizzy that I remember leaning against the concrete walls as I walked so I wouldn't fall. I approached the visitation area, and before I even got to the window, I recognized a man who was a customer at the cleaners—a business lawyer.

As soon as he saw me, he shouted, "Get the Colonel! Get the Captain!"

They walked me past the visitation area and right into an office area and put me in a chair. I can still remember the look on that lawyer's face— the kind of look a person would have if he saw a poor, wounded animal suffering and knew there was nothing he could do to help it. As soon as the Captain (or whoever stepped around the corner) took one look at me, he said, "Call an ambulance." Then he turned around and started yelling at the guards.

I remember one guard saying, "He didn't look like that back in the cell block! The lighting is so dim in there."

I thought, *Look like what?* When I looked down at my arms, they were as orange as a pumpkin, and my skin looked all dry. When I rubbed my arm, the skin just rolled back like it would after a terrible sunburn or something. I found out later that it was from severe dehydration.

The next thing I knew, I was on a stretcher and an EMT was inserting an IV into me, right there in the office. As soon as that fluid entered my body, it was like a cool stream of life and freshness flowing through me. It was far more pleasant than anything I had experienced in a long, long time. I was soaking it all up like a sponge—*literally*.

They took me to the hospital where I was diagnosed with Hepatitis B. They assigned officers to guard me and chained my ankles to the bed. They wanted me to use a bed pan, but I refused. Since I now had an IV in each arm, I would call the guard to unlock me, roll the IV poles to one side of the bed, and use one in each hand like ski poles to hold myself up and roll into the bathroom.

A Foot-Long Chili Cheese Dog with All the Fixin's

As time went on, I began to earn the trust of the hospital guards. Sometimes they would leave me unchained. The type of Hepatitis I had was only contagious through blood transmission, so I was also allowed visitors. I had full access to the phone, so I was back in business. Some of my old friends started coming to see me, and when I was able to eat again, they brought me food. Naturally, they were always smart enough to bring something for the guard in my room also.

One of my favorite foods was the foot-long chili cheese dog from Dairy Queen. Friends would show up with dogs, fries, and drinks, and spread them out for everyone to take and eat. The foot-long they set in front of me was special, though. Under my dog and in my bun would be a nice new syringe, a bag of meth or MDA, and maybe a little cocaine. While eating in my bed with the table across my lap, I would discreetly drop those items into the Kleenex box I kept by my side, then casually pull out a tissue while shoving those items to the bottom of the box.

In the evening, the night guard would walk down to the nurses' station for a cup of coffee. I'd seize the opportunity to roll with my IV poles into the bathroom, Kleenex box under my arm. I remember looking down at my arms with all those tubes in me, trying to find a vein to do a shot, and thinking to myself, *This really isn't good, but hey, I'm about to go to prison. This may be my last chance.*

After four or five weeks, I started getting better . . . and I didn't want to. I was down to one IV and thinking that if a man had to do time, this was the way to go! I knew alcohol was hard on the liver, so I asked an old friend to bring me a pint. He slid it in the cabinet when the guard wasn't looking. The old saying goes, "An apple a day will keep the doctor away." Well, I was thinking, *A few swigs of liquor a day will cause the doctor to stay.* Then I got really careless.

One day, I kept seeing a TV commercial with a trailer for a late-night movie *Riot in Cell Block 4.* The thought of a good prison movie had a new allure since I knew that was where I was headed sooner or later. I decided it would be cool to do a big old shot of MDA and watch *Riot in Cell Block 4.*

The guard on duty that night was an older guy who enjoyed drinking coffee and flirting with the nurses. He was almost never in my room at night, so I got bold and took it a step further. One of my main hot dog delivery guys had brought me some marijuana, and I was dying to smoke it. Since this guard rarely came into my room and had "never" used my bathroom, I figured I could smoke it in there, turn on the exhaust fan, and he would be none the wiser.

I did a big shot of MDA, smoked a big fat joint, and settled in to watch *Riot in Cell Block 4.* Just as the movie started, the old guard opened the door, pointed his finger at me, and said, "I just want you to know, I could smell that mary-wanee all the way down at the nurses' station!"

I thought, *Surely that exhaust fan doesn't blow out in the hallway, does it?*

Within minutes, four uniformed police officers busted into my room like they were raiding a house. They tossed everything and never found my stash in the bottom of the Kleenex box, but they found that stupid pint of liquor.

They immediately called my doctor, who directly came up there and signed my medical release, and I was on my way back to jail. But they didn't take me back to cell block #1, where I had been before. Can you guess which one they sent me to? Cell block #4. I kid you not!

Cell block 4 was a cell block for sick inmates. It was like some kind of quarantine cell block. This was around late June of 1977, and I don't remember ever having heard of AIDS. After seeing what AIDS does to people, however, I now realize that is what most of the men in cell block 4 were suffering from.

Not only that, it didn't take me long to realize they had put me in a cell block with a bunch of perverts. I was in the back cell playing cards with the "house man," an informal, self-appointed position in the jail system much like a leader in a gang. Three men came to the cell door and said, "Send the new guy over when you finish the game."

I'm thinking, *Send me over where?*

The house man looked at them and said, "No, not this one. Besides, look at him. He's all jaundiced and sick." One man stepped into the cell, looked into my still-yellow eyes, nodded in agreement, and left.

The next thing you know, I heard the sounds of several men raping another young guy a few cells down. I wish I could tell you it was the only time I would hear those sounds, but it would not be so.

13

"I Hear that Train a-Comin'"

'VE OFTEN HEARD inmates speak of being "railroaded" by the system. Some men have "13 ½" tattooed on their right hand, which stands for 12 jurors, one judge, and a half a chance, to put it politely. I don't know how many of them are just complaining about their situation, or how much truth there is to it, but they didn't just railroad me. They ran me over!

To give them the benefit of the doubt, maybe they just figured they were doing what they had to do. From what I understand, they told my lawyer that they did not have the medical facilities at the jail to take care of me, which was true, and they weren't set up to provide the kind of security necessary to keep me clean and out of trouble at the hospital, which was also true. So they wanted to get me into the prison system as fast as possible so I would be sent to Jackson, where I could get the proper medical care. I'm not sure if they really believed that one or not.

Welcome to the Big House

Now I did not know any of this as I was sitting out in the open day room, so I would have a fighting chance if the Sodomites decided to come after me, when the guards showed up saying I was going to court. They walked me before a judge, and the D.A. started reading off the charges. Seven years for MDA, seven years for meth, seven years for this, seven years for that. In all, there were five seven-year sentences and a one-year sentence.

The judge said, "Recommendation accepted," and I was declared guilty. I was never even asked how I pleaded. The probation was never addressed. I was on my way to Jackson.

Jackson prison's official name is Georgia Diagnostic and Classification Center. It is in Bibb County in Jackson, Georgia. It is a maximum security prison where all inmates entering the prison system are sent. There, they test you and classify you to whatever security level they deem fit and then send you to the prison they think is most appropriate. The security is very high, as all criminals convicted of any crime move through there. Even Georgia's "death row" and the electric chair are at Jackson.

Because they never knew the health or mental state of an inmate coming into the system, they were set up to handle every imaginable issue or problem. My dad learned all this from his business lawyer friend. He said they planned to revoke the rest of my seven years' probation, which I had received only four months earlier, and get me into the system. The judge also said he would make sure that after Jackson, I would be sent to Stone Mountain Prison, where I would be close to my family so they could come see me.

When I got to the Jackson infirmary, they put me in a room by myself. I don't know how many days or weeks I stayed there, but it felt like an eternity. A dripping faucet in the room echoed with every drop. I tried everything to shut that thing up—toilet paper, clothes—anything to soften the sound. It would help for a moment or two, but as soon as the water soaked into the clothes and puddled up, the maddening *drip . . . drip . . . drip* would start echoing again.

I had seen movies where they would use "Chinese Water Torture" on prisoners by dripping water on their foreheads. I'd always thought that seemed ridiculous. I mean, what could dripping water do to a man? I promise you, a dripping faucet 24 hours a day, seven days a week, in an otherwise silent environment could indeed drive a man insane. I never saw one doctor or medical professional of any kind. Day in and day out, the guards simply slid my food under the door. Then one day, the door opened and they let me out. I had no complaints. I just wanted out of that room.

They told me to fall in line with a bunch of men and stay single-file against the wall. The place was huge, and I'd never been in the "big house" before, so curiosity got the best of me. I stepped away from the wall so I could see past the men and check things out. As soon as I did, a guard hit me upside the head with a billy club and yelled, "Against the wall!"

I thought, *What in the world is wrong with these people? They're treating me like I'm some kind of criminal! They must have me confused with somebody else!*

Going through intake is a humiliating experience. By the time it's over, everyone looks just alike—a line of bald men wearing white jump-suits, rubbing their heads because it feels so strange to have a crew cut. They sent me to Cell Block E. It was one of those long, two-tier cell blocks like you see in movies. I was on the top tier in a cell five feet wide and nine feet long with a bunk, a cement toilet and sink, and a metal cabinet. It was August in central Georgia. There was no fan, much less air conditioning. The heat was stifling.

The fronts of the cells were bare bars, so you could talk to the men in the other cells. When I told them I was going to Stone Mountain when I left there, they laughed at me. "Man, no judge can say what prison you're going to, and they know it. You belong to the man now. You're 19 years old, and with your record, there's only one place you're going—Alto!"

In 1977, there were two notorious prisons in the state of Georgia. One was the Georgia State Prison in Reidsville, where they sent the baddest of the bad. It was where they filmed *The Longest Yard* with Burt Reynolds. It was known in those days for hard labor and prison riots, but they didn't send teenagers there. The worst place a young man could be sent was a prison in north Georgia called Alto. In the system, it was referred to as "Little Reidsville." It was known for fighting and punking (raping), and I wanted no part of that!

I often would think of Randy being there on death row, but of course, they did not allow death-row inmates to be out in population. Then one day, it happened. I was standing in line "against the wall" on my way to chow. There were little windows the size of a cement block where you could see out into the visitation area. Lo and behold, there was Randy, talking through the glass to his parents. I knocked on the window. As soon as he glanced my way, a big smile came across his face, and his parents began waving at me. It was like two old school buddies running into each other on some college campus or something.

I read my first book while I was there. Can you imagine? I graduated high school with flying colors, even took my SATs while fried out of my mind, and had one of the highest scores in the class, yet I had never read a book. This book was called *Please Make Me Cry*. It was about a girl junkie who was so hardened that she couldn't cry until she ended up in David Wilkerson's Teen Challenge ministry and met Jesus, who softened her heart.

It didn't make much sense to me. I mean, how could she meet Jesus when everybody knows He died on a cross? She must have been doing more than heroin to think she met Jesus! She must have done too much LSD or something. The last thing I would want to do is have my heart softened in this place and start crying! And what was the big deal about crying anyway? I remember thinking to myself, *When was the last time I cried?* I couldn't remember.

In the evenings, I would look over at G House. Big sprinklers would come on, spraying the roof of the building in an attempt to cool it down at night. I could only trust there were sprinklers on our roof, too, but if so they didn't seem to do much good. At night, things would quiet down. You could easily talk out of your cell toward the big windows and the sound would bounce back, allowing you to carry on conversations with the men around you without even raising your voice.

Some of the men had been through Alto when they were younger and were now going back to prison for their second, third, or maybe even fourth time. They would school me at night on what to expect and how I needed to act when I got to Alto. They had no doubt that my parents had been lied to and that I was headed there.

They would tell me things such as: "Mind your own business." "Don't get involved in gambling or drugs. You'll get killed quick that way." "Don't act like you're tougher than you are because *that* is a sign of weakness." And: "Find your homeboys."

"So what is a 'homeboy' anyway?"

"That's the guys from your area. It gives you something in common. You band together with your homeboys so you can watch each other's backs."

The one thing they kept stressing, though, was that I had to prepare myself for the most important moment in my life. This one moment was going to determine the rest of my life because how I handled myself at that precise moment would determine whether I would continue through life as a man or as a punk. And no man who was "punked out" could ever go back and face his wife. If I failed that moment, they warned, by the time those boys at Alto got through with me I would never be of any use to my wife or child ever again.

There was never any doubt in those men's minds that I was going to face that moment and that it would happen as soon as I was placed in population.

They said, "As soon as you walk in that dorm, somebody is going to test you. They will probably just tell you to give up whatever you're carrying in your hand, and this is what you say: 'So, it's going to be like that, huh?' Then drop your stuff and just plow into him. There may be four or five of them standing around to intimidate you, but don't even look at them. If you make eye contact, they may take that as a challenge. You just plow into him no matter how big he is!"

Then another man pointed out, "You don't have to *win*. You just have to fight!"

I wanted to say, "You're kidding, right?" But I knew they weren't. Of course, I was thinking that these convicts didn't know anything for sure, but that I did need to be prepared. I decided to get down on that nasty floor and start doing some push-ups. To my surprise, I could not even hold up my weight, much less do a push up. I still got dizzy when I stood up.

There is a track at the yard in Jackson. When they let you in the yard, most men just walk around and around in a big circle, but a few jog or run. I thought, *That's what I need to do.* I started to jog and made it about three steps before my legs turned to rubber and I collapsed. As I lifted myself up, I thought, *Oh, God, please don't let me go to Alto.*

During all of this, I actually had a good attitude considering the circumstances. For some reason, I've never had a hard time accepting the consequences of my actions. Sure, I was "railroaded" through court, but I was guilty. I was going to have to serve seven years' probation anyway, and the other five seven-year sentences plus a one would run concurrently. I was assured of this by all of the professional convicts who surrounded me. And, sure, I had almost died in jail, but I was the one who was shooting dope. I had brought it all on myself, and I knew it.

Something Happened that Changed Everything

Then something happened that completely and totally changed everything. Under the prison system in 1977, a con was eligible for parole with one-third of his time served, which for me would have been 28 months. If you were denied parole, you still earned a-day-for-a-day for good behavior. That meant I would serve 42 months. Now if you got busted for drugs in prison or stabbed somebody or whatever, they could revoke that earned time, and you would serve all seven years. In fact, you could catch a new case for drugs or assault and end up with more time than you started with, which happens to a lot of people. But, of course, that wasn't going to happen to me. I was going to make parole in 28 months. I believed that with all my heart. But there was one huge problem: *Time wasn't passing!*

Time is relative. We've all heard that "time flies when you're having fun" and the example that five minutes passes quickly when you're on that special date, but it can seem like an eternity when your hand is on a hot stove. Unless you have been through what I'm about to tell you, you will not really be able to understand. Even if you're reading this book in a prison somewhere, you will have to think back to the very first time you were locked up for a length of time. A lot of factors were working against me in those first months.

First of all, when you're young, time passes much slower, and when you first experience something, it seems to take much longer. For example, the first time you drive somewhere, let's say about 100 miles away, it seems like a long trip. The trip back may even seem shorter, but if you make that same trip four or five times, it will seem much shorter.

Well, I was young. It was my first time in prison, which is bad enough, but I had been very sick—very much like having my hand on a hot stove, so to speak. Time was passing so slowly that I would mark off days on a calendar and sit there in disbelief, checking it over and over again. When I finally checked off 100 days, I just couldn't imagine how 100 days could possibly be *that* long. Knowing that at the very least I had 740 more days to go was beyond comprehension.

I shared my agony and amazement with the men in the cells around me. They said my first mistake was marking off days on a calendar—that I had to quit thinking about it, learn to flow with prison life, and not worry about it. So I put my calendar under my mattress and tried not to think about it. At first, I couldn't do it. I kept pulling that calendar out and tormenting myself. Finally, I resisted looking at it. Then I resisted again, and again, and again, and again. Over and over, I wouldn't look at it.

I fantasized about pulling that calendar out and marking off a whole month at one time! Finally, I decided it was time to pull the calendar out and celebrate the passing of time. Was it going to be a whole month? Probably not, but surely 20 days. Worst-case scenario, I would be able to mark off two weeks; two weeks would be a great victory! That's half a month! Well, almost half a month. I was lowering my expectations so the victory would seem that much sweeter!

I yelled out to the guys, "Hey! What's the date?"

"Oh, man, you're back at that again? Let it go!"

"I *have been* letting it go. What's the date?"

"August 26th."

I said, "Man, I'm serious. What's the date?"

Another guy yelled out, "It's the 26th. Now shut up!"

As I looked at my calendar, panic began to set in. It had only been four days! I just couldn't believe it! While I was reeling in the reality of the situation, a guard nonchalantly walked by and placed a slip of paper on the bars, which is how they delivered mail. But this was not mail. It was a yellow piece of paper that looked as though it had been printed on a computer. I unfolded that sheet of paper and read: "Probation Revocation: August 25, 1977." Further down: "Time Served: 1 Day."

I thought, *Okay, they revoked my probation yesterday, so it has been one day. But why did it say, "Time Served"?* I continued to read, and all of the dates were laid out. Five seven-year sentences and one one-year sentence to be served concurrently. Time beginning August 25, 1977. Discharge Date: August 24, 1984.

I yelled out to the guys, "Man, they have messed up my time! They are showing I have only served one day!" Of course, several derogatory comments came back about how the system was all screwed up, but one comment caught my attention.

"You didn't have a probation hold on you, did you? Because they did the same thing to me!" He went on to explain that when they put a probation hold on you, your time stops that moment until it is released, whether through reinstatement or, as in my case, revocation.

The only analogy I can give is of anesthesia. If you have ever been put under anesthesia and they tell you to count backward from 100, you realize after a few numbers that you're going under and have no hope of stopping it. Or maybe you have injected some drug that just consumed you in some overwhelming feeling. Well, it was as though I were receiving an injection of pure, unadulterated hatred and resentment toward the court system and everyone in it. If I could just figure out who decided not to bother revoking my probation back when they said they were, and who just fooled around waiting to revoke my probation until yesterday like it was no big deal, I would kill him—and if it was more than one person, I would kill every last one of them.

I entered a state of mind that was so deep, so dark, and so filled with resentment and hatred that I desperately longed for an enemy to project my hate upon. I needed a release, and it felt as though the more pain I inflicted, the more relief I would feel. You may be thinking that it was unreasonable to respond with that kind of hatred, and I agree. It was not a natural response as I had unwittingly allowed some very unnatural forces access into my life that were just beginning to show themselves.

I don't know how long it had been, but as I was lying in the dark, the little dim light in my cell came on. A guard walked up to the bars and said, "Cole, pack your stuff. You're going to Alto."

I remember looking up at him and saying, "Yeah, well, that figures!"

14

Alto Prison Blues

The movie *The Shawshank Redemption* is the most realistic prison movie I have ever seen. Alto was no work camp. It was a prison very much like Shawshank, where it was considered a privilege to break the monotony by going outside to work on a roof or something like that. What really got me about that movie was when "Andy" (Tim Robbins) played a record of some lady singing over the loudspeakers and all the men froze for that moment. Only a man who has spent years experiencing nothing but steel, concrete, and other men could possibly understand the impact that a woman's voice singing can have on a bunch of convicts. Whoever inspired that movie has done time in a place just like Alto.

All the characters in that movie are really there. Everybody from Red, who could get anything, to the rapists referred to as "Booty Bandits" in Alto, to the really old convict with the most time running the library. They are all there. Even the part where all the men pass time by watching the new arrivals show up on the bus.

"So it's going to be like that, huh?"

As the bus pulled into Alto, it was kind of like it pulled into a big cage, and the gate closed behind it. All around the cage, convicts were lined up, shoulder to shoulder, yelling at us.

"Fresh meat! Fresh meat!"

"Boy, I can hardly wait to get ahold of you!"

I remember thinking, *I thought this was a prison for teenagers.* These guys were huge, and not one of them looked like a teenager to me. They looked more like professional football players, only meaner.

They opened another gate and walked us into a cell house kind of like Jackson, except this one was dark, dingy, and even nastier. The first thing I noticed was looking through the bars into shower rooms and seeing guys shaving their legs!

I thought, *Oh, boy! I'm sure enough in the valley of the Sodomites now!*

But it wasn't long before I realized they were nothing like those guys back in cell block #4. They were just young homosexuals referred to as "sissies" who could not survive out in the prison population, so they lived and worked in this one building. They did all the cleaning, cooking, and serving the food to the cells. This dark, depressing building was their world.

Then I came to find out another alarming truth about the system. When charges are dropped, they are not erased. They know charges are often dropped in plea bargains or for lack of evidence, etc. For example, I always had my gun charges dropped, but I was guilty. The way the prison system looked at those dropped charges was, "Where there is smoke, there is fire."

So what do you suppose they were thinking when they were determining where I should be placed in that prison? Their thinking was likely, *He's got a car theft charge, so if he can make it over the fence and get to a car, he's gone. And if that car has a gun it, then there's no doubt he will be shooting at us because he has already assaulted one police officer.* At least it seems likely that's what they were thinking, and it probably was considering where they placed me.

There were some buildings down by the vocational school, but you had to have five years or less to be placed down there. There also was a drug dorm in the main building, which I definitely should have qualified for. But everyone was trying to get into the main building because they actually had hot water. The whole main building was kind of like something to strive for, a good reason to try to stay out of trouble in hopes that some-day you might get moved there.

The worst place to go was the oldest building, called the annex build-ing. It was an old Tuberculosis hospital. Back in the day, they would sort of quarantine people with TB up in the mountains to die, to keep the disease from spreading. Right above the main doors of the annex, engraved in the cement were the words "Tuberculosis Hospital." In fact, they actually handed out medicine for Tuberculosis to everyone on a regular basis, just in case.

The higher up you went in that building, the greater the security, be-cause the severity of the crimes the inmates had committed increased. The two worst dorms at Alto were 13 and 14, which were both on the top floor of the annex building. I was placed in 13. Every person in there was a violent criminal with more than five years—everyone, that is, except me. Remember, I had only been looking for my wallet when I got the assault charge. Of course, no one else knew that. I did have one thing going for me, though: My newfound hatred looking for a release.

I stepped into that dorm with all of my belongings in a pillowcase—soap, shampoo, snacks, and cigarettes. Sure enough, there were about four guys standing there. As soon as the guard locked the gate behind me and walked away, one of the guys stepped forward and said, "You might as well face it right now; I'm taking your stuff."

I responded, "So it's going to be like that, huh!" and just tore into him. The next thing I knew, I was picking myself up off the floor and realized I still had ahold of my pillowcase. I had forgotten to drop my stuff, but it seemed like that was for the best because as soon as I stood up, the four guys walked off.

All these other kids were like, "Put your stuff in my box! Put your stuff in my box!" You could tell they were like a bunch of hungry vultures wanting to get ahold of my belongings.

Very calmly, a guy walked up and said, "Don't worry about it, man. We've all had to go through it. The guards will bring you a footlocker up here soon to put your stuff in. Until then, you can put your stuff in my box. So where you from?" It turned out that the guy in the bunk above him was from the same area I was. They called him "Cannon Ball," and you could see why. He looked just like one. It was disappointing to find out I was only the third "homeboy" from my area—not exactly a force to be reckoned with in a dorm of 120 guys. And "Cannon Ball" didn't seem to be into the whole "homeboy" thing anyway.

But there were plenty of them who were. The dorm was sectioned off in areas like Cabbage Town, Techwood, Capital Homes, Union City. Believe it or not, the biggest population was Augusta. I don't know what was going on in Augusta, Georgia, in the 1970s, but they must have locked up every teenager in town.

I walked with these guys down to eat chow, and when we got back we found that someone had broken into my new friend's box and stolen all of our stuff. There was also a footlocker by my bed. Someone told me that all those guys from Augusta ran a store. In the prison economy, any time you get something on credit, it is understood that you had to pay "double back." You couldn't carry cash, but if you had people who would send you money, it was put into your account and you could spend up to $16 a week. I figured I would get $5 worth of soap, toothbrush, toothpaste, and, most importantly, a box of roll-your-own "Top" tobacco. That way, the next week I would come off the books for $16. I would pay them their $10 and still have $6 for myself.

So the big day came to go shopping at the store. I took my trusty pillowcase and filled it with my $16 worth of supplies. When I came around the corner headed back to the dorm, there were all these guys standing along the covered walkway. For a moment I had a flashback to an old cowboy movie I'd seen where the Indians captured this guy and made him walk between two lines of Indians while they beat him, and if he could make it to the other end, he could go free. I brushed off that feeling,

As I walked a little way down the line, I felt an arm go around my neck and felt the pressure of this person pushing on the back of my head while another guy grabbed my bag and started trying to tear it out of my hand. I knew exactly what was happening. I had seen professional wrestling where they would get a guy in the "sleeper hold" until he was unconscious. But wrestling was fake, right? Well, I can tell you one thing—the "sleeper hold" is for real. That was my first experience with it, but I've seen many men choked out and I consider myself very fortunate all they wanted was my store goods.

This did cause a serious problem, though. Now I didn't have the money to pay all those boys from Augusta. When I told them what happened, one guy said, "All right. I'll see you at Dead Man's Curve in the yard." Dead Man's Curve was a curve that went around the end of a building right at the end of the yard, a total blind spot in the prison. It was an area of a few hundred square feet, out of the sight of any guard tower or office window, so it was where guys met to settle any "beef" they had. If you were fortunate enough to get a seat on the wall, you could comfortably pass the afternoon watching one fight after another—sometimes two or three at a time.

So I met the guy out there, and we just walked up to each other and went at it. I had so much anger and hatred in me that I didn't even feel it. My only fear was that he would realize how weak I still was from being sick. I had to live that whole week with nothing, and then the $10 I owed became $20. So the next week, I ganged up with some of the guys in the dorm so we could walk the "gauntlet" together and make it through. But since I could only come off $16, I had to give up everything for a second week. I also had to go to Dead Man's Curve for another round because I was $4 short, which now doubled to $8.

Then a new guy came in. A different guy challenged him, while the guy who had challenged me quietly walked up to befriend him and offered to let him put everything into his box. My original friend broke into it while they were at chow. Are you getting the picture? It was all a scam! They were all in on it. Even the store guys were in cahoots with the robbers. It was all a game being played over and over, with the same guys playing different roles but always dividing the loot. When you realized how well you had been played, it was hard to be mad because you were so awestruck, especially when you realized it was nothing personal. It was more of an initiation and a test. I fought, so I graduated.

"A War Going On Between Good and Evil"

Now try to imagine a simple, long, rectangular room with bunks lining each wall, and two rows of single beds down the center referred to as "skid row." Each bed is 18 inches from the next, so there is no room for two men to walk by each other without turning sideways. There is an old black-and-white TV at each end, turned all the way up and showing mostly static. Almost every "cut" between bunks has a radio turned up full blast. And there are 120 men between the ages of 17 and 21, full of testosterone and energy. There was so much noise that you literally had to yell in each other's ear to talk, like you were at a rock concert.

When shower time came, you would unlock your box, take out your soap, set it on the bed, put the lock back on your box, and when you turned back around, the soap would be gone. You would be shaving, looking in the tin mirror, and when you looked back down your shaving cream would be gone. In the middle of this chaos, five guys would gather in the center of that dorm, open their Bibles, and study. I was about five rows away from them and could clearly see them read the Bible, then lean over and yell into each other's ear while pointing to something on the page. This would go on for a while, then something amazing would happen. These five guys would join hands and drop down to their knees to pray, and the whole dorm would go silent. It wasn't like someone would make an announcement like, "Hey, they are praying!" It would just happen!

Then, when the silence came, boots would start flying through the air and strike those guys in the head. I mean, stuff would be flying at them from every direction. Then guys would run up behind them and slap them in the side of the head. Once, blood was coming out of a boy's ear after being slapped so hard while he prayed.

I remember sitting there thinking, *There really is a war going on between good and evil!* Of that, I had no doubt. I was so confused, though, that I actually thought their praying was a sign of weakness, that somehow they were the ones who couldn't handle it. Of course, nothing could be further from the truth. It is my prayer that somehow God will get this book into the hands of one of those boys and that they will contact me. I would love to know what significant things God has done through their lives. To this day, I have never personally witnessed any greater example of Christian courage.

Of course, I wasn't thinking like that then. I was so filled with hate that I would sit and stare at some big guy and fantasize about cutting his throat. I never thought about hurting someone smaller than me. It was always someone bigger as my hate had grown to the point that I not only desired to inflict pain. I wanted to receive pain also. Sometimes I would look over at someone and they would be staring at me, and I would wonder if they were fantasizing about killing me.

I told a guy named Mark about this once, and he told me he did the same thing. Mark was a skinny, nerdy-looking guy, and someone did something really bad to him, but I never asked him what. We both started writing poems as a release, but as we talked about our fantasies flowing from our hate, we wrote one together and called it *Dark Shadows and Evil Deeds*. I think it is a pretty good expression of where I was spiritually at the time. I'll share it with you, but I'll spare you all the profanity, because it was filled with it. It was over 36 years ago, and I can still remember it like it was yesterday.

Dark Shadows and Evil Deeds
My mind is floating,
Through a dark foreboding space,
Dark shadows and evil deeds,
Plotting murders without any trace.

And hate and greed, and plunder,
Can all find its place,
In my memory, my memory,
It just will not erase.

Yell and scream,
Rant and rave,
No one cares,
You won't be saved.

Your pain is real,
But your fear more true,
And alas, poor fool,
There's nothing you can do.

A night, a day,
An endless chore,
Hate and blood,
And little more.

Get loose, get free!
Ha! What a joke!
Now I can see
The lies you've spoke.

So I let my mind float
Through this dark, foreboding space,
And love dark shadows and evil deeds,
Plotting my murders without any trace.

And let hate and greed and plunder,
All find its place,
In my memory, my memory,
It just will not erase.

I have to admit that leaving out the cuss words does take away from the true nature of the expression, but it is not my desire to expose you to that nature. I just want to give you a picture of where drugs lead. It is nothing to play with, and neither is your freedom.

For Reflection . . .

The Wages of the Sin of Sorcery

So how does a child who will fight to defend others who are being called names journey into "dark shadows and evil deeds, plotting murders without any trace"? Well, it's a sin referred to as witchcraft [*mekashep*] in the Old Testament, which referred to cutting up herbs and brewing them for magical purposes. In the New Testament, it is referred to as sorcery [*pharmakeia*], which of course is where we get the word pharmaceuticals from, and it's only going to get worse. In Revelation 9:21, the trumpet judgments of God are being released on the earth yet men will not repent of *"their murders or their sorceries"* [*pharmakeias*].

Who would have imagined that you could invest in marijuana companies on the New York Stock Exchange? And yet that day has come. I can't remember the last time I've helped an addict who was on cocaine or meth. They are all on narcotics obtained legally at medical offices referred to as "pill mills" operating all over Georgia under the guise of a pain clinic. CNBC has been running a documentary titled *The Colorado Pot Rush* that shows people legally making candy filled with hash oil and selling it over the counter in plastic bags while Bayer would be sued if they failed to place a "Keep out of reach of children" label on a bottle of aspirin.

On June 23, 2014, 11:00 a.m., CNBC reported there was a huge announcement of a major breakthrough at the Marijuana Conference that they could now "personalize" your pot, that investor money was pouring in, and I quote, "We can now send you on a personal path" in your marijuana experience. Mark my words: Soon one of those paths will claim to lead you to God.

There is a saying that "sin will take you farther than you want to go, keep you longer than you want to stay, and cost you more than you want to pay." It will take you so far there is no way to return. A man can't return and give back all the happiness that he has robbed his family of while living in sin. When a child is aborted, there is *"no place for repentance."* You cannot return to that child. Whether you are playing around with drugs, or living in full-blown sin, friend, please think about what I am saying.

Seeking the Answer to Fix Myself

I was finally accepted into the drug dorm, which was in the main building above the infirmary, so the guys would tunnel through the wall somehow and go through the ventilation system and steal pills without being detected. This was their drug program! In eight months, we had one meeting for one hour, and only six people attended. Of course, being a part of that program looked good on your record for the Parole Board, but what a farce!

I had already been going to college while in dorm 13, but now the atmosphere was more conducive to study. Truett McConnell College offered classes at Alto, and the Pell Grant paid our tuition. I decided to take psychology because I knew I was messed up, so I was going to figure out how to fix myself. Then one day I would go home and help all of my old friends, and the next time we would get this drug thing right. I was convinced there was a way to make the drug business work. We just had to figure out how to control it, and to do that, we had to figure out how to control ourselves. No more night watchmen in the bushes, etc.

So as I began to study psychology it was obvious that they were really good at defining the problem—that if a person had this or that issue, he would react this or that way in this or that situation. But I kept expecting answers to follow, and there really weren't any. Sure, there was this study, and that theory, and you could try this or that, but there were no solid answers to man's condition. I was looking for a definitive solution: "Here is your problem, and this is the answer." It just wasn't there.

15

Stone Mountain Prison

I⅃T'S A LONG story, but eventually I did get transferred.

When all this began, my lawyer had asked the judge to send me to Stone Mountain because it was the closest state prison to Atlanta. Little did we know that it was every convict's dream to go there. Everyone put in for it, kind of like they put in for the drug dorm at Alto. It was a work camp, but when you drove out of the gate to work, you were in Stone Mountain Park.

It was the only prison I ever heard of where all guards and convicts wore street clothes because they didn't want the park visitors to be uncomfortable. Almost everyone working in the park was a convict. The whole place was built by convicts. What an atmosphere to do time in!

It was a lot smaller than Alto—only two dorms upstairs and a shop and some classrooms downstairs. As soon as I walked into the dorm and told some of the guys I had been transferred there from Alto, the "house man" came to see me. He said, "Don't even think about bringing that Alto mentality in here. We're not interested in those mind games, and if you start stealing anything around here, we are not interested in fighting you. We are grown men, and if we have a beef with you, then we will just kill you." I looked at him and said, "Thank God!"

It really was completely different. I never saw one fight while I was there. These men went out and worked hard and then came in and just chilled at night. There was only one problem. Since I had transferred from Alto, I was considered a security risk, and the guards wouldn't let me go out in the park!

I didn't mind at first because after all the men went out to work, it was quiet. They gave me the job of cleaning the dorm, but as the months rolled by, it got old. There were no windows to see out of and no yard. Over a period of six months, I stepped outside only a few times—to take out garbage.

At night when the guys came in, there was always plenty of pot to smoke. Many of the guys had ways of getting it in the park. You could have cash in this prison, and some guys had plenty of it. There was a leather shop downstairs, and this biker actually ran a business making Harley Davidson saddlebags for motorcycles. He paid guys to turn them out.

It wasn't long before I had my own little drug-running business going. Because I had spent all those months taking care of the building, the guards gave me free rein to walk around, so I could easily move drugs from one dorm to the other, etc. I made friends with the cook and we would go out to the kitchen at night, get into the dough they had for biscuits the next morning, roll it out, sprinkle cinnamon and butter on it, roll it up, cut it in sections, throw it in the oven, and melt sugar to pour on them. *Voila!* Homemade cinnamon rolls. I'd take them back to the dorm late at night and sell them to all the guys who had the munchies.

World Religion 101 as Taught by the Devil's Advocate

I also continued going to school. Mercer University offered classes at Stone Mountain. One of the classes was "World Religion," and I thought, *Huh? Maybe religion has some answers.* The teacher began by telling us that Christianity was a very small and insignificant religion when you look at the whole world. The only reason that people around here are Christians, he said, is that they have just been raised that way and that we would be wise to expand our horizons to obtain more of a worldview.

He began to teach on Hinduism because it was a "much larger" religion. When we got into the whole reincarnation thing and the caste system, I said, "You know, it sounds to me like this whole thing was made up to control the people. If you're poor and starving, you need to behave yourself and accept your condition in hopes that you will come back as something better next time."

He said, "You're right. All religions have been made up by man to serve one purpose or another."

When we started studying Buddhism and found out about Tantric Buddhism, which involves the worship of sex, that pretty well sealed the class. When you take a bunch of lost convicts and tell them there is a religion with a "bible" that teaches you over 600 ways to have sex, that's it. Class over. They're all ready to convert!

That teacher truly was the devil's advocate. Personally, I believe that class did more to keep me away from the One True God who has the only answers to man's condition than the drugs themselves. The only religion he said that we should never bother looking to was Christianity, which had the only Book with the answers we were looking for, yet now we were convinced always to search in another direction. May God have mercy on his soul!

Evidence of God: A Miracle for Snuffy

Yet, there was evidence of God in that place. The man whose bunk was right across from mine was the meanest-looking man I had ever seen. His eyebrows were always furrowed down like he was angry, and he had a pug face like a bulldog, but when he spoke, he was as sweet as he could be. They called him "Snuffy," and legend had it that he once was as mean as he looked, but something life-changing had obviously happened to him.

Snuffy claimed that Jesus changed his life, to which the men responded that he was just crazy and had some kind of breakdown that made him nicer. One day Snuffy said, "You know, Fonzie [that was my nickname in there because they said I reminded them of Winkler's character the Fonz;

I never saw the resemblance], I can prove that I'm not crazy. Can you prove that *you're* not crazy?"

I thought about it and said, "I guess not."

With that, Snuffy pulled out his release papers from the Milledgeville mental institution and said, "See, this proves I'm not crazy. If I was crazy like everybody says, then they would have never let me out! And you need to come to church with me."

I said, "Well, I might one day."

He said, "You need to come tonight. There is an ex-convict coming to preach!"

I said, "An ex-convict! Whoever heard of such! I don't think you need to be listening to any ex-convict preachers, Snuffy. You need to stay in here with us." I was genuinely concerned for his well-being. He was like a little pug-nose puppy.

I was lying on my bunk reading a book when the dorm door opened and the guard yelled, "Church call!" Something just grabbed my heart. It was obvious. I just lay back down. The guard opened the other dorm door and yelled, "Church call!" and the only way I know to describe it was that I was being drawn or wooed toward the door.

Of course, Snuffy was prancing all around my bunk, panting like a little puppy, wanting me to go with him. The guard yelled, "Last call for church call!" and now I was holding on to my bunk. I knew for a fact that if I got up and went to church, something was going to happen to me, so I just kept holding on. Snuffy finally left, and when the guard slammed the door, that pulling force just let go.

I jumped off my bunk, looked at the guys across from me, and said, "Whew! God almost got me that time!"

Snuffy wasn't the crazy one; I was. I was the lunatic. And if that wasn't enough, I witnessed a miracle happen to Snuffy. He could not read a word, and everyone knew it. Guys would write letters for him, and he was always asking us what postings on the bulletin board said. When he signed out for work, he never signed his name. He made his "mark," so the guards knew he couldn't read. But he always carried his Bible to church as though he could read. Every now and then, he would flip through it and just stare. You could tell he wanted someone to read it to him, but nobody ever would.

One night, I looked over at Snuffy. He had his Bible open and was weeping uncontrollably. I said, "What's wrong, Snuffy?" He looked at me through teary eyes but couldn't speak. I started asking everybody if they might have read some letter to him with bad news in it or something, but no one knew what was wrong. All during the night, I heard him weeping, and I was thinking, *Yep, he's got mental problems. He's having another breakdown.*

The next morning he was still crying when he left for work. I was worried about him all day long. I really didn't expect to see him come back in. I honestly expected the guys to come back from work and tell me that Snuffy had a breakdown and they took him back to Milledgeville. But he came back in and without saying a word walked straight over to his bunk and opened that Bible. When he looked down at it, he collapsed on his knees and started weeping again. I thought, *As soon as he's not looking, I'm going to hide that Bible.*

Then Snuffy pointed at his Bible and said, *"Are you not more valuable,"* and then he started crying. I looked at his finger, and he was pointing right to those words. Snuffy could read! Of course, since I was still continuing my psychological studies with Mercer University I was thinking there was some logical explanation. Maybe Snuffy knew how to read when he was a child, but because of some abuse or trauma he had suppressed those memories, but now they had resurfaced. There was only one problem with my theory. It turned out that Snuffy still could not read anything except the Bible!

Looking back, it seems like the whole prison would have gotten saved, but none of us knew what "saved" meant or that's what we needed to be. I do remember more and more people going to church after that, but as for me, I saw no reason to. I'd always known there was a God, and I wholeheartedly believed God gave Snuffy his wish, but as the World Religion teacher had put it: There was nothing special about the Bible. I figured that if Snuffy had been from the Middle East, then God would have let him read the Koran. Plus, Snuffy needed God's help. He was like a little snub-nosed puppy with mental issues. As for me, I had no problem. As a matter of fact, I had a plan.

Getting Out: Of Marriage and Prison

Finally, after six or seven months, they let me go to work in the park. I was on the masonry detail. We built stone barbeque pits all over the park, poured the foundations for the water slide, built the putt putt golf course, and laid the sod. It really helped me a lot. I had gotten to the point at which even my dreams were limited to prison life. I needed to see cars driving and families together with smiles on their faces.

My wife had been a real trouper through all of this. She had spent every single Sunday for years coming to see me, but doing time had taken its toll on both of us. I guess it was early 1979 when I got my divorce papers. Soon afterward, I made parole, and the experience was nothing like I had expected.

16

Welcome Home

WHEN A MAN dreams about getting out of prison, it's kind of like when people think about going to Heaven. They don't really think much about what they are going to do when they get to Heaven, they just know they want to go. Well, I really didn't know what I was going to do when I got out, but I just knew it would be the most awesome experience of my life. I just imagined stepping through that gate and being overwhelmed with joy and a feeling of freedom, for I had been waiting so long!

But just as I had experienced depression when I finally reached my goal in the drug business, when I stepped through that gate to freedom . . . *nothing*. I mean complete and total emptiness. My mom and Karen picked me up, and though I tried to act happy, on the inside I was in shock and dying. A deep depression was setting in. How could that be?

Satan Welcomes Me Home

When I walked into my parents' den, there was a letter from an old friend who was now stationed at Fort Hood, Texas. I had written to tell him the great news, and being the good friend he was, he sent me a letter with a couple of grams of cocaine in it to welcome me home. I know that in his mind that's what a friend does for a friend who just got out of prison. But, as I look back I see that it was as if Satan himself was waiting for me to walk through the door.

My plan was to work at the family dry cleaners, spend time with my son, pay child support, and slowly rebuild my drug business. I knew the MDA guy would be more than happy to front me anything I needed to get going again, and this time I would sell only meth. No more MDA, which takes you too far to function, and certainly no more cocaine, with paranoid delusions and customers hiding in the bushes and running from imaginary policemen with mustaches in grocery stores. Nope, no more jumping through windows for me. From now on, it was going to be family and business while speeding my brains out so I could do a great job at both 24 hours a day.

One problem I had was that I knew way too many people. So while I was in prison I put together an organizational chart. People ran in groups, so I laid out the groups and identified a specific person who would be the safest to deal with and designated him to sell to that group. For instance, I knew a guy named Fat Bear, who knew a whole slew of people who were a few years older than me. Fat Bear was a down-to-earth guy who loved to smoke pot, do meth, and work hard. He hung gutters for a living, which was conducive to doing drug deals on the job, and loved to come home at night and get high. You couldn't drag him out of the house to go party. His idea of going out was to go hunting or fishing, and I have never heard of anyone getting busted in a deer stand.

Not only that, but he was huge (thus the name Fat Bear), so no one would mess with him, and yet no one would ever have a reason to. He couldn't stand snitches, and he would never cut anyone's drugs or rip anybody off because, like me, he was not in it for money. He was in it for the high, but to stay high the way we enjoyed it, you had to be in the business. Yep, Fat Bear would be perfect, and I identified about 10 others. One would take care of this area, or that town, and one would take care of all the bikers, etc.

Also, no more home phone. This was the day of the beeper, and every pay phone had a nine for the seventh number. For example, 770-427-9327 was one of the pay phones I frequented, so when you beeped me, the seventh number had to be something other than a nine, but I was going to dial nine. For example, you could beep 770-427-**6**327, but I was going to dial 770-427-**9**327. This way, if the police got a hold of someone's beeper number, they wouldn't know which numbers were being called, and this forced customers to go to a pay phone. It was a security measure.

I had a huge problem, though. When I came home, cocaine was waiting on me and instantly sunk its teeth into me once again. I was consumed by it. It is the only drug I've ever done that had my mind, while I was in the process of injecting it into my arm, already thinking about the next shot. Every dime I had was going to cocaine.

So I called my blood brother, Tommy, whose father had introduced me to the cocaine connection before I went to prison, to see what was going on with those guys. Tommy said that his father had continued in the cocaine business after the "Blow" connection had come to an end, and moved the family down to Ft. Lauderdale and that I should come on down. These were the days of the "Cocaine Cowboys" of Miami. So many people were being killed that Dade County had to have a refrigeration truck to put all the bodies in because the morgue was overflowing.

Then he told me some troubling news. Steve, the marijuana connection, had become a preacher while I was in prison, or at least that's what he had heard. I said, "Now, Tommy, you know better than that. You and I both know Steve is in the business somewhere, and he would never use a church as a front. That would be just plain wicked, so I don't ever want to hear you spreading any more rumors like that about Steve."

He said, "Okay, I'm sorry. I won't do it again."

A Biz Op in the Sunshine State

No too long after this Tommy called me and said that his older brother, Dennis, had been shot 5 times and killed by the Miami police and that his father wanted me to come down. Apparently, because I had been to prison and refused to snitch on anyone I had proven myself. He needed someone he knew he could trust to take Dennis' place. I was both flattered and excited. What an honor to be asked to stand in the place of a man's son who was killed in the line of duty (so to speak)! So off I went.

They had quite a system in place. They would send out five to seven souped-up open fishing boats well beyond the 24 nautical miles in which the coast guard patrolled to pick up a load. Sometimes the shipment would be transferred into one boat (or as many as three boats) that traveled in the center. An aerial advertising pilot would fly up and down the coast towing his banners, while at the same time spotting the coast guard. Then, when the timing was right, all the boats would enter national waters at the same time with the empty decoy boats on each end where they would be most susceptible to the coast guard. It was a shell game.

They could actually drive a boat into the canals of Ft. Lauderdale, right up to Tommy's place. Then at night, they would all take coolers and fishing poles down by the boat and start slowly transferring the drugs into the coolers for transport into Tommy's condo. If anyone was watching, it just looked like several people partying while night fishing, which was not an unusual sight by any means.

I was excited about becoming a part of this great organization. When I got down there, however, what I found was confusion and chaos. I didn't understand it then, of course, but looking back it was obvious. Here was a large family who had lost a son and a brother, and there was supposed to be a grieving process. But drugs change the way you feel so that the grieving process cannot take place. These powerful emotions deep down in a mother, or a father, sister, or brother become twisted, looking for a way out.

What I found was a family sitting around a big dining room table with what looked to be about a kilo of cocaine sitting in the middle of it, and everyone was freebasing cocaine. This was about the time when comedian Richard Pryor had caught himself on fire freebasing, and I'm surprised that whole house didn't explode. One minute they would be toking on the pipe and laughing and the next weeping because Dennis was dead. Then rage would set in, and someone would want to take a gun and go out and start shooting cops to avenge his death.

One of the brothers, Richard, announced it was time to go take care of some business. I jumped in the car with him, and the first stop was always to visit the place where Dennis had been killed. While driving through Miami, loaded down with drugs, the throttle stuck wide open! We were flying through the city, and he was slamming on the brakes every now and then to sling the car around another corner. I was yelling, "Just turn the key off! Just turn the key off!" and he just kept yelling, "Yee-ha!" like a wild man and then started heading back to Ft. Lauderdale. We almost made it to Tommy's, but he lost control and we went airborne, landing in a canal! As we climbed out of the car, Richard seemed thrilled about the whole situation. I had just one question: "Was that an alligator that just touched my leg, or what?!"

It turned out that they were getting more than cocaine from South America; they were getting Quaaludes by the tens of thousands. Since everyone knew that I had no interest in any kind of downer, we all thought this would be a great area of business for me because I would not use any of what I was selling. They gave me a suitcase full of Quaaludes, and the plan was that Tommy's mother would come to Atlanta and spend time with a friend while I sold them. I would then pay her, and she would serve as the runner between their family and me.

Of course, I was still addicted to cocaine, so I started trading the Quaaludes for it. I did manage to get all of their money together. When I called Tommy's mom so I could drop off the money, she said that she wanted to wait a few days while she went to visit someone else. I said, "I really wish you would let me drop this money off now." I couldn't tell her that the reason was that I was afraid I would spend it on cocaine. Well, she refused, and that's exactly what I did.

Never in my life had I messed up somebody's money. I had built a reputation of trust, but I simply could not control myself. When it was all said and done, I had no Quaaludes, no car, no money, nothing. When I went to buy that last bag of cocaine, I was close to Cumberland Mall. I left that apartment walking and soon just stopped on the side of the road and did a shot. When the paranoia set in, I would take off running. The faster I ran, the faster the imagined footsteps behind me ran. I could feel murderers and robbers coming out of the darkness to kill me and take my cocaine. Then I would eventually calm down only to do it all over again.

A Pointed Talk with God

By morning I had run all the way to my parents' house, which was about 18 miles away, but I did not run there in a straight line. There is no telling how many miles I ran that night. It was daylight when I got there and my parents were gone to work, so I was just going to go in the house and crash. But, instead, I decided to go out in the nearby woods and have a serious talk with God.

There was a place in the woods where we had a tree swing when I was a kid. It was where I smoked my first cigarette as a child, and it eventually became our little hangout where we drank beer and smoked pot when all of our parents were home. I walked to that area and began to reflect on how it all began, well over 10 years before. I remembered how I felt as a kid, just wanting to smoke a little, joke a little, and have a good time, and back then it seemed so innocent. Not anymore. I needed help. I had become someone I did not want to be.

So I began to scream at God. Now that I know the Lord, I would never, ever speak to Him the way I did, but I guess He just looked down at me as a parent looks at a little 2-year-old pitching a temper tantrum. I demanded that God come down there and speak to me. I screamed, "I know You're up there!" as I threw rocks at Him, crying. "You get down here right now. I don't know why You hide Yourself, but I need You right now. I won't tell anybody what You look like!" On and on I went until I had nothing left in me.

When I finally walked out of those woods, I remember thinking I felt better. When I walked in my parents' house, the first thing I noticed was all the furniture looked lower—as though I had grown a foot taller. I thought, *That's weird*, and passed out on the couch. I should have slept for a month, but I woke up in just a couple of hours and felt great. As I stood in the shower, it hit me that I had absolutely no desire to do cocaine, and to this very day I have never desired it again.

When my parents came home, I apologized for running off to Florida. I told them I was ready to get my life back on track. I remember my dad looking at me and saying, "Well, you look real good, son," which was nothing short of a miracle. He began to tell me how relieved he was to see me in my right mind and looking more like my old self.

He told me of a night not long after I got home from prison. He said that he had awakened in the middle of the night and walked downstairs to get a drink of water in the kitchen. As he walked by my bedroom door, I was just sitting in the dark, and when I looked at him my eyes flashed orange. He said my pupils were oblong, like those of a tiger or some wild beast. He said he knew that he was in the presence of pure evil but did not know what to do about it.

Now if you knew my dad, you would know this was quite a story. He was not a spiritually-minded man or superstitious in any shape, form, or fashion. He was the most normal, straight, honest, hardworking business-man I have ever met.

After this and my obvious deliverance from not only cocaine but all the after-effects of depression and exhaustion that should have followed, I actually considered asking God to take away the desire for all drugs, but I was terrified at the very thought. When you get into drugs, it's not a habit. It's a relationship in the deepest sense, and I could not bear the thought of life without it.

For Reflection . . .

For a person to end their relationship with drugs they have to go through the same five stages of the grieving process that people have to undergo after the death of a loved one: denial, anger, bargaining, depression, and acceptance.

Let's say a husband and wife are having dinner and receive a call that their teenage daughter has been in a terrible accident and is not expected to live. The first stage is denial. "Oh, no, this can't be! I'm sure she is going to be fine."

Then, on the way to the hospital, anger sets in and the shifting of blame begins. "I told you we shouldn't have let her go out with her boyfriend tonight!" "What do you mean? I told you I didn't like that boy from the beginning."

Then the bargaining starts. "Please, God, just let her be okay! I promise from now on we will have the whole family in church every Sunday."

When they arrive at the hospital, their daughter has been pronounced dead. Now depression sets in. A complete and total feeling of hopelessness and powerlessness overcomes them. The parents can't even imagine life without their daughter.

Then somewhere on the other side of depression comes acceptance. While they will always miss their daughter, life goes on.

Now let's apply this to the drug addict, and please remember that alcohol is a drug by its very definition. A person whose child dies obviously cannot remain in denial for long because of the overwhelming facts. It is hard to deny your child has died as you look upon them lying in a casket, but an addict can live in denial for decades justifying their actions.

If someone even mentions the addict may have a problem, they immediately go into the anger stage and the shifting of blame. "How dare you insinuate I have a problem when you know I only do it at such-and-such times?" Or, "I wouldn't even do it if you would quit such-and-such." My favorite classic is, "Well, if you're going to accuse me I may as well do it!"

Even in the face of hardcore evidence, such as when I became sick in Canada after running out of drugs, I denied that I had a problem. It had to be some kind of flu or that Canadian north wind (in July!).

God help you if someone comes along to reinforce your denial with some scientific mumbo-jumbo. "Well, you know how it runs in the family. It's a genetic thing." Or, "After all, he's been diagnosed with Bipolar Disorder." Yeah, no joke! So was I. Any drug addict who goes through the tests will show Bipolar Disorder, which just means they have mood swings ranging from mania to depression. It's what addicts refer to as getting high and then crashing. I can't say that Bipolar Disorder doesn't exist, but all of us were not using drugs because we were Bipolar—we were showing up Bipolar because we were using drugs!

Next comes the bargaining stage. "Well, I know I can't continue jumping through grocery store windows, so I'll quit shooting cocaine and just smoke pot." "I'm on probation so I'll get a job, settle down, and just get high on weekends." "Oh, I know! I'll quit when we have the baby!"

Then, if an addict can just live through all of this without well-meaning people enabling them, they can reach the depression stage—that place where they realize it will never work. It is hopeless and they are powerless. There is no use trying to bargain because their lives are completely unmanageable. It is referred to as the first step in the 12 steps of recovery because until an addict reaches this place, they will never let go.

Finally comes acceptance, and right here is where an addict needs to turn his or her life over to God. If not, they are just an addict without drugs and will probably relapse. But with God comes new life. When a person loses a child, they will always miss them. When God delivers a drug addict, that addict's only regret is that they waited so long.

Going Back to Church . . .

I managed to pay Tommy's family back and decided it was time to go to church and thank God for my deliverance from cocaine and allowing me to live through Alto. I was never raped, stabbed, or seriously injured, and I thought it would be a good thing to show God how much I appreciated it. So I would go to a church to say, "Thank you." But which one?

My parents had told me the story of my being christened as a baby in a Methodist church in Toccoa, Georgia, where I was born. My dad said that he went to that church because that's where all the businessmen and politicians went, but something very strange happened. When the pastor christened me, he raised me above his head and walked around the sanctuary proclaiming that he was holding in his hands a future pastor and speaking of all these things I was going to do. I would love to know what those things were, but my parents didn't take it to heart because they just thought it was part of the ceremony.

My parents said as soon as they walked out of the church, all of those businessmen started teasing my dad and making fun of the pastor, saying things like, "Boy, that pastor didn't know whose kid he had a hold of then, did he?" because my dad had a reputation for throwing big parties. They just thought it was hilarious that the one time this pastor ever did something like that, it was with my dad's kid, of all people.

Of course, given my behavior, over the years it continued to be a family joke. So since I had heard of the Methodist church, that's where I decided to go. As I listened, I could tell the preacher was about to make a point when, all of the sudden, grotesque visions came into my mind. When I got a hold of myself, he was talking about something else. Then, just as he was about to make another point, it happened again! And I don't just mean my mind was wandering. These were depraved visions that I had never had before—the blood in the syringe and sexual acts I had never thought about much less participated in!

I began to ask myself, "Why in the world am I thinking about these things in church of all places?" I scooted up to the edge of the pew, leaned forward, and with all of my will made up my mind that I was going to hear what this preacher was saying. He was talking about birds and was just about to make a point when it happened again. Then the reality of what was going on began to sink in.

My mind went back to those five boys in Alto who would kneel down to pray and all would go silent, and then people would begin attacking them. I realized that the same spiritual battle that I had witnessed taking place in that prison was now raging inside of me!

17

"Well, I Guess It's Just Time."

ABOUT THIS TIME, another huge event occurred in my life. Mike, the drug store burglar, had a little sister named Dani. I remember the first time I ever laid eyes on her. It was at my 16th birthday party. She was a little hippie girl with a velvet jacket and a velvet top hat on, and she was drop-dead gorgeous. I was immediately attracted to her, but I was dating someone else, and Dani was dating a friend of mine, so I never pursued her.

She's the One

When my wife and I were married and having our son, she and my friend were married and had a son. We were all young and wild. Their marriage had about as much of a chance of making it as mine did, and by this time it was pretty much over for them. When I became involved with Dani, it was not a decision I took lightly. I carried a lot of guilt and pain over what had happened with my wife and child, and I knew that another man's family was nothing to play with. But I also knew she was the one, and she is definitely the one thing I got right. We have now been together for 32 years, and we are more in love now than we have ever been. To God be the glory!

Dani was the first person I had ever met who could keep up with me. She came from a family of pretty wild folks, so I knew that she could keep her mouth shut. And while she was not easy to deal with, I knew I could trust her when it really mattered.

It's amazing how drug addicts think that people can't tell what they are doing. One day, Dani went to pick up her son at a Christian school he was attending, and his teacher saw right through her and knew that she needed help. The teacher prayed with Dani and got her to open up and share some of the burdens on her heart about what was going on and even brought Dani into her home.

Of course, now I understand what the lady was doing, but at the time I didn't. All I knew was that Dani said she had prayed with some Christian lady and was moving in with her, and that she was going to change her life. Then Dani really freaked me out when she said, "I'm praying God will save you." I thought then she had really gone off the deep end!

"The Devil's Been in My House"

One night soon afterward, I was watching *60 Minutes*, and they did a special on a cult called the Moonies. It said they targeted troubled youth, and especially young, pretty girls. They had all these parents on there talking about how it seemed like a good thing at first, that these Moonies would take in these runaway girls and act like they were going to help them, but then the girls would disappear.

Of course, I was as high as a kite, so I jumped up off the couch and thought, *Oh No! The Moonies have gotten Dani! I've got to rescue her before it's too late!* I took off over to the lady's house (a sweet Christian woman, I'm sure) and sat in the living room trying to convince Dani to make a run for it before the lady realized I was there or we might both disappear.

Dani was trying to tell me that she was a sweet lady and that I should meet her.

"Oh, no! Not me!" Just being in that house made my skin crawl. Of course, now I realize it was the Holy Ghost, but at the time, all I knew is whatever was in that house was greater than what was in me. I heard that lady walking down the hall, and I took off out the front door.

Dani said the lady walked into the living room, looked around, and said, "The devil has been in my house."

Over time, I managed to win Dani back and woo her away from the "religious fanatics," but I did it from a distance. You couldn't have dragged me back into that lady's house. Now I pray that kind of anointing rests upon me and my family and floods all of our home all the days of our lives!

A Guy in a Trans Am and a Clever Ruse

I was working at the dry cleaners all day and did deals all night long. When you go weeks with no sleep, paranoia begins to set in—not as bad as with cocaine, but bad enough to make you crazy. There was one problem: Just because you're paranoid does not mean that the police aren't there! You're just not sure which ones are real, and which ones aren't.

There was one who was obvious. I was standing at the cleaners one day when this guy, Rodney, just walked through the front door and said he wanted to buy some meth. I knew who he was, but I had never dealt with him. I also knew that he had been busted recently. He had a guy with him I had never seen before, driving a Trans Am. Now, you just don't do that. It was obvious this guy had been busted and now had brought a narc to the cleaners so he could bust me to cop a plea and get out of trouble. I told them I hadn't messed with any drugs in a long time and didn't know anybody who did.

Then I would be at a game room where Dani and I loved to play *Stargate* and that guy would be three machines down. Or I'd go to one of the pay phones that I frequented and there he would be in the parking lot with a group of people. One of my regular guys who usually purchased a half ounce of meth at a time suddenly wanted a quarter pound. I said, "Let me guess. You have a new customer who drives a Trans Am."

"How did you know?"

This guy had come out of nowhere and was suddenly everywhere.

Through a series of events, two of my main suppliers were down at the same time, so I was about to be out of meth for the first time in four years.

I didn't like the thought of that, so I came up with a plan. I had met a guy in prison named John, who claimed to have a meth connection down in Clayton County. He had been after me for quite a while to get something going. I didn't know the people, so I needed all the cash up front. I was $2,500 short and running out of time. After using every day for over four years, if I ran out, there was no telling when I'd wake up again. I needed to move fast.

I called Rodney and said, "I know your friend in the Trans Am has been wanting to cop from me. Tell him that if he will front you $2,500 so I can go cop in Stone Mountain, then when I get back I will sit down with him and we will talk business." Sure enough, he got the money, and we met. He looked all nervous and uptight and was talking 90 miles an hour.

"So you're going to cop methamphetamine, huh? So how much are you going to get? So where are you going in Stone Mountain?"

I just looked at him and motioned for him to hand me the money. When he did, I mouthed, "I'll call you later," and drove off.

I drove over to my friend Danny's home and got out of my car with a baseball cap on and a London Fog coat thrown over my right shoulder since I was always too pumped up and hot to wear a jacket during the winter. That coat provided all kinds of pockets, which I filled with drugs. I carried it with me everywhere I went.

I already had Tim, who was about my size, waiting for me in jeans, boots, etc., like I was wearing. After a few minutes, I sent him out the front door with that baseball cap on and my coat over his shoulder. Danny's house was way down a hill. If you were anywhere up on the road, you would be looking down on his roof. I knew that, even if they had night goggles, they would not be able to see his face with the baseball cap on. So he got in my car and started driving to Stone Mountain.

I exited Danny's basement in the dark and went across his property, across the creek, up through the property behind him, and back up on the next road over where John was waiting. We took off to Clayton County to cop, and Tim went on a ride to Stone Mountain, just in case this Trans Am guy really was the police. Let's face it—I still didn't know for sure. Maybe I was just paranoid, but I had no intention of ever speaking to him. I just needed to use his money for a day or so.

I went to Clayton County and copped, and everything went fine. As John and I were in a hotel room cutting it up, about to go flip it, Tim was taking a little drive around Stone Mountain before coming back to Danny's house. When he got off at the exit, a police car was sitting in the gas station, and it pulled out behind him. The officer pulled him over and when he looked at Tim's license and shone the light in Tim's face, he turned and walked toward the back of the car, speaking into the radio attached to his shoulder: "This isn't even him."

The officer spent a few minutes on the radio but was too far away for Tim to hear what he was saying. When he walked back up to the car window, he handed Tim his license without saying a word. Then he got in his patrol car and drove off.

Of course, Tim waited a while to contact me, but there was no doubt now. The guy in the Trans Am was a narcotics officer. Many people had done business with him, and I had just used the police's money to carry on my meth business. I'm sure all the serial numbers had been recorded so that when they busted me and my connection, the money would be used as evidence. I wasn't concerned about the $2,500 I had given those people, for I felt sure that the money would not find its way back to my area. But what about all the money people were handling all around me? There was no telling how many people this guy was building a case against.

When I got the money together, I went to a Waffle House bathroom, put it above a ceiling tile, and called Rodney.

I said, "Man, I'm sorry, but please quit trying to get me to do things I shouldn't do," and told him where to find the money. I figured they would know it wasn't the exact same bills, and while that didn't prove anything, it wasn't a good thing, either.

Everybody's Getting Busted . . . According to God's Word

Then it began to happen. People started getting busted all over the place. Some would not get a bond, and some would be right in and out, which made you wonder if they were going to work with the police, like Rodney. But I didn't personally do business with any of them. It looked like I was only going to lose one of my 10 men. I had tried to warn him about the Trans Am guy, but he wouldn't listen.

Then they busted one of my top suppliers. There were four of them, and they got every one of them in one night. I had warned all of them about that Trans Am guy, but they wouldn't listen, either. I kept thinking if everybody would just listen to me, we could do this thing right.

I was at the Journey's End Motel, bagging up meth and thinking about how smart I was. I would always take the Gideon's Bible out of the drawer and lean it against the curtains to make sure there wasn't even a little bitty crack for someone to peek in. I would always have the plain back of the Bible facing me, because the front of the Bible that said "Holy Bible" made me feel strange. And on this night, I did something strange.

When I pulled the Bible out of the drawer, I opened it up. I had never done that before. I mean, why would I? When I opened it up, my eyes fell on a scripture that said, "A haughty spirit precedes a fall," and I thought, *What am I doing?* I closed the Bible and leaned it against the curtains, but I kept thinking about that scripture.

I knew what it meant—that when a person was haughty and thought he knew everything, that was when he would get into trouble. I thought it was amazing that I would look in the Bible and read that because it described perfectly what had happened to all of those people getting busted. I tried to tell them what to do, but they just wouldn't listen to me. They thought they knew everything, and now they had fallen. It was like God was telling me where all those people went wrong.

I was still working at the dry cleaners and seeing my son often. Since I didn't use any drugs when I was with him, as soon as I dropped him off at his mother's I was always ready to get high. Some people who grew up in my subdivision lived in some apartments about a mile from there. I wasn't in business with them. They were just people I had known all of my life who liked to get high, so I would go by there after I dropped my son off so I could do a shot. I would let them have some, too, so they were happy to let me come over. One night I went by and all the parking spaces near their apartment were full, so I just pulled over with two wheels in the grass and went in. When I came out, a security guard told me I couldn't be parking in the grass. Of course, I told him no problem, that it wouldn't happen again.

"God Put Those Drugs down My Pants"

Then one night I babysat my son, and by the time his mother got home, I wanted to get high bad. I also had several deals waiting, so I was in a big hurry. When I drove over to those people's apartments I didn't see any parking places, so I pulled back up in the grass again. I was only going to be in there for a moment. I ran in, did a shot, and when I came back out, my car was gone. I thought that was awfully quick for a security guard to see my car, call a wrecker, and have it towed off. The problem is that when you do meth, it is hard to keep track of time. You may think it's only been minutes when in reality hours have gone by. So I figured maybe it had been longer than it seemed.

When I went back into the apartment, they told me that this security guard was strict and notorious for having cars towed off, but that it had seemed awfully quick to them as well. They knew what wrecker service the apartments used, so we called them. Sure enough, they had my car. I called one of the people who had been waiting for me so we could do a deal, and he came and picked me up and dropped me off at the wrecker place.

While we were driving, he told me about more people getting busted. Of course, I told him about how they should have all listened to me and they wouldn't be in that position. I even gave him a Bible lesson on how a haughty spirit precedes a fall, but I guess some people just have to learn the hard way.

It was about 1:00 or 2:00 a.m. by the time I got to the wrecker office. When I walked in, I spotted a man who seemed out of place, but I figured maybe he was waiting on his car, too. The wrecker service sat behind a small office park right on Highway 41. As I pulled out and drove through the office park, I saw tail lights come on from a car parked in the dark between the buildings. I knew right then it was a police car.

All of a sudden, cop cars were coming from everywhere! One stopped, and a police officer swung open his door and yelled, "Freeze!" I had a hole cut in my floorboard so I could drop drugs out of it during a chase, should the need ever arise. I pictured myself flying down Highway 41 and dropping the drugs on the bright, lit-up highway; they would see the drugs come out from under the car. But if I dropped them right there in that dark office park and took off, they would all be jumping in their cars, focused on me, and probably run all over the drugs. Of course, if they started shooting, that would be bad, but I didn't think they would. There were so many of them, they would be in danger of shooting each other.

I hesitated for a second and then dropped the package through the floorboard and took off. Sure enough, the police all just poured out onto the highway behind me. It looked like the O.J. Simpson chase, except it was nighttime, so all the lights were really something to behold. I figured that if I could just put a few miles between me and those drugs, then even if they found them, a good lawyer would be able to raise enough doubt in a trial to beat the charges. I mean those drugs *way back there* could have belonged to anybody. No officer could honestly testify that he saw me with those drugs. Oh, yeah! I was going to outsmart them again!

When I got up by a bowling alley, I pulled into the parking lot and was quickly surrounded. The cop told me to get out of the car, place my hands on the roof, feet back, and spread them apart. He began to search me and asked if I had any weapons or syringes that might stick him. I proudly told him that I didn't have anything. When he grabbed me around my waist, I felt him grab something in my pants. I looked down, and there was a huge bulge just under my belt. I knew exactly what it was. It was the package of drugs that I dropped out of my floorboard! It was so big that the officer couldn't pull it out. It was so big I couldn't have shoved it down in there, either.

I knew God had put those drugs down my pants. I even had a calmness come over me because I knew that I was up against a Power so much greater than me that there was absolutely nothing I could do. I'll never forget standing there with my hands on top of that Chevelle with those policemen trying to pull that package out of my jeans. I looked up at the stars in the sky and said, "Well, Lord, I guess it's just time."

It was so overwhelming that I wasn't even upset. As I sat in the back of the patrol car, watching them tear my car apart and find another stash that I hadn't even thought about and the pistol in my glove box, I added up the charges in my mind. Then my little Bible lesson that I had preached on the way to the wrecker service came to mind about how *"a haughty spirit precedes a fall,"* and now where I had been blind, I could clearly see.

I was the man with a *"haughty spirit,"* and I had just been set up by Almighty God Himself, who had spoken to me through the Bible. Of this I had no doubt.

18

Round Two

MADE THE newspapers this time. Just a simple article that a drug task force had been formed and that Grant Cole had been arrested. As I said before—"Just because you're paranoid doesn't mean they aren't really there."

When God sets you up, He doesn't leave you any room to wiggle. I kept my cars in other people's names in case I ever had to run, so I couldn't be charged with something simply because it was in a car that belonged to me. But when a package is down your pants, let's face it—you're not going to convince 12 jurors that you don't know how it got there. And if I were to tell them God put it there, then I would not only still go to jail but I'd probably end up with a nice padded cell.

Of course, God never would have done that if I hadn't been guilty, and now that I know God, I can tell you right now He only did it to save the lives who were destined for Hell if He didn't intervene—my life for sure as this was the same time that my unseen copilot was running me into cars.(I only mentioned one of three wrecks that night), but there may have been many other lives that God saved as well. I wasn't thinking like that then. All I knew was that it was time for me to go back to prison, and there was nothing I could do about it.

I was guilty. I knew it, obviously God knew it, the police knew it, everybody knew it. The only question was: "How bad is it going to be, and how can I make the best of it?" The only pleasure I'd had so far was to let them know there was no way I was going to be one of their snitches—that there were still true believers left in the business. I even had a typed-up card stating what I thought about snitches and how they should be ostracized by the community as a whole from both sides of the law. I had it laminated and placed it in my wallet behind my license, so that if I were ever arrested, the police would find it. It worked. As the officer was searching my wallet, he found it, read it, and passed it to the other officers. We will call him Officer Relentless.

Back to Jackson

I held off as long as I could to try and get the best deal. They were picking the jury when I finally agreed to plead guilty to what they said was their final offer—two 12-year sentences and one 1-year sentence. Eight years to be served in prison and four years on probation after my release. Once again, I was sent to Jackson.

There is absolutely nothing to do at Jackson while you're waiting to go through diagnostics but read and write letters. I had burnt myself out writing letters my first time in prison, so that left reading. I thought, *I'm going to read the Bible and see what else God has to say.* So I found a Bible that was much thinner than the big, thick ones in the hotel rooms. I really didn't know what was up with that.

I had heard guys make comments about how they couldn't stand reading the Bible because all it said was "so-and-so begat so-and-so." I opened it up and it said, *"The book of the genealogy of Jesus Christ, the Son of David, the son of Abraham. Abraham begat Isaac, Isaac begat Jacob,"* and I thought, *That really is what it says!* But it didn't take long to realize there really aren't very many "so-and-so begat so-and-so's" in there.

As I continued to read, I was dismayed because I could not understand it. I had always excelled in school. *Why could I not understand this book?* I sure understood the first verse I ever read: *"A haughty spirit precedes a fall."* Where was that verse anyway? I didn't even see it in there. I began to talk to the guys in the cells around me, and they explained that I only had the New Testament, but that was okay because the "old" part didn't matter anymore.

I thought, *Well, that's just great! The old part is the only part I can understand.* I started thinking that could not be true because that was the part God spoke to me through. The whole experience was very troubling to me, so I just kept reading from time to time.

Then something strange happened. The arresting county requested that I be returned to them, so I was going back. The jail was overcrowded, so I was to be boarded out to the Douglas County Jail. Douglas County had just built a new, state-of-the art, maximum security federal jail and had plenty of room. The federal government was also boarding their inmates there due to overcrowding. My cellmate was a guy facing federal time for manufacturing methamphetamine. We quickly became friends and made a deal.

A Bible in One Hand, a Meth Recipe in the Other

He wrote out the entire formula for manufacturing sulfate-based methamphetamine, as well as the contact information for a man in a chemical distribution company in Texas. I was to call this number, ask for the man, and say a code word to let him know I was referred by my cellmate. The man would get my order ready, and when I went to pick it up and pay the company, I was to also tip the man at least $5,000 in cash the first time (after that, he said I may want to tip him more).

I was to rent out a storage unit not too far from there under a false name and have other containers waiting to transfer the chemicals into. Due to Reagan's War on Drugs, the feds had started randomly putting tracking devices in containers of chemicals at manufacturing plants, so they could turn them on from time to time to make sure everything was going where it was supposed to go. There was no way for the man at the distribution company to know if the barrels he sold me were being tracked or not. If they were, they would just track them to a storage building full of empty containers. Of course, I was going to have to move fast during all of this.

In return, I would find girls to write to him and maybe go visit him while he was locked up. Of course, in the federal system there was no telling which state he would end up doing time in, but wherever it was, I would send him money so he could go to the prison store. Then when he was released, I would front him enough meth so he could get his lab going again, and if I got busted again, he would take care of me while I was in. We had a deal.

I was still reading my Bible, and by now I was in the book of Luke, still not understanding anything until I got to Luke 11:46, where Jesus said, *"Woe to you also lawyers! For you load men with burdens hard to bear, and you yourselves do not touch the burdens with one of your fingers."*

I told my cellmate, "Finally I understand this thing, and I agree with Jesus!"

He said, "What do you mean?"

I said, "Did you know that Jesus can't stand lawyers, either?"

He said, "Really? Let me read that!" And he started trying to read the Bible some, too.

Then, to my surprise, they informed me that I was going back to Jackson. To this day, I have no idea why they took me back and placed me in the Douglas County Jail. A lot goes into moving inmates around, and I remember thinking to myself, *This makes no sense, and it seems strange that for no logical reason I'm now walking out of a federal jail when I'm not even doing federal time, with a Bible in one hand and the formula and connection to manufacture meth in the other.* And, of course, I was thinking that of the two the latter would once again make all my dreams come true.

When I got back to Jackson, they put me in "F House." From my cell, I had a clear view of "H House," which was death row, where Randy was. During this time, his mother had become a leader in the movement to abolish the death penalty because she was convinced that apart from the drugs, her son would have never mutilated his ex-girlfriend's mother. In other words, Randy was guilty of using drugs and maybe should spend the rest of his life in prison to protect society if he ever made the mistake of using drugs again, but the murder was out of his control. I guess she figured that since she knew her son was not capable of doing what he did, maybe some of the other men on death row had done things out of their control also. When she began to investigate, she found drugs at the root of almost every case on death row. Of course, the other side of the coin is that over 80% of all people in prison are there as a result of drug- and alcohol-related crimes, but they didn't mutilate people.

While I was there, they executed Ivan Ray Stanley on July 12, 1984. From my cell, I could see the huge generator they pulled up and plugged into the side of the wall at the end of the building. Some guy said that was because Georgia Power refused to sell them the power to execute someone, but I don't know if that's true or not. It was an eerie feeling to sit there in a prison cell and hear that generator rev up real high and then bog down as they threw the switch.

The generator continued to idle a few minutes and then began to rev up again, and then bogged down a second time. All the men were talking about how mean that guy must have been to have that much electricity flow through his body and still not die the first time. As for me, I was just trying to imagine what my friend Randy must have been thinking while all of this was going on. Ivan Ray Stanley had committed his crime in 1976, which was the same year Randy committed his. That would mean Randy's number would be coming up soon. Very soon.

19

"What We Have Here is a Failure to Communicate"

THIS TIME THEY sent me to a work camp in Meriwether County. If you have ever seen the movie *Cool Hand Luke*, then you have a pretty good picture of the Meriwether work farm. It was a very small, very old prison. There were only two dorms, each holding 68 men—just a single room with bunks lining each wall with a shower area at the end.

The warden there didn't act like the warden in the movie, but he was all-powerful. He had a big house on the hill overlooking the camp. From what I understand, he was the warden, road superintendent, mayor, chief of police, and a large land owner.

Work Camp: Don't Work, Don't Eat

When I first got there, I thought, *This is where they get that old saying, "Tall as a Georgia pine."* The pine trees towered over 100 feet tall and were only a few feet apart. As a result, they were perfectly straight and had no limbs, except on the very top. It was a pulp wooder's paradise, and pulp wood trucks continually ran up and down the highway.

They had a farm that raised cattle and such, but the main focus of the camp seemed to be building roads from nowhere to nowhere. First, they would pulp wood the land and clear it for the most part to build a road. Then the convicts would be brought in to remove every root and stone by hand. Then trucks would bring in gravel, which we would spread by hand.

They had a tar truck that was pumped by hand. The man who turned that crank had been doing it for five years, and his arm was as big as my waist. I kid you not—28". You may remember in *Cool Hand Luke* where the men had to spread sand on the tar fast enough so the guard's shoes wouldn't stick to it as he walked down the freshly tarred road. At Meriwether, we had to sling sand fast enough for a dump truck to roll across that tar in low gear for miles.

When we came in from work and entered the front door of the camp, we saw the pillars on each side of the door with big metal rings on them. They used to tie prisoners there and whip them for not working hard enough. The guards said they hadn't used them in a long time, and that we should be grateful that we had it so easy in these modern days! The Meriwether Courthouse still had a hangman's gallows in the dome of it. I was hoping they hadn't used that in a while, either.

It was the only prison I've heard of that didn't have visitation on Saturday because by the time Saturday came, no one could get out of bed anyway. By then, we had to recuperate. If our families had seen what we looked like by the end of the week, they would have been crying "cruel and unusual punishment," but men would actually hide their injuries for fear they would be shipped somewhere else.

Oh, yeah. It wasn't difficult to get a transfer. I have no idea if the warden was a believer or not, but he sure applied 2 Thessalonians 3:10, which says, *"If anyone will not work, neither shall he eat."* And eat we did. The guys on the farm would kill a cow or a hog, and we would have fresh ham and eggs for breakfast, and steak and potatoes for dinner. They had to feed us good to work us like that, and if you were lazy, we certainly didn't want you on our crew, and the warden had no use for you.

When you work hard with men like that, you build a bond with them. I never saw one fight the whole time I was there. That's not to say everybody necessarily got along with everyone, but you grew close to the men who worked beside you, and if someone got on your nerves, you were too tired to argue, much less fight.

When I first started working like that, my sweat was brown and smelled like a mixture of hydrochloride and ether. It wasn't long before I was drinking eight quarts of ice water a day and would go a whole day without urinating a single time. My sweat was as pure as water, and I was feeling clean, strong, and healthy. I started thinking it sure would be nice to do a big old shot of meth about right now. I was sure it would be just like the first time.

Meth for Performance Enhancement

One of the main reasons the men didn't want to be shipped anywhere else had to do with the attitude of the guards at night. It seemed that as long as we worked hard, then whatever else we did really didn't matter. Men would come in from detail and have a cold beer or glass of liquor, and pot was everywhere.

Now this is where the "failure to communicate" comes in. I interpreted this to mean everything goes as long as we worked hard enough, and I was going to "speed" up the productivity of this whole operation with a little help from my faithful friend, Fat Bear. It was the only prison I had ever been in where they didn't open your mail, so it was easy. He would just take a gram or two, mash it flat between the paper, and mail it to a guy in there who didn't mind taking the chance, and I would turn him on when it came in.

The only problem was that you couldn't put a syringe in an envelope. One of the old timers there, Sam, had been there long enough to get to drive one of the tractors. He pulled in to a drug store, walked right in, and bought a bag of insulin syringes—wearing prison clothes, mind you! So, of course, he earned a shot from each batch. Then we made a waiting list so that after me, my carrier, and Sam got our shares, the rest would go to whomever was next up on the list.

Some of the guys there had a lot of time, most of which they had already served in some prison like Alto or Reidsville before they were shipped to Meriwether. For instance, Sam had life. He had been high on PCP and was going to rob someone to get money to buy more. He randomly went up to someone's house and rang the doorbell. When the lady answered, he was so high and nervous that he accidentally pulled the trigger and killed the lady.

When you just randomly ring a doorbell and kill someone, you are not getting out for a very long time. He had already been down 14 years. There was another guy there, called "Chain Saw," with a lot of time. He had murdered his wife and children.

I really missed my son and still felt guilty over the way I had failed my now ex-wife, so the thought of a man killing his wife and children rubbed me the wrong way. When his name came up on the list, I just bypassed him. I tolerated the guy, but I certainly wasn't going to let him have any of my precious meth.

We all worked together in the hobby and craft shop. Sam and Chain Saw worked a lot with leather. Sam taught me how to make some awesome churches (believe it or not) out of bleached stone walls, pine cone shingles, Popsicle stick pews, carpeted, and trimmed in match sticks that I would sell in the visitation room. I have one in my office today—30 years old and just as sturdy as it can be. Though I had given up trying to understand what the Bible said, I sure could build a church.

As time went by, Chain Saw started noticing that some men had come up on the list two or three times to do a shot while he hadn't done the first one. So he snitched on me. They didn't catch me with anything, but he had told them where we had the syringes stashed in the metal frame of a table in the hobby shop.

To my surprise, the warden didn't like this at all. We definitely had a "failure to communicate," because I thought the message was *work hard and do as you please.* Apparently not.

They sent the syringes to the crime lab, and tests showed that the residue in those syringes was the same type of meth I was in prison for. While they could not convict me on new charges, they still shipped me off to the prison I would have gone to if convicted because they knew I was guilty. Of course, they had to ship off Chain Saw too, because the men would have killed him.

It had to be God . . . or the Devil

I was transferred to the Rivers building in Hardwick. If a prisoner attacked a guard, stabbed someone, or caught a new case as I almost had, this was where they sent you. It was a prison for prisoners—the worst of the worst. No hobby and craft shops here. You were searched each time you walked in and out of the dorm and counted every few hours, and yet the court system ran continually in this prison. They averaged 52 felonies a week from the prisoners' committing crimes.

As I was being searched and checked in, I came very close to catching a case for assault on a counselor. I was trying to explain that I had not been convicted of a new crime, but only snitched on, so I didn't belong there. You expect a different attitude from a counselor than you do from a guard, but this counselor sarcastically said, "Well, a bit dog always barks," as if to say that my complaint proved I was guilty.

To that I said, "And this dog is about to bite you!"

I was just about to punch him in the face, but at that very moment I heard someone yell from behind me, "Homey Jack!"

I had never been called "Homey Jack" by anyone in my life, but I knew that voice. It was my old friend, Randy, who had been on death row the last eight years.

I said, "What are you doing here?"

He said, "Man, they commuted my sentence to life. What dorm are they putting you in?"

I said, "Dorm 7, south building." To that, he let out this big, hearty laugh that was so familiar to me and then walked off.

I thought to myself, *How can a man do the things Randy has done, and go through the things he has gone through, and be exactly like the friend I remember from high school, right down to the way he looks and walks and the sound of his laugh?* It was strange. The guard escorted me to Dorm 7 and told me to go find bed 46, which would be my new address. As I placed my stuff on my bed, who do you think came walking up with a big smile on his face? Randy.

I said, "Man, you're in this dorm?"

He said, "You're not going to believe it." He sat down on the bed next to me, unlocked the metal drawer under it, pulled out a joint, lit it up, and passed it to me!

Now seriously! What are the odds? I sat there trying to grasp all of the "coincidences" that had to take place for this to occur in the lives of so many people—even the man who just left that bed that morning. Where would you even begin to figure out the odds of the two of us ending up in beds right next to each other? Impossible! It had to be God! Or the devil? I didn't know which, but I certainly knew that it was no coincidence.

Due to his mother's continuous efforts, Randy's death sentence finally got commuted to life. On a regular life sentence, you were eligible for parole in seven years. I had never heard of anyone actually making parole in seven years, but at least you were eligible. When your death sentence was commuted to life, then your first chance for parole was after 25 years. Most likely you would never be released, but once again, at least you were eligible. There was some glimmer of hope.

Randy had only been there a few months, but he seemed to know everything about the place. They had put him in charge of the library, which they always seem to do with the men who are never getting out. He expedited my enrollment into Massey Business College, got me into the drug program to help with my chances for parole, and, after much study, put together a workout plan for the two of us. Randy was flourishing. After eight years on death row, this was a dream come true for Randy. Of course, being "Homey Jack" to a man everyone knew came from death row didn't hurt my status among the prisoners either.

While resting after we had been working out one day, Randy said, "Okay, Homey Jack."

I said, "What?"

"Ask me anything you want to. Let's get it over with."

I said, "Why did you do it?"

He said, "I don't know." Then he just sat there, obviously telling the truth, waiting for my next question.

He did not remember that we had planned to meet at the Dairy Queen and fight after arguing. He watched *Barnaby Jones* on TV that night, and the show began with a shooting. After that, everything was very methodical. He got up, went to the closet, retrieved his shotgun, and walked out of the house. He said that he really wasn't thinking about anything. He wasn't mad or forming any kind of plan.

He walked one block over and headed for his ex-girlfriend's house. It was an old farmhouse with a barn and a lot of land. Her mom let us have a big high school party once out in their field. I remember going into their house and noticing they had several bolt locks on their door. I thought it probably made them feel safer, being two women living alone back in those woods, and that it would take a bulldozer to knock that big old solid wood door down. I actually thought to myself, *They don't need all those locks. Nobody is coming through that door!*

Randy said that as he approached his ex-girlfriend's house, he could see the back of her mother's head as she sat on the couch watching television in front of their big living room window. As he watched the barrel of the gun raise up, pointed at her, he panicked as he realized what was about to happen, and pulled the trigger.

He then walked over to that big front door and pushed on it. He said it felt like it wasn't latched and that he was surprised as the whole frame came loose with it obviously displaying strength way beyond his natural capabilities.

He said there were times when he would be screaming on the inside to stop and then he would grow tired and just watch.

After it was over, he threw the shotgun out in the woods and went home and cleaned himself up. Pretty soon, he saw police cars flying down the road and knew his ex-girlfriend must have come home and found her mother. Knowing she would be devastated, he went down to her house to console her.

I sat there, bewildered. Was this guy making this up? How could this old friend who seemed so normal do something like that? I kept thinking about how he "watched the barrel of the gun go up," and that "he panicked as he realized what was about to happen." Could a person really be that out of control?

I wanted to ask more questions, but I just let it go. All I know is that I never felt any kind of danger from him and never saw him do one thing that would indicate any kind of mental problem in any shape, form, or fashion the whole time we were together, which was almost 24 hours a day.

An Eye-Opening Dream

During this time, I had a dream concerning my son that caused me to wake up in a panic.

The first time I went to prison, he was a baby and had no idea what was going on. This time he was seven years old, and we had grown close. I couldn't just tell him I was "out of town." He would think I didn't care. So while I was out on bond, I took him to that same Methodist Church that I had gone to when I first got out. I didn't know anything about dedicating babies or anything like that, but without realizing it, that's what I did. Not officially before the congregation; it was just me, God, and my son on the back row.

I had the strangest feeling that I wouldn't live through prison this time, so I just asked God to watch over him and to protect him from the mistakes I had made. I was asking God to be his Father since I wasn't going to be and to give me the words to explain to him what I had done and what was happening in a way that wouldn't mess his head up.

After church, I took him to White Water Park, which had just opened, and spent the day with him. I did the best I could and tried to tell him, "this is what I did," and that he should not follow in my footsteps. Even in my lost, drug-induced state, I knew that was not going to add up in his little mind because the truth is that it doesn't add up at all. We can help our children by sharing past mistakes we have made and explaining where we found the answers so they won't have to make the same mistakes. But to tell your child not to do what you are doing—that's the true definition of hypocrisy, and I knew it.

Well, in this dream, my son was saying, "Everyone tells me drugs are wrong, but I love my dad and he does them. He loves drugs so much that he is willing to go to prison for them, so I'm going to find out for myself," as he injected the drugs into his little arm.

I sat straight up in my bed in a sweat. Never had I been so glad to realize it was just a dream and yet so terrified because I knew that it was a dream that could very well come true.

I thought, *I have got to do something about myself, but what?* I had been going to the drug program and learned that drug addiction was a disease, so what could I do? I didn't have the power over a disease. Only God controls things like that. Obviously, it was His decision that I had the disease in the first place. So just as a person with diabetes has to learn to live with it, so would I. (I'm glad to report this is not true, but we will come back to this subject later)

I began reading some books on "behavior modification" and "the power of positive thinking," and before long I was convinced that I could "moderate" my drug behavior and deal drugs in a "positive" way. A new plan began to develop. Was this Plan E or F? Or was it J or K? I'm not sure, but what other choice did I have?

Not too long after this, I made parole in October, 1985.

20

Home Sweet Home . . . Again

MY WIFE, DANI, had been living with her brother Tim and his wife while I was incarcerated. She worked as a bartender at an upscale pool hall called *Player's Retreat*. I knew better than to try to parole to their house because both Tim and Dani had records.

One time when the police were arresting her brother Mike, who was a suspect in a bank robbery, the officers were roughing him up, so Dani came to the rescue. During the scuffle, one of them pulled Dani's hair (she had beautiful hair), so she kicked the officer in the privates and was charged with Obstruction of a Police Officer.

You had to watch out for her feet. Once when she was sitting on the couch and I was standing in front of her yelling down at her, she kicked me right in the face without even getting up. Another time we were in her car arguing, and she put her back against the door, turned those feet toward me, and went to work. She kicked me so hard and so fast that she pummeled my body right out of her passenger door window, then pulled my pistol out of the glove box and threatened to shoot me.

Yeah, I could hardly wait to find Dani. She was my "pretty lady," and I had really missed her. Life was never boring with Dani around.

"Clean" for a Year—NOT!

Of course, I could hardly wait to see my son. Children are amazing. He acted like I was never gone, but I began to notice something about myself. Going back to prison was much easier than the first time, and adjusting to freedom was becoming more difficult.

I was working at the cleaners, going to a required drug program every Thursday night, and being tested regularly. My parole officer showed up constantly, but we got along. I was spending time with my son and seeing Dani. It seemed all should have been well, but I had this emptiness on the inside.

I hated that feeling, and I wanted some relief. One of the things they taught us in the prison drug program was how long each drug stayed in your system so that it could be detected in a urine test. I remember thinking, *Why in the world would you teach a bunch of drug addicts in prison this stuff?* The only reason I could think of was so we could use drugs and avoid detection at the same time, so I decided to take them up on it.

I knew marijuana was off limits because that stays in your system up to a month. Meth was off limits, too, because that lasted eight to ten days and I was tested every seven. That left cocaine, which only stayed in your system 72 hours. I'd had no desire for it ever since I'd had that talk with God out in the woods by my parents' house, but I believed I had this disease of drug addiction, which needed a treatment, so I took my medicine as much as I hated it.

And hate it I did, but that empty feeling was gone—at least for a little while. I used one Friday, and then the next Friday, and then I used on Monday. I thought to myself, *Am I setting up a pattern? The first time I went seven days, the next time three-and-a-half days. Surely not. That's ridiculous! I've only used three times.* Then, one-and-a-half days later, I used again and knew I was going to have a dirty urine screen. I needed a plan, and I needed one quick.

One of the employees at the cleaners was a Christian and was always talking about church and stuff, so I figured she and her husband were straight. After I got off work, I went and knocked on their door. When I entered, I noticed the man had been reading his Bible . . . . To make a long story short, I actually talked that nice man into peeing in a bottle for me.

When the Christian man got tired of doing it, I got the man who worked at the Texaco next door to the cleaners to take over. I even talked customers into peeing into a bottle for me. Once when I was particularly desperate, I managed to talk a complete stranger walking down the sidewalk at a shopping center to go into the laundromat bathroom and pee in a bottle for me.

Then one Thursday night when I went to the drug program, the lead psychiatrist had an announcement to make and an award to present. He announced that I was the first parolee ever to come to that program and stay clean for one full year. He presented me with a certificate.

After this, the leader would turn to me often during the meetings to give advice to the newer members of our group. One night, a new guy poured his heart out about all the terrible things he had done to support his cocaine habit. The leader said, "Grant, why don't you tell us how it was that you overcame your cocaine addiction?"

So I did. I told him the whole story of how, out of desperation, I went into the woods by my parents' house and started yelling and crying out to God and that when I came out of those woods, I'd never had the desire to do cocaine again. The leader looked at me in disgust and said, "I am so disappointed in you. I actually thought you would have something beneficial to offer this man." After that, he seemed to ignore me in every session.

I thought: *What a farce this whole thing is! I've been given an award for staying clean for a year while I was probably the only person who actually stayed high 51 of the 52 weeks, and then the only answer that I knew for a fact worked, he rejected.* Not only did he reject it, but it was obvious he did not like God. I thought: *This guy has all these diplomas on his wall, but if he doesn't like God, then he's the dumbest guy in the room!* I couldn't help but wonder how much they were paying this guy!

Jesus said, *"If the blind leads the blind, both will fall into a ditch"* (Matthew 15:14). That is a perfect description of that drug program.

The War Is On!

Things went along like that for quite some time, until the spring of 1987 when Dani let me know she was pregnant. Abortion was out of the question in the minds of both of us, so for the second time in my life I wanted to quit using drugs. And just as it happened the first time I had attempted to quit, I found myself in the middle of a battle.

For Reflection . . .

When you're submitted to the enemy and living in sin, there's no reason for a struggle; but when you want to quit, your master will often show his true colors. Often I've heard people say, "Well, I tried to change my life, but things actually got worse." They interpret that to mean the Christian life doesn't work, when in reality, the enemy just doesn't want to let you go and is making one final attempt to steal, kill, and destroy you and everything in your life.

Disgusting Myself

What I'm about to share with you is true. I cannot give you every detail because the people involved have asked me not to. I will honor that, but I can tell you enough to make the point I want to make.

Not only could I not stop using drugs but I actually found myself doing things that were totally contrary to my intentions. The war was on. On one particular night, I had done something that so disgusted me that I went over to Fat Bear's and poured my heart out. It bothered me so much that I tore the money up that I had made and left there determined to go to someone's apartment to straighten things out.

As I opened the door and entered the apartment, I realized I could not feel my legs. It was as though I was not walking but floating through the apartment. I was actually talking to myself, trying to convince myself that everything was okay, that I was just high. The people that I had come to confront just sat there in silence as though they were under some kind of spell. It was so strange because they should have been preparing themselves for a fight because they knew I was upset about what happened earlier.

Then it seemed as if I were about four feet behind my eyes. It was like looking out of a window at the end of a four-foot tunnel. As I watched my hands, I began to freak out because I knew I was about to do something that I absolutely did not want to do. Then when I began to do it, I heard a voice begin to speak the purpose of what I was doing to this person. It was hideous. Pure evil. I would never, ever want to be any part of doing what this voice said was being accomplished at that moment, nor could I ever imagine any human thinking like that.

When the deed was done, I dropped what was in my hand, and the first thought that came into my mind was, *This is what happened to Randy.* No, I did not kill anybody, but it just as easily could have been a knife or an ax for that matter. There is no unsolved crime that I need to confess. But I can tell you this: Simply murdering someone would not be as wicked and insidious as what that thing had spoken over that situation, and in the name of Jesus, it will never be fulfilled. That curse has been broken by the grace of Almighty God. Of course, all that is true now, but at that time I didn't know what to do.

I walked out of that apartment and drove away, trying to come to terms with what had just happened. I thought back to the old Wolfman movies I had seen as a kid. The Wolfman was a good guy who didn't want to hurt anyone, but he knew he would when there was a full moon. So he would try to make sure that he was locked up in some room when the time came, so he wouldn't be able to get out. I thought: *That is what I have to do. I have to be locked up.*

So I went to the building where the drug program was and waited in the parking lot for morning to come. When the leader of the program arrived and got out of his car, he asked, "What's wrong, Grant?"

I cried, *"Help!"* but no sound came out.

21

When an Unclean Spirit Comes Out of a Man

H E TOOK ME inside and gave me a drink of water. As soon as I could speak, I said, "You have to put me in jail." I told him that I had been using and was out of control. I fully expected him to pick up the phone and call my parole officer, who would immediately rush to have me picked up. I let him know that Dani was pregnant and that she was going to need help while I was incarcerated. He didn't seem to understand the gravity of the situation. Of course, I wasn't telling *him* all the details, either, but it should have been more than enough to have me arrested.

He said, "Okay, I'll call your parole officer, and I need you to take a urine test." I can't remember the whole conversation, but I can remember exactly what it felt like while I was giving him the sample—like freedom. I was confessing in a way that was going to be documented. There was no turning back. I was experiencing relief as I was giving him the infallible evidence that would put me back in prison! That way, everyone would be safe.

Then he told me to go to work and he would call me later. I couldn't believe it! I had spent what seemed like my whole life running and hiding from these people, and now I'm begging them to lock me up and they won't do it. I went to work, expecting the police to pull in at any minute. I don't recall how long it was, but sometime later he called me and told me to come to his office.

A Glimpse of Hope

He told me he had talked it over with my parole officer, and the two had decided they wanted me to try a new drug program that was having great results. It was called SAFE Recovery Systems. SAFE was an acronym for Substance Abuse Free Existence. It was a top-notch program, but very expensive. The 28-day program would cost anywhere from $30,000 to $45,000, depending on the treatment plan they developed for me.

All of the sudden, I felt a glimpse of hope. I mean, for $30,000–$45,000, I figured these people had to have some answers! If those people didn't have the answers, then *nobody* had the answers. I said, "Let's do it, but where am I going to get 30-45 grand?" He said some grant money was available. I had a few thousand, and maybe my parents would give me a few. Then I found out that while I would live there, I would still be able to work at the cleaners during part of the day. I said, "Oh, well, let's do this!" I mean, if these people could help me quit doing so much meth, I could easily sell enough drugs out of the cleaners to pay for the program!

The day I was to enter treatment was one of the most horrible days of my life. I was sick, tired, and sweaty. My car broke down. I had a flat tire on I-75. Everything that could go wrong did go wrong. When I finally made it down there, I passed out in the parking lot, but somehow I made it inside.

While I was in the front office, I read all the stuff on the walls. There was a glass cabinet with a framed article on cocaine that I believe was from *LIFE* magazine. It talked about how cocaine was unusual in that people often went into convulsions while initially getting high on the drug rather than when they were coming down. They had interviewed 300 cocaine users who had experienced these convulsions and lived to tell about it, and they all reported the same experience. They either did not remember anything at all or remembered hearing the words, *Come with me, me, me* repeated three times. Sometimes the hallucination would be accompanied by a large hand and sometimes not. Then the article went on with some mumbo-jumbo, feeble attempt to explain how all of these people could experience the same hallucinations.

I just stood there staring at this article. I mean, there it was. *Come with me, me, me!* When the lady came to get me, I pointed at the article and said, "That is no hallucination! That is the devil himself!" She didn't seem surprised that I had experienced it.

I expected to get some book and lecture where I could take notes and get a $30,000–$45,000 formula for success. Instead, we sat in a big circle, and they kept talking about "powerlessness" and "surrender" and how we had to "give up" and quit trying to "control" our addiction. It made no sense to me. If I quit trying to control my addiction, then I would just spin out into oblivion.

I was impressed with the depth of understanding the people attending the program seemed to have. I actually thought some were undercover counselors the administration had planted for some soon-to-be-revealed purpose. Many were doctors, dentists, and nurses who started using the drugs they prescribed and administered, and their livelihood depended on their recovery.

One doctor had started injecting narcotics. He had a pilot's license and his own plane. He was flying home from a vacation with his wife and children, who were sleeping in the back. It had been a while since he had done a shot, and he knew that he wouldn't be able to do one until after the drive home from the airport. So he decided to do a shot while they were asleep because, of course, he had been hiding his addiction from his family. When he did the shot, it blurred his vision, and when he landed, he touched down so hard it busted the plane's landing gear off. They went sliding down the runway on the belly of the plane. After that, he decided to get some help.

There were some people from Hollywood in the program, and some rich kid that must have come from some really important family. He was the youngest in the program, and while anonymity was important to everyone, he was essentially top secret. Everyone used first names only, but this kid's anonymity was so important they even used a fake first name.

There was a truck driver who was a meth addict. He had nodded out and run his truck off the road. Apparently it was not the first time. He was so sick and tired of being sick and tired that he got out of his truck and dropped to his knees on I-75, fully expecting to be run over.

A car slammed on its brakes, and a man got out and yelled, "What are you doing?"

The truck driver threw up his hands and said, "Take me to a drug program!"

I liked him immediately.

"My Demons Know Your Demons"

After about a week, a new guy came in. When he sat down in the group, it was like something with wings flapped inside of me. He grabbed his chest, looked straight at me, and said, "My demons know your demons!" He was a spooky guy and did not last long in the program. He kept talking about how his favorite movie of all time was *The Exorcist*, and that got me thinking.

When *The Exorcist* came out, I was about 16 years old and working at Joe's Steak House. Stores were still closed on Sundays back then, and *The Exorcist* was the first modern high-tech horror movie ever made. A bunch of us went down to Lenox Mall on a Sunday to see the movie. The line went all the way through the mall. We started waiting in line at 10:00 a.m. We brought in a cooler, so half of us drank beer while holding the place in line while the other half went out to the parking lot to smoke pot and do Mescaline, LSD, MDA, speed, and you name it. Then we would rotate.

This went on all day long until we finally got in at about 6:30 that night. We were so high, and that movie had a tremendous effect on all of us. My girlfriend at the time said that she kept seeing people's heads spinning around out of the corner of her eye. She was really upset. I had never connected the two before, but now I began to think about how she shot herself not too long after that. Had we picked up something in that movie? Is that why my demons knew that weird guy's demons? I didn't know, but I couldn't help but wonder.

"No" to Drugs to Quit Drugs

Then one night after group, the head guy called me into his office and said, "Grant, we are very concerned about you. You have not made any progress in this program after nine days of intense therapy."

I said, "What do you mean? What is supposed to be happening that's not happening?" I was stunned.

He said that was beside the point, but he believed they had identified what was wrong with me. He went on to explain that there is a part of your brain that releases endorphins that cause a person to experience pleasure, among other things. They believed that because I had managed to get high pretty much every day since I was 12 years old, now that I was 30 my brain had become conditioned to release endorphins only when chemically stimulated. He said it was a condition that was especially showing up in cocaine addicts because cocaine causes that part of your brain to release more endorphins than any substance known to man. That's why cocaine is so addictive. That is why you experience such severe depression when you come down from cocaine—because that part of your brain has no more endorphins to release after being stimulated by cocaine. All drugs do this to one degree or another.

He said there was a good chance that, for the rest of my life, I would never be able to enjoy the touch of a woman, the color of green grass, or the feel of a breeze on my face unless I first stimulated myself with a chemical.

I thought, *Man, it was not supposed to be like this! I just wanted to smoke a little, joke a little, and have a good time, and now I've permanently destroyed my life.*

But then he said that there was hope—that some pharmaceutical company had developed an experimental drug that was designed to "jump start" that part of a cocaine addict's brain to help cure the damage that had been done. He said that the drug was cost prohibitive, so the only people who were paying for it were pretty much Hollywood movie stars battling cocaine addiction. He told me that he would refer me to a study so I would not have to pay for it. He said that I would be a perfect candidate for the study.

Something told me not to do it, which surprised me. Normally I would have found it exciting to do some experimental drug—especially being supervised by experts. Shoot, sign me up! But I felt so strongly that I just point-blank refused right there. He told me that I could take time to think it over, but I said, "No, I'll pass." It just didn't make sense to me to use drugs to try to quit using drugs.

He said that it was a waste of my time and money, and their grant money, to keep me in the program if I couldn't make any progress. He said, "When you go back to the apartment tonight, you have to write out your first step." By the time I got off work the next day and came to group, I had to explain and present in writing how I was "powerless over my addiction and my life was unmanageable." If I could not do that the next night then I would have to leave group, go to the apartment, pack my stuff, and leave. Of course, he added, my parole officer would be informed that I had not been able to make it through the program.

Meeting Jesus on the First Step

When we got back to the apartment, I began to wrestle with the first step. I sat at the dining room table and had no problem with the "my life had become unmanageable" part. After all, I had turned myself in and asked to be put in jail so I wouldn't hurt anybody; Dani and I were about to have a child; I was about to be kicked out of a drug program for which I was paying a $1,000 a day because I didn't want to get on another drug on top of all the other drugs; and I couldn't even take the first step because I had fried my brain! Oh, yeah, my life had become unmanageable! I got it.

But I had a harder time with the "powerless" part. What did it mean to be "powerless," and how in the world could that be a good thing? It just didn't make sense! But it *must* make sense because all those other people got it! Why couldn't I? What was I going to do? *"Please, God, help me!"*

As I said those words, I dropped my head into my hands, closed my eyes, and saw a bolt of lightning flash across a dark sky. As the lightning flashed, it was as though I was in the air, looking down on Jesus Christ hanging on the cross. I was slightly above and behind Him, to His left. His head was hanging down to the right, so I could not see His face. Water or sweat was dripping off of his face and hair, and He said, "Forgive him, Father, for he knows not what he does."

At that moment, something huge welled up inside of me like I was going to projectile vomit, only there was no nausea or anything like a physical sickness. It was more like I was being inflated with air, and if I did not open my mouth, my body was going to explode.

When I opened my mouth to release what was inflating me, it looked like gasoline fumes shimmering on a hot day, if you have ever seen that, or like the camouflage the Predator wore on the movie of that name with Arnold Schwarzenegger. As it was coming out, I could see that it had a backbone, but not like a man. It was like the vertebrae of a bird and it had wings, but not like the wings of a bird but rather like the wings of a fly.

I can't say what it looked like in its entirety because my whole head was between my legs as I sat on the chair, so I never looked up. I just saw it floating out of my mouth, and as it did tears began to gush out of my eyes right along with it. I reached up on the dining room table where there was a box of Kleenex. There were boxes of Kleenex all over that apartment because somebody always seemed to be crying about something that had been stirred up in therapy—everybody except me, that is.

Until now. I was ready for the box of Kleenex. And when I pulled it down in front of me and reached into the box, it was filled with my tears, just as if I had held it under a water faucet. So I just reached up and set the now soaking wet box of Kleenex back on the table and remained bent over, watching the tears pour out of my eyes. In a matter of seconds, they had soaked the carpet and were actually splashing in the puddle that had formed.

All I could think was, *It's true! It is really, really true! There are living beings that can live inside of people!* My next thought was, *Wow, I feel so much better!* It wasn't like a good feeling came. No, it was the absence of severe pain that had been there so long that I didn't even know it was there. I was amazed at how easy I could move my arms. I thought how could a person live like this and not realize it? *It has been a constant struggle to even move all this time!*

As a side note, I had just experienced powerlessness. *Why can't I? What am I going to do? Please, God, help me!* That is powerlessness. But of course I was not even thinking about that! I had bigger issues going on here than worrying about writing some paper for some drug program. I stood up and paced around the apartment, in disbelief that the other four guys were still asleep! How could anybody sleep through all of that? Then, all of the sudden, I became so sleepy that I almost did not make it to my bed.

When I woke up, everyone was gone. I looked at the clock: 9:30 a.m. I was late for work. Everything looked lower again, like I was taller, just as it had when I came out of the woods delivered from cocaine. I was still amazed at how easy it was to move.

I stood in the shower, soaping up the washcloth and thinking about what had happened. I didn't have another vision. I was just recalling the memory of what the vision had looked like. (There is a huge difference between a vision and imagination.) I thought about those words, *"Forgive him, Father, for he knows not what he does,"* and another demon welled up inside of me. I didn't see anything at all this time, but as it came out, I hit my knees on the floor of the shower. I looked down, unable to tell how much water was pouring from the shower and how much was pouring from my eyes.

When I came out of the shower, there was no resistance to movement at all. The only analogy I can think of for it was—if you have ever thought you were about to pick up a heavy box, but when you went to lift it, it was empty. That's what every movement was like. When I grabbed my can of deodorant to put it on, I just slung it across the room. I thought, *Dear God, should I try to drive?*

I started driving carefully, and everything was fine until I got off of I-85 onto I-285. The traffic was heavy, so I would guess we were all moving at about 25–30 miles an hour. Once again, I thought about what had happened. When those words came to my mind, *"Forgive him, Father, for he knows not what he does,"* another one welled up inside of me, while at the same time I looked up into the sky beyond some clouds. Although I did not see anything other than the sky, there was this incredible, magnificent, terrifying, awe-inspiring power projected right at me, and yet I knew it was just the tip of the iceberg of what was beyond those clouds. I just dove to the right into the floorboard to get out of its way while this thing was coming out of my mouth.

Realizing How "Nothing" Everything Really Is

Once it was released, I heard myself whimpering like a little puppy while I was hiding in my floorboard, and then I remembered that I was driving! When I sat back up, my car was stopped in the middle of I-285. Cars were stopped in a big circle all around and people were just staring at me. I looked back at them and started yelling, "Don't look at me! I am nothing! And you're nothing! These cars are nothing!" I pointed at some large buildings and yelled, "And those buildings are nothing!" I waved my hands around as I yelled, "Everything is nothing!"

I started driving again, and as I pulled up beside those people and looked over at them they would look the other way, as if they were afraid of me, and I'd say things like, "That's okay! You're nothing! I'm nothing! Nothing matters compared to what is beyond those clouds!"

For Reflection . . .

I want to take a moment to make a point here. If I'd had any idea of why Jesus died on that cross or what salvation was, I would have been saved right there and that would have been it. I would have been born again right then. But I had no idea what these things meant. What

I knew at that point was that Jesus died on a cross, demons are real, and so is God. That's it. If I had ever read or heard that Jesus actually said, *"Forgive them, Father, for they know not what they do,"* I had no memory of it. At that point, I just thought it was something He said in a vision just for me at that time.

This is the point: It doesn't matter if a person is ready to be saved or not. Tell them *how to be saved* so that when the time comes they *can be.* Hosea 4:6 says, *"My people are destroyed for lack of knowledge."* How true that is! When I'm witnessing to someone who obviously is resistant, I'll say something like, "Okay, I know that you are not ready, but there is one thing that every person on planet earth needs to know."

I have never had anyone say, "No, I don't want to hear the one thing that every person on planet earth needs to know."

I'll say, "It's this one simple thing: Jesus Christ died on the cross to pay for your sins, and if the time ever comes when you want to turn to Him and leave your old life behind, then ask for that forgiveness that Jesus paid for. Ask Him to forgive you and to come into your life, and He will."

If you have ever shared the Gospel with someone who refused to pray with you, don't be discouraged. You just gave that person the most important information they could ever know—*how to be saved.* I wish I had known. It would have not only saved *me* but it would have saved a whole lot of people a whole lot of trouble.

A Visit from the Evil One

By the time I got to the cleaners, I was still blown away by what had happened. I thought, *I can't just walk into work like this! They are going to think I'm crazy and on drugs!* So I pulled into a shopping center, got out of my car, and walked around, trying to come to terms with just how "nothing" everything really was.

The day at work was pretty uneventful, except that I could certainly move a lot easier and everyone said that I looked much better than I had been. I didn't say a word about what had happened because I figured everyone would think I had lost my mind for sure. When it came time to go to group, I had no clue what I was going to say because I was supposed to present my first step in writing.

The group session started with the usual question, "Did anyone experience anything since we last met that we need to discuss before we move on?" One of the girls raised her hand and launched into this huge event that had happened in the girls' apartment the night before, which set the stage for the whole meeting. As we were leaving, the leader said that I could make my presentation the next night.

The apartment we stayed in had three bedrooms with five men. The house leader had the room in the middle, and on each side of him was a room with two men. We had our typical little meeting and went to bed.

The next thing I remember is I woke myself up screaming, and sat straight up in bed. I looked to the left and saw the house leader and the two men from the other room gathered at our bedroom door. I thought, *I wonder what's going on with them?* Then I looked over to my roommate's bed (the rich kid who was there under a false name) and saw him flapping back and forth in a very unnatural way. It was so fast and so violent that a person just couldn't flap back and forth like that. I remember thinking, *Now that looks like something out of an* Exorcist *movie!* Then I fell back onto the bed and did not wake up again until morning.

Once again, everyone was gone when I woke up, and once again, I was going to group totally unprepared. They asked the question, "Did anyone experience anything since we last met that we need to discuss before we move on?" The truck driver who had fallen on his knees on I-75 threw up his hand. He was white as a sheet and clearly troubled.

He said, "Last night, I had a dream that was so real I can still smell the swamp and feel the temperature of the air!" He said that he was walking through a swamp on a path about a foot wide. He knew that if he made one step to the right or left he would plunge into the water filled with terrifying creatures. He described the fog, trees, and moon and how it reminded him of a "Wolfman" movie, which really struck me because it was feeling like the "Wolfman" that had led me to turn myself in.

He said that as he was walking a wolf suddenly rose up out of the water, bit his leg, and tried to drag him into the swamp. It terrified him so much that when he awoke, he jumped out of bed and started kicking his leg to get it off. He paced back and forth once or twice, trying to gather his thoughts, and then his roommate (the doctor from the plane) started gurgling like he was drowning so he shook him awake.

The doctor said that he was having a dream that a dark shadow was pressing down on him like someone sitting on his chest. At the same time, this dark shadow had its hands around his neck, choking him to force his mouth open so it could flow down his throat. When his roommate shook him, it let go.

So both of them were out of bed, freaking out about what had just happened. They were making so much noise that the house leader came out of his bedroom to see what was going on. While they frantically tried to explain what happened, they heard me scream. They came to my doorway and saw the rich kid flapping back and forth on the bed.

The rich kid spoke up then with tears in his eyes. He said that he heard me scream and then something grabbed him. It was so strong that it started shaking him like a dish rag. He said that when it let go, he sat up and looked out of the window by my bed. He said the devil was looking in at him, and he heard a voice say, "I will get you the next time you are alone."

He said that he had called his family and begged them to come and get him, but they didn't believe him and refused. He started crying and asked us to promise him that we would never leave him alone and move him to another apartment. He asked us to gather his belongings for him or just throw them away. He said he would never step foot in that bedroom again.

I sat there speechless. Before this, good and evil had been some distant forces in my mind—like when those kids at Alto would pray, everything would go silent, and then people would start throwing things at them. That seemed like the "forces" of good and evil at battle, but now things were personal. I had experienced the struggle hearing that preacher at church. Then the "Randy" experience happened. I had seen Jesus Christ on a cross, saying, *"Forgive him, Father, for he knows not what he does,"* and now I had creatures coming out of me and actually staying in an empty apartment all day waiting for us to come back.

I guess they were watching while we had our meeting. They watched while we went to sleep and then tried to get us. It was mind-boggling, and something told me to be quiet. Somehow I just knew that this was a discussion that needed to quiet down as soon as possible—that we did not want to make this experience the focus of our attention. I felt as though I now knew some deep, dark secret that no one else on earth would possibly know or believe. Once again, the presentation of my first step was forgotten.

A day or two later, the phone rang at the dry cleaners. It was Dani. "I'm having the baby!" She wasn't due for at least two more months.

I said, "Do you want me to come and get you?"

She said, "I'm having the baby right now!"

I said, "Dial 9-1-1!"

She said, "I can't, you stupid idiot! You're on the phone!"

I said, "Hang up and call them!"

She screamed, "Oh no! There's its head!"

22

"We're Making Progress Now"

HUNG UP the phone and immediately called 9-1-1 in case Dani could not and gave them the address and took off. I arrived at the same time the ambulance did. By the time we got there, Dani had already delivered our baby boy: Gregory Shane Cole, 4 pounds, 8 ounces, born September 1, 1987. The birth certificate states that he was delivered by Dani Cole. What a woman!

Being premature, he spent a few days in the hospital but was fine. I never had to present my first step because everyone recognized immediately that I'd had a "breakthrough," as they called it. I couldn't help myself. I just had to ask the leader, "So you reckon that thing in my brain came unstuck?"

He said, "Well, whatever has happened, you're making progress now."

"The Loneliest Person I Ever Met"

I was surprised by some of the things that the people in the group told me—that they had actually gone to the leadership and asked that I be released from the program because they were afraid of me. I was blown away. Why in the world would anyone be afraid of me? I was the nicest guy I ever met!

One of them said that every time I walked into the room, he immediately wanted to get high, and with that several nodded their heads in agreement. When I thought about it that actually made sense. I'd always wondered how I could walk into a prison dorm full of 100 strangers who all looked exactly alike with shaved heads and dressed in prison uniforms and be connected to the main drug dealer literally within minutes. It had become clear that it was a spiritual thing. "My demons knew their demons."

Now, you may be thinking, *Okay, Pastor Grant. You experienced deliverance, so now you're one of those guys who thinks he sees a demon behind every tree!* Well, I want you to know it is not that way at all. Demons are *everywhere*— not just behind trees.

The objective of this SAFE recovery program was that by the time you completed the 28-day regimen you would have completed the fourth step and be set up to work the rest of the 12-step program successfully for the rest of your life. By this time, we were on step four, but the problem was, I really didn't understand step one, which is, "I accept that I am powerless over my addiction and my life has become unmanageable."

As I said before, I knew my life had become unmanageable, but now that I had been delivered, I should be able to "manage" everything just fine. I mean, those demons must have been the problem all along. Right? *I* certainly couldn't have been the problem.

As for this "powerlessness" business, I still didn't pick up on the fact that it was that confession to God that "I could not do it" and that cry for "help" that had opened the door for God to move in my life in the first place. It seemed to me that with those demons gone, I was back in control. *They* were the problem.

Step two was: "I came to believe that there was a power greater than myself that could restore me to sanity." Now, that one I got. There was definitely a Power greater than myself that could do anything He wanted to. Of that I had no doubt. I just hoped that if He ever "peeked" at me again from behind a cloud I wasn't driving any faster on I-285 or a whole bunch of us were apt to be killed!

Then the third step was: "I made a conscious decision to turn my life and will over to the care of God as I understood Him." I don't even remember our working on that one. Personally, I don't believe that man has the wisdom to write the 12 steps. I believe they are a gift from God, and the fact that man has so twisted them is just further proof that they didn't originate in man.

People have taken "God as I understood Him" to mean that He can be any old higher power that you want to trust in—another religion or something really kooky such as a tree, a door knob, or the group itself. The fact is, I have the power to "chop down the tree" or "turn the door knob," and the group is supposed to realize we are all "powerless," so how can any of those things be a *higher power*?

We are to turn our lives over to "God." Big G. There's only one, and the truth is we are all relating to God as we understand Him. That does not change who He is. He is the same yesterday, today, and forever. It is our understanding of Him that is at different levels. It is my prayer that I understand Him more every day, and most days that is exactly what happens. Praise God! Why people are so afraid to say that Jesus Christ is the Way, the Truth, and the Life and that no one comes to the Father except by Him is beyond me.

So even though no one ever helped us with step three, we ended up on step four, where we were to "make a searching and fearless moral inventory of ourselves." One of the classes was really great. The leader challenged the class to name one single character defect that did not come from self-will.

Many are self-explanatory—selfishness, self-centeredness, self-pity, etc. Of course, stealing, lying, cheating, and all addictions result from self-will. I certainly wasn't shooting dope to change the way *you* feel. It was to change the way *I* feel. As a matter of fact, there is only one reason any person gets high—to change the way they feel. See, if you do any drug and it does not change the way you feel, then you just got ripped off. The question for an addict should be, "Why do I so desperately want to change the way I feel?"

The way you know you're in self-will is when you think or say, "I," "me," "my," or "mine." Pretty simple.

Someone called out, "Anger is one. I'm angry because someone else did something."

The leader responded, "There is that word 'I.'" And the reason I'm angry is that whatever they did affected "me." Then we talked about anger for a while. The most severe anger is guilt because then "I'm" angry at "me."

Then someone said, "Loneliness is not from self-will because you're focused on the person you miss—not on yourself."

The leader said, "Say that in the first person and then you'll understand."

The person said, "'I'm focused on the person I miss.' Okay, I see now."

Then I spoke up and said, "You know, that is the only character defect we have talked about that I don't have." (By that time the dry erase board was covered with them.)

One of the guys spoke up and said, "I don't believe that."

I said, "No, I'm serious. I've never been lonely in my life—not even when I'm alone. I don't even know what it feels like."

Then another guy said, "Grant, you may be the loneliest person I've ever met." I was stunned.

Then another guy said, "Well, I know I'm lonely." He grabbed his chest and said, "The emptiness I feel is almost unbearable at times!"

The revelation hit me so hard that it had to be God! All of a sudden, I realized that the unbearable emptiness I felt was not the desire for drugs! It was loneliness! I had been covering up the feeling of loneliness with the feeling of drugs so long that I thought the emptiness I felt when I came down off the drugs was the result of not having drugs. That's why I had always suspected that God created me as a drug addict—because that feeling never went away. I thought that I was born with a desire to do drugs—that I needed them to be complete, whole, and full. But it was loneliness!

Right then and there on the spot I was having an identity crisis. As with most drug addicts I had become a legend in my own mind. I was a tough guy. I was an ex-convict. I couldn't be lonely! I was a modern-day Al

Capone, and you know Al Capone wasn't lonely! Man, I'd had demons in me! I was bad to the bone! You mean to tell me I was nothing but a weak little wimpy drug addict who couldn't handle being lonely?

Oh, No! You mean to tell me that I got Karen busted. You mean to tell me that my son has grown up without me. That I left my ex-wife out there by herself. That I have broken my parents' hearts. That I have spent years of my life in prison. That right now I've got Dani and a little bitty baby boy who need me, and I'm not there because I'm in this drug program . . . all because I'm lonely!

"How Can A Man Change Self-Will?"

I got up, walked out of that program, went and got me a shot of dope, and spent the night with Dani and Shane. I spent the whole night telling Dani about how all character defects come from self-will. I was drawing all of these circles on paper and thinking about how our behavior is on the outside—that I had been trying to change my behavior when that wasn't even the problem. Even society had been trying to change my behavior by putting me in prison, when in fact my behavior was controlled by this severe feeling of loneliness. But that wasn't the real root problem, either. It was this stinking "self-will" at the center of it all, and how could a man change his will? That was the question.

The next day I went back to the program and asked, "How do you change your self-will?"

The leader said, "You have to move into self-worth."

"Okay, what is that?"

"You have to realize that you're only a part of things and not the thing itself. You're like a grain of sand on a beach—one of many, but a good grain of sand."

I thought, *You have got to be kidding me. What a bunch of mumbo-jumbo!* Oh, I understood that I was just a part of things, like a grain of sand, but I was not a "good" little grain of sand. I was a dirty, rotten, no good, self-centered, lonely grain of sand. If I had only known how close I was to salvation at that moment.

For Reflection . . .

See, what these people understood about self-will is absolutely true. You can trace back every character defect to "self-will." It is what the Bible refers to as your sinful nature or "flesh." We all have it. Billy Graham refers to sin as a "disease in your heart." A disease is a "destructive process at work in a living organism." So when people call drug addiction a disease, by definition that is correct. It is a sin that is a "destructive process in a living organism," in this case that living organism was me. The problem was with my interpretation of it, and I've seen many people interpret it the same way.

When you are told that you have a disease, there is a tendency to think you have no responsibility in the matter. As a matter of fact, my attitude was that society doesn't persecute someone for having cancer or leukemia, so why were they persecuting me? There was nothing I could do about it (and truly there's not), but God has made a way for you and me to be healed and delivered.

And self-worth is involved in our "recovery" from the disease of sin. Our self-worth is that we are a sinner and need a Savior. The cure for the disease is that God loves us so much that He gave His only begotten Son to die on a cross to pay for all of those things we have done and experienced in the flesh.

Moving from Sinful Self-Will to Self-Worth

So how do we move from sinful self-will to self-worth? Romans 2:4 says that it is by the goodness of God that we are led to repentance. To repent means to " return" or *turn away from*, so when we become sick and tired of self-will and all of the loneliness, greed, lust, anger, resentment, and sin that go along with it, then we should pray because the goodness of God is what has led us to that place. When you reach that place, ask Him to forgive you because Jesus Christ died on the cross to pay for your sins. Ask Him to come into your life, and He will change your will. It is such a radical change that it is referred to as being *"born again."*

Second Corinthians 5:17 says, *"If any man be in Christ, he is a new creation. Old things pass away, and behold, all things become new."* That *"new creation,"* that *"born-again"* experience, takes place when the Holy Spirit of God comes into your life and sets you free from that self-will, and all the character defects will begin to *"pass away, and behold, all things become new."*

And what are the "things" that become new? Your self-will, which is being crucified and replaced with God's will. Have you ever noticed that God's will is *always* the opposite of self-will? God says that it is better to give than to receive. To love even your enemies. To do good to those who despitefully use you and persecute you. Love the Lord your God with all of your heart, soul, and mind, and love your neighbor as yourself.

This new focus on God's will, instead of your own, will bring with it *"new"* characteristics, referred to as the fruit of the Spirit. The selfishness of your self-will is replaced with the *"love"* of God. Your misery, depression, and loneliness are replaced with the *"joy"* of the Spirit. Your hatred, anger, and fear are replaced with a *"peace"* that surpasses understanding. Your anxiety and resentment are replaced with *"patience."* You become *"kind"* and *"good"* and generous to others. You become *"faithful,"* and others will begin to depend upon you instead of you always depending on others. You will become *"gentle"* and gain *"self-control,"* victory over self-will. And the Bible says, *"Against such there is no law."* Oh, how wonderful it is to be set free from the law!

Seeing the Dream as a Nightmare

`One of the girls in group that night started pitching a fit because she was not allowed to see her husband while I had gone to spend the night with Dani and Shane. It just wasn't fair! I said, "You're right." I went and packed up my stuff and left the program. I had a wife and baby to take care of.

Dani was living with a friend at the time, so of course we needed to get our own place to live. But I was broke. I was recovery-poor. I was still working at the cleaners, still empty on the inside, which I now understood to be loneliness. I had no idea what to do about it, because apparently my loneliness had no bearing on whether I was alone or with a thousand people. I needed money fast and I needed to self-medicate, so I just did what I had always done. I came up with a new plan, but there was a problem.

In the short time I was in that program, everyone seemed to have lost their minds. When I went over to a customer's house I noticed that his car was all crashed in on the side. Ronnie and his wife told me that he had nodded off while driving and had run into a guardrail. They had a little boy about two years old. I asked where he was while this was going on, and they just looked at me like that was a strange question. They said, "Well, he was in his car seat. He was fine."

I sat them down and had a heart-to-heart talk with them about how maybe it was time they quit. "I mean, you guys are married, and you have a child. You need to settle down."

They said, "Well, you and Dani just had a baby!"

I said, "I know. And you're right. We all need to quit." So I left without selling them anything.

I went to the apartment of another customer, who lived on the second story. As I walked up the steps, I saw broken glass all over the sidewalk, and when I looked up I saw that their window had been broken out. They were really excited to see me, and their two children were running wild around the apartment as always. You could tell they were ready to get down to business.

I said, "What happened to the window?"

The husband laughed and said, "Linda got mad at me last night and snatched the phone off the wall and threw it at me. I ducked and it went right through the window!"

And she said, "Yeah, but Tony grabbed that television and threw it on top of me while I was sitting in that recliner!" I looked over and saw about a 27" TV sitting on the cabinet.

I tried to picture the scene that must have taken place. I just couldn't imagine a man picking up a 27" television and throwing it on top of his wife! I asked, "Where were the children?"

Tony said, "Oh, they were in bed."

And Linda snapped back, "No, they weren't!" and they started arguing again.

I said, "Look, you guys need to quit this stuff. Y'all need to settle down! I can't imagine you throwing that television on top of her!"

She said, "Yeah, he picked that thing up over his head and slammed it down on me!"

With that, I walked out the door, and as far as I can remember, I never went back.

I'd had a dream that I was going to make life better for all of us—that we were all going to smoke a little, joke a little, have a good time, and make plenty of money on the side; that we would be free to spend more time with our wives and children because of all the easy money we were going to make. But now it seemed that my dream had become a nightmare. Or had it been a nightmare all along, but I just couldn't see it until now? Maybe they had not just lost their minds. Maybe I had just lost my demons.

This scenario played itself out time after time. I found myself in a place where I could give every customer at least 10 reasons why they should not buy drugs from me and give myself 10 reasons why I shouldn't sell them for my sake, my freedom, and my family.

I kept thinking about the words of Jesus, *"Forgive him, Father, for he knows not what he does."* Had I been blind all this time? It sure "looked" like it.

While thinking on all these things as I walked through the dry cleaners, I stopped and said to myself, "That's it. I'm done. I quit." At that exact moment, the drive-through bell rang, and I knew that something was about to happen.

There was no logical, natural reason to think that. The drive-through bell constantly rang at the cleaners. It was the busiest cleaners I've seen to this day. No this was spiritual. I knew when I heard the sound of that bell that it was ringing for me, and something big was going to happen. Really big.

And it did.

"When an unclean spirit goes out of a man, he goes through dry places, seeking rest, and finds none. Then he says, 'I will return to my house from which I came.' And when he comes, he finds it empty, swept, and put in order. Then he goes and takes with him seven other spirits more wicked than himself, and they enter and dwell there; and the last state of that man is worse than the first. So shall it also be with this wicked generation." (Matthew 12:43-45)

23

Crossroads

THERE WAS A group of criminals in the South who had become known as the Dixie Mafia. It was not a self proclaimed title by any means. Some believe they were a myth, and they would be the first to tell you there was no such thing, but they were very real. It was of group of older men, most of whom were third or fourth generation criminals. Of course, they raised their children with the expectation they would carry on the family business. They were much like a family in the sense that they were a close-knit circle, so they didn't need to bring in new people. Thus the name Dixie Mafia.

Some of the families' roots were in bootlegging back during Prohibition. There was a time when they traveled the county "punching safes" until the newer generation of safes became more trouble than they were worth. They were counterfeiters until the Federal Reserve began printing bills so advanced that it became cost-prohibitive. Where the money went, they went, and in the 1980s, the money was in meth.

Since they were in it for the money and not for the high, they had their wits about them. They weren't diving through grocery store windows thinking the police were after them and so forth, so they were a force to be reckoned with. The same would not hold true for the next generation they were attempting to raise up in a new environment. Their kids were getting into the whole drug scene and all that went with it.

Dealing with the Dixie Mafia

One father-and-son team became well-known. They were the focus of a bust which had all the elements of a good story, so it became well-publicized. They owned a used car lot, which was a popular front used by these old men. It gave them a legal appearance as they drove cars from one location to another, but the business was not about the sale of cars. It was about what was *in* the cars.

Big John and his son, Little John, had a car lot across from a very large and well-known church in the area. The FBI set up surveillance in the bell tower of the church where they had a great view of the lot and everything coming and going. When you coupled that unusual circumstance with a very large drug bust of a father-and-son team, you had the makings of a great story, and the media ran with it.

After they were released from prison, Little John and I ended up making a connection, but he was just like the rest of us: He loved the high. And because of the people his father was involved with, there was plenty to get high on. When his paranoia set in, he always thought the police were in some high place watching. I always figured that came from the church bell tower incident.

Little John kept telling me that the police had set up surveillance in a house up on a hill above where he lived and had been watching him with binoculars. When I told him he was just paranoid, he dragged me out into the yard, handed me a pair of binoculars, and told me to look up at the house. When I focused in on it, sure enough, standing right in the big front window of the house was a man with a pair of binoculars, looking right at me looking right at him. It scared the daylights out of me!

A month or so later, a man out walking his dog saw Big John and said, "I kept seeing your son out in the back yard watching me with a pair of binoculars, so I went and got a pair of binoculars so I could watch him, too!" He laughed and just kept walking.

One day, Little John came to the dry cleaners. We were standing outside talking when all of the sudden some guy came out of nowhere and hit him in the back of the head with an iron pipe so hard he fell to his knees. Then the guy's girlfriend came around the corner with a baseball bat and was about to attack Little John from the other direction. I grabbed the baseball bat from her and pushed her away before she had a chance to hit him.

When I turned around, the guy had Little John in a headlock, and Little John was stabbing him in the ribs with a knife. I was amazed at how controlled and calm he was. Little John could have easily been killing the guy, but he just stabbed him enough to make him let go.

Now Little John's father had a reputation for cutting people. He carried a straight razor and had once cut a man so fast that he didn't even realize it until his intestines were falling out. So I figured like father, like son. Fearing I was about to have a murder take place right there in the dry cleaners parking lot, I snatched the knife out of Little John's hand. About that time, I looked up and saw my dad and another businessman who owned a dry cleaners come walking out of the back door, about 70 feet from where all of this was happening. They took one look at that scene and walked right back in the door.

Yes, things were not as they used to be. This was all part of what brought me to the place where I said, "That's it. I'm done. I quit," and then the drive-through bell rang. I walked up, and there was Little John at the drive-through.

He said, "I've talked to Big John. They want to meet you. Come to the house when you get off work," and then he just drove away.

The words that got me were, "They want to meet you." I knew right then that Little John had opened a door where all of my dreams could come true. As I walked back to press clothes, I felt very much like the day I walked out of the Douglas County Federal Jail with a Bible in one hand

and the formula to manufacture meth in the other. I was at a crossroads, and I knew that it was no accident.

It was just too much to resist. I had to go check it out. When I went over there, it was as if I had known them all my life. They welcomed me in. Big John was there, of course, and I met his wife Martha. There was a really old man there named Jim who was pretty much blind. There was another man there who could apparently steal anything from anybody at any time.

To prove the point, they told me a story of how he had once stolen a house. No joke. I guess it was some historical house that had already been scheduled for relocation so it had been raised off its foundation and prepared for transport. This man went and stole the heavy equipment necessary and then stole the house in the middle of the night—not for any profit because no one had any use for it. The best I could tell, he stole it to prove the point that there was nothing too big for him to steal. In other words, if you needed something stolen, he was your man.

I learned a lot of stories about Little John's childhood—like the one about how when he was a little boy Little John walked up to the local hardware store, saw a Red Flyer wagon, and wanted to buy it. The man at the counter said something to the effect of, "That wagon costs a lot of money, son."

To that, Little John said, "No problem. My dad has plenty of money drying on the line right now. He has piles of money at our house as big as this counter!"

After a while, we finally got down to business. They showed me a bag of meth, and when I checked it out, it was that "cold shake" from years before. As far as I was concerned, there had never been any better. This was no homemade stuff. In my estimation, this had "biochemist from Berkley University" written all over it. If there was ever a time to quit, it certainly wasn't now.

I said, "Oh, man! I was not expecting to cop. I have no real money with me."

They said, "No problem. Little John has vouched for you. Take what you want, and let us know when you have the money to do it again." I was off and running, and Big John and I became very close very fast.

He still loved to sell cars (well, anything, for that matter), but they would not issue him a business license due to the episode I mentioned above. His new front was that of a house painter. He would leave the house in the morning dressed in clothes covered in paint and drive a van just like a painter would, but it wasn't paint in those cans. We would ride around, and he shared with me his concerns about the kids—not just his, but other older guys in the business who still had car lots as a front. They had raised their kids to be in their business, but this whole drug thing was getting the best of them. They were using far too much, and spending way too much money. The whole thing was getting out of hand.

Of course, I still had my concerns about how my customers seemed to have lost it also. Everybody except Fat Bear. One day, I told Fat Bear, "Man, you're the only one who hasn't changed on me!"

He said, "It's interesting you said that," and showed me an award that was just presented to him at a high school reunion. Fat Bear had been voted the "Most Unchanged Person Since Graduation."

But of course, the devil had an answer to this dilemma also. I met a man named Roger, and when we started talking, it was as though I was meeting myself. He said he felt the same way. He talked about how whenever he found a good connection they would often shut down the rest of their business, realizing that he was the only customer they needed. I couldn't count how many times that had happened to me.

The great thing was that his customer base was centered downtown in the Buckhead and North Druid Hills areas, where I was not known.

And it wasn't just him. There were other high-level dealers from Cartersville, Adairsville, and other places where I was not known. The money was flowing like never before. First it was freezer bags full, then briefcases, and pretty soon suitcases.

"Did I Just Confess that I've been Worshipping the Devil All these Years?"

Right in the middle of all this, an old friend walked through the door of the cleaners—Steve, the old marijuana guy from years before. Remember how I said when Tommy told me that Steve had become a preacher I didn't believe it. The first thing I noticed was how clean cut and young he looked. The second thing I noticed was those eyes. They seemed to burn a hole right through me. I thought, *Oh, boy! He has gotten into something weird!*

He told me that he had become a pastor of a church called the Milford Church of God. I thought, *Why is he telling me this stuff? It can't be true!*

Then he added, "Are you clean?" Of course I told him I was, but I knew those eyes could see right through me. Drugs are the only sin I know that will take a person so low that they will look into your eyes and tell you a lie, even when they know, that you know, they are lying.

To get rid of him, I told him that if I ever decided to go to church, it would be to a church called Mt. Paran Church of God that I had visited while I was in the SAFE recovery program (which was true).

He said, "Well, Grant, that's who we are. The Church of God. They are Mt. Paran Church of God, and we are the Milford Church of God. We are the same denomination"

I was thinking, *Why won't this guy leave me alone? Aren't all churches, "churches of God"?* I had no idea that Church of God was a denomination or even what *denomination* meant. I didn't even like the sound of the word "denomination," and his eyes were freaking me out.

He talked me into going to lunch, which was a bad mistake. Now I was sitting directly across from him, face to face, eye to eye, at a small table in Wendy's. I kept thinking, *I wish there was a sun visor I could pull down to block the light from his eyes.* I almost wore a blister on my backside because I was shifting back and forth in my seat so much! Man, I sure was glad when that lunch was over.

Now there's only one problem with a suitcase full of money. You can't really buy much without drawing attention to yourself. So, of course, I came up with a plan. While it wouldn't be cool to pay cash for a house when you worked as a laborer at a dry cleaners, I could get away with buying a mobile home. Remember my old friend Richard? Well he and a friend of his had bought a mountain up in Emerson and built their dream homes up there. I figured I'd get them to sell me some land for cash, move the mobile home up there, and then slowly build a dream home for Dani and me.

So I bought a mobile home in Kennesaw. Dani, Shane, Jason (Dani's son from her previous marriage) and I moved in, and she was pregnant again. This time, we were going to have a baby girl. Shane was only 9 months old. Both times before when I was to become a father, a war had broken out between the devil and me, and this time was no different.

I had reached the point where I had blown every vein in my body. For some reason, I couldn't bring myself to settle with snorting the meth or just simply eating it. It was like I was addicted to the needle or something. I would try and try to get a vein. The blood would coagulate, and I'd have to throw the shot away. Sometimes I would spend literally hours and waste hundreds of dollars' worth of meth trying to inject some into my body.

On one such morning, I was in the bathroom, frantically trying to do a shot. I was late for work, which made me feel guilty. As I threw away shot after shot, I thought about how selfish I was to be wasting money on myself like that when we were about to have another baby. I had blood running down both arms, and I was cussing myself and asking God, "What is wrong with me?"

At that moment, I heard a voice say, "Bow down. Worship me, and you can do that shot." I knew exactly who and what that was—but I had no idea that it was attempting to fulfill Mathew12:44-45 and that the unclean spirit was trying to return from which it came, and I'm sure he had seven more spirits right along with him. All I knew was that I was at a crossroads again, and this time I knew my very soul was at stake. I was not going to take the wrong turn this time, but I was not prepared for the words that came out of my mouth.

I said, "You mean to tell me that I have served you all these years, and you have the power to let me do this shot, and you have withheld it from me? That's it! I will find a way to get away from you!" I was so mad that I kicked the bathroom door open, and as I marched out of the house, I was just a-cussing the devil, telling him how stupid he was for revealing himself like that, because this was *it* for me—I was done! I would find a way out from under him if it was the last thing I ever did.

As I drove up the road on my way to work and began to calm down, I thought, *Did I just confess that I have been serving the devil all these years?*

24

The "Scientology Rundown"

So that whole day at work I wondered how many people had actually accepted the devil's invitation and had never told anyone. I mean, surely the devil had extended that invitation in one form or another to many. I had no illusions that I was any big shot in the grand scope of things. If the devil offered little ole me some type of deal, then what about the leaders of those drug cartels? What about some of these old men I was dealing with? What about their ancestors?

Exiting the Highway to Hell

What about some of those famous rock musicians? I loved the hard-driving music of the hard rock band AC/DC. One night, Dani and I poured liquid LSD into a syringe full of meth and shot it right before going into an AC/DC concert. The show began with the lowering of a giant golden bell over the stage. A man walked out on stage and began hitting the bell as the band sang the song *Hell's Bells*. I had never noticed that the song was actually a calling together of demons. And not just demons. The lyrics go: "If you're a friend of evil, you're a friend of mine, Hell's Bells!"

We had seats close to one of the many entrances to the auditorium at the Omni. While the bell was ringing and the stage was commanding most of the people's attention, a guy dressed like the grim reaper walked out of the breezeway and raised his hands out over the crowd, obviously praying over everyone or conjuring. I expected a spotlight to shine on him as part of the show, but it never did. I looked around, and there was a grim reaper at every entrance, praying over the crowd. When the song was over, the reapers slipped quietly back into the darkness.

As I watched Angus Young, the band's guitar player, it was obvious to me that the way he continuously contorted his body was not natural by any standards. The climax of the concert was the song *Highway to Hell*. The crowd of 18,000 now stood on their seats with both hands high in the air and singing with all of their might: *"No Stop Signs, Speed Limit, Nobody's gonna slow me down, Like a wheel, Gonna spin it, Nobody's gonna mess me around, Hey Satan, Paid my dues, Playin' in a rockin' band, Hey Mama, Look at me, I'm on my way to the promised land, I'm on the highway to hell!"*

Right then, I grabbed Dani and pulled her down in the floor between the seats, yelling, "Not us, honey, not us! I'm sorry I brought us into this place!" She nodded with me in agreement. We had brought Dani's brother, Todd, with us, and I pulled him down there, too.

There are some things you just don't do, and knowingly making an agreement with the devil is one of them. I had been doing drugs so long that the very thought of life without them was beyond my comprehension, but the words of Jesus kept coming to mind: *"Forgive him, Father, for he knows not what he does."*

Well, Jesus couldn't honestly say that of me anymore.

A Dianetics Detour

I may have been blind, but I was beginning to see. It was time to get out, and get out fast. When I went home that night and looked through the mail, there was an advertisement for a new drug program! I stood there looking at it and thought, *This has to be God!* The timing was perfect, and how would anybody else know that I was ready to quit? (I'd forgotten about the devil.)

The program was called the "Scientology Rundown." *Well, that sounds scientific!* When I arrived at the Scientology organization on Ponce De Leon, it was nothing like I had expected. All these people were walking around with little while collars on like Catholic priests wear, and I thought, *Science and religion. What a great combination! The best of both worlds!*

The place had the atmosphere of a doctor's office, church, huge library, and media center all rolled into one. When I informed them that I was there for the drug program, they said that I had to be prepped before I could begin. I had to read this book and take a course before I could experience the great Scientology Rundown that would set me free.

The first book to read was *Dianetics* by L. Ron Hubbard. He taught that every human being was born perfect, and that it was our environment that messed us up. Our brains, he said, were like a calculator that always comes up with the right answer. If you were to tape down the 7 key on a calculator, though, then every answer would be wrong. The wrong answer was no reflection on the calculator; the problem was with the person who taped down the 7.

So if I had a problem, it was no reflection on me. We just had to figure out why my 7 key was stuck, so to speak, and fix it. Then I would be successful like John Travolta or Tom Cruise who, among others in the rich and famous set, owed their success to L. Ron Hubbard. You see, they, too, at one time had their button stuck, but of course most people would never know about it because all of your secrets are safe with Scientology.

They said that most of the problems a person experiences are just a matter of false beliefs and could be fixed by simply applying truth. In my case, a particular course for $5,000 would really help prepare me for the "Rundown," which would set me free. Then there was a seminar for $1,500, and a weekend course for $2,500, etc., etc., etc.

I'm not going to say too much about their teaching. If you know the Word of God, then you would quickly recognize Scientology as just another New Age form of Universalism but one that is packaged in a very unique way. If you do not know the Word of God, the teaching does have the power to deceive, and I want no part of that.

I gave those people at least $30,000, and they knew that I was dealing drugs to pay for it. But that was okay with them because in Scientology there are no absolute truths. They have a formula so you can figure out just how right or wrong something is on a "sliding scale," so taking my drug money was justified according to their beliefs. I fell for it hook, line, and sinker.

For Reflection . . .

When treasury agents are trained to detect a counterfeit bill, they are not taught what counterfeit bills look like because there can be millions of different kinds. A treasury agent is taught to recognize the true bill. They become experts on the exact color, design, texture, and type of paper a true bill is made of so they can easily spot a counterfeit.

That is why it is so important that we learn *"the truth."* The devil has millions of lies out there, but once you become an expert on *"the truth,"* they are easy to recognize. For example, if there is no absolute truth, then there is *no* truth. Truth is absolute by its very definition. Oh, how Scientology loves to redefine things.

Josh McDowell, a great teacher (not Scientologist), defines truth like this: Truth means to adhere to or to coincide with the original. For example, if you go to the grocery store to buy a liter of Cola, then how do you know if it is a "true" liter of Coca Cola? The way to test it is to compare it to the original liter at the Department of Weights and Measures in Paris, France. If the liter of Coca Cola adheres to and coincides with the original liter, then it is a true liter. If it does not, then it is false.

I teach this principle in prisons this way: Let's say that shouting "Hallelujah" was against the law. So I shout "Hallelujah," and the police kick the door down and ask, "Who just shouted 'Hallelujah'?"

If I answer, "Not me. I said, 'Tim Buck to ya!'" then I just lied because what I just said did not adhere to and coincide with what I originally said

John 1:1 says, *"In the beginning was the Word, and the Word was with God, and the Word was God"* . . . *"and the Word became flesh"* (verse 14).

So Jesus Christ, *"the Word became flesh,"* is the original. That is why He could say, *"I am the way, the **truth**, and the life. No one comes to the Father except through Me"* (John 14:7, emphasis added). So if I want to know spiritual truth, then I compare it to the original Word—what is referred to as the Bible. If it adheres to and coincides with the Word of God, then it is true. If it does not, then it is false.

It is amazing how someone will discover some ruins or dig up some relic and present it as though it proves the Bible is true. No, it doesn't. They have it backward. The Bibles proves what that thing is they just discovered.

When people say they have made some new discovery that proves that something in the Bible is not true, that is the epitome of stupidity. That would be like someone marching into the Department of Weights and Measurements and demanding that they make a public apology because he found a liter bottle of Coca Cola at Walmart that was different from the original liter that has set the standard since the beginning.

The Heat is On

Of course, I did not understand any of this. I was dry cleaning 12 hours a day, running a drug business 24 hours a day, studying Scientology, and trying to work my way up the "Bridge" so that not only would I be a "clear" in this lifetime but I would become like God, after a few more lifetimes. (Don't ask—it's a Scientology thing!) All the while, I was trying to maintain a relationship with my sons, be a husband to Dani, and now our new miracle baby, Chelsi, who was born premature on March 23, 1989, at 2 pounds, 10 ounces, so she needed much attention.

Once again, things began to spin out of control. One night as I was walking out of the dry cleaners about to do a deal, I saw this huge, clean-cut, nicely dressed guy coming up on me. He pulled out a pistol. I thought he was an undercover policeman, so I didn't go for my gun. Then a car with three masked bandits came flying up with shotguns and Uzis and proceeded to rob me.

I had heard of a crew that had been going around robbing drug dealers, but they hadn't hit anyone in my circle. I figured this was probably that crew. I was out of my mind. I was looking at this guy, who had to be at least 6'5" and huge, and I don't mean fat. He had a .45 pointed right at me, and I just started cussing him out.

I said, "You guys are just a bunch of sorry so-and-so's who don't have enough business about yourselves so you have to go around robbing people!" I pulled a small personal bag of marijuana and a wad of cash out of my front pocket and handed it to him.

Then, out of my mind once more, I started thinking about how that just happened to be the best marijuana I had ever smoked in my 22 years of smoking marijuana and here these people just walked up and took it! So I started cursing him out some more as I pulled a personal bag of meth out of one pocket and shoved it in his face. I had a leather pouch of cash in the back of my pants, chained to my waist, and quite a bit of meth ready to distribute, but I stopped right there without giving it to them and said, "That's it!" as I pointed my finger in his face.

I looked over at the skinny guy in a mask with a sawed-off shotgun. I could tell he had greasy, sandy-blond hair and pock marks from bad acne on his forehead. I looked him straight in the eye and said, "That's it!" They all got in their car and took off.

I turned to the person I was about to do a deal with, who was petrified, and told him off. Then I went over to Big John's and told him all that had happened.

He said, "Well, I can tell you one thing: That was not the crew that has been robbing these other dealers. I know the man who brought that crew into town to straighten out a situation, and they have decided to stay and take down some more scores to make the trip worth their while. If that crew had taken you down, you wouldn't have had a chance to say anything.

They would have beat you down, stripped you clean, and taken everything you had. No professionals are going to leave a mark with a wallet!"

I said, "Well, somebody is running their mouth, so just be careful. If they know about me, they may know about you."

The next day, Big John's curiosity got the best of him, so he went over to the house of the man he knew had brought the crew in. He said as soon as he walked in, he knew it was them. There sat a huge, clean-cut guy on the couch with two other men. Then he looked into the kitchen and saw a tall, skinny guy with greasy-looking, sandy-blond hair and a pock-marked face. The man didn't realize I was in business with Big John and apologized for robbing me!

I said, "Well, did they offer to give you my money back?"

Big John said, "You need to let that go and be thankful it wasn't worse, and whatever you do, don't be telling people you cussed those men out." Of course, I had a few choice words about that. He said, "Listen, the key to every smooth robbery is intimidation and fear. If you attack these men's reputation, then they will come back and hurt you to prove a point. They won't have any choice, and it will be your fault." I didn't like it, but I let it go.

One of Big John's partners, Bobby, who had a car lot and much to do with the meth business, was into surveillance equipment. He decided to use the same tactics against the police that they used against us. Little did I know they had me under surveillance also. There was a new person I had allowed into my circle who had introduced me to Roger, who was making me a fortune. Bobby's daughter presented me with a recording of the new person's telephone, which they had tapped.

Don't ask me how, but she had not only a recording of these people talking to what sounded like the police but also the tones from the number they dialed. When you held the recording device up to another device she had, it would dial the number based on the sounds. Sure enough, it dialed the police, but not just any police. It was the same department of the same cop (Officer Relentless) who had sent me to prison the last time.

Of course, I immediately told this new person that I had quit the business, warned Roger about him, and never went back over there. Now I knew the heat was on.

If I could just hold on a little bit longer I would be ready for the great "Scientology Rundown" and be set free!

By now, we had moved Cole's Cleaners to a shopping center. I was meeting several people out in front of an Ingles grocery store. One had ordered a couple of ounces of meth, but when I went out to his car, all he had money for was one ounce. So I slipped the other ounce down the front of my pants and started walking down the sidewalk toward the cleaners.

Just as I was about to walk in the door, a van swerved up and a bunch of policemen jumped out, yelling for me to put my hands up against the wall. I looked over, and more police cars were coming from the back. Cole's customers who had pretty much watched me grow up were pulling in, watching all of this go down, and I was thinking, *My poor old parents are going to be so embarrassed.*

The normal procedure for a search and pat-down is that they have you put your hands against the wall and pull your feet back so you are leaning against your hands, which makes it far more difficult for you to attempt any fast moves. Then one police officer stands behind you and frisks you down, which includes reaching around the front of your waist and checking your crotch area, just as they had done that night at the bowling alley when they easily found the pouch full of dope that God had miraculously placed there.

So here I stood with an ounce of meth down my pants, which I had placed there this time, being arrested by the same cops who found the last bag. It should have been easy to find, but so many policemen were crowded around me. One stood to my right and slid his left hand into my right pocket, naturally pulling away from my crotch, and another stood on my left side, sliding his right hand into my left pocket, which naturally caused him to pull away from my crotch. Another stood behind me, emptying my back pockets.

All three of them came out of my pockets with fists full of cash (and a little personal dope), which seemed to cause a lot of excitement. These three officers took the money over and placed it on the hood of a police car and started to count it all, while another officer pulled my hands behind my back and put cuffs on me. They had been so rough emptying my pockets that it had pulled my fly open.

There I stood, with my hands cuffed behind my back, and an ounce of meth hanging out of my fly. I kid you not. I looked down and saw the plastic bag and thought, *How can this be when I know for a fact that when God wants you busted, you're busted!* Of course, I knew that as soon as they took me downtown they were going to find it.

As they walked me over to the car, they started playing the "good cop, bad cop" routine. One cop was reminding me about how Georgia had just passed a law that allowed life sentences to be given for drug charges, and was saying stuff like, "I guess you haven't been reading the papers? If I was in your business, I sure would be! Our county is proud to be the first county in Georgia to give life sentences to drug dealers, but I don't guess you know anything about that!"

Then Officer Relentless, who was obviously in charge, held up his hand as if to tell the "bad cop" to back off. He quietly came up beside me and started saying things like, "Grant, I know that you care about Dani, Jason, Shane, and Chelsi. I know about the encyclopedias that you bought for Jason. No man spends thousands of dollars on his children's education unless he truly cares about them. I know that somewhere down in you that you want to do the right thing."

I was thinking two things. First of all, I was impressed by the true power of the "good cop, bad cop" method. Everyone knows about it, yet it still had a tremendous effect on me. That didn't mean I was going to fall for it, but I was still impressed. I mean, there you are in a terrible situation. Your whole life is about to be taken from you by this overwhelming, hostile authority, and right in the middle of this chaos up walks this island of safety—the only man who cares and who has the power to help you. It is very effective.

The second thing was: How in the world did this cop know I had bought a set of encyclopedias for Jason? He even had all the children's names memorized! How much did this guy know?

It turned out that while they were busting me, they were simultaneously raiding my house, so I guess they were communicating with each other. Shane was 3 years old and Chelsi was just a baby, so they didn't realize what was going on, but Jason was 12 and was home from school sick (of all days). Jason was always very intelligent, which is why I wanted to make sure he had all he needed to study. He truly was gifted. Remember, there was no Internet back then so he needed encyclopedias.

Then the good cop said, "Aren't you getting tired of this, Grant?"

About that time, my dad walked out of the cleaners to where we were, and the cop said, "I know your parents have to be tired of it."

My dad took one look at me with these sad eyes and said, "Son, your fly is open."

I thought, *You have got to be kidding me!* I was just waiting for any one of the many cops to look down at my fly and they would easily see there was an ounce of meth hanging out of it!

I said, "Dad, I can't do anything about it right now with my hands cuffed behind my back!"

Then the cop said, "Grant, the guys down at the precinct have been taking bets on whether you will finally do the right thing and cooperate with us. The right thing for Dani, Jason, Shane, Chelsi, your dad here, and your poor mother. All you have to do is agree to work with us, and I'll take those cuffs off right now, and you can just walk right back into the cleaners and go back to work."

There was no way I was going to become a snitch, but I knew that if I could just get those cuffs off and get rid of that ounce of meth, they really didn't have that much on me. I knew I couldn't look too anxious about cooperating or they would know something was up. This was the same cop who, during the last bust, had found that laminated card in my wallet stating my thoughts toward snitching.

Just for the record, now that I'm a law-abiding Christian man, I will not hesitate to help the police, but that is not snitching. Snitches choose to live a certain way, but then when trouble comes, they refuse to accept responsibility for, and the consequences of, their actions by shifting blame and living a double-minded life. It's the same as being a crooked cop, or a pastor who preaches the truth and lives a lie. It's just not right.

So I beat around the bush for a few minutes as though I was considering his offer and finally I said, "I am getting sick and tired of being sick and tired. I never thought I'd see the day that I would say this, but if you'll take these cuffs off right now and let me walk back into the cleaners . . . ." I nodded over at my poor, heartbroken mother standing on the sidewalk. "I'll work for you."

Immediately, he said, "You got it. You're doing the right thing. We will be in touch." He unlatched the cuffs, and, very quickly, they all jumped into their cars and took off. I guess they wanted to reduce the risk of any of my customers seeing what was going on so I could be more effective in the field. I remember looking at my dad, and he knew good and well I was up to something. Wavering doesn't run in my family.

25

Where Is L. Ron Hubbard
When You Need Him?

WALKED BACK into the cleaners, stashed the dope, and thought to myself, *This is unbelievable. How did I just get away with that? And if those cops ever ask me for any information, I'll just pretend like I don't know anything or I'll make up stuff until I can go through the Scientology Rundown and be set free!* Little did I know they weren't looking for any information. They already had it.

Working (for) the Cops

To my surprise, as soon as I walked into the cleaners the following morning, Officer Relentless came through the back door and said, "Let's go, 'Buddy' [my street name], it's time to pay your dues."

I said, "What do you mean? I can't go anywhere right now. I have to work."

He said, "We had a deal yesterday, and it's time to keep your end of it."

When I walked out the back door, I saw the same van from the day before. The door opened and I saw that it was full of plain-clothes cops and surveillance equipment. Immediately, they handed me a beeper and said,

"This is your new beeper, programmed to your number so you will still get all your messages. It is also a transmitter, so we can hear every conversation that you have. We have two targets to start with this morning."

The first one was a man who owned a liquor store. They said that he was about to have a shipment of marijuana come in, and they wanted him, the shipment, his money, and his liquor store. They were going to take it all.

I said, "Well, I don't deal pot anymore, so I don't even know the guy."

They said, "We know, but he knows of you and that you deal with Big John, so we feel sure he will deal with you."

Then they said, "But the one we really want is Big John."

I said, "What do you want to bother him for? He is just an old man." As soon as I said that, every cop froze and just stared at me in disbelief.

Officer Relentless said, "Don't try to play games with us. We know everything. We even know that we missed an ounce of meth on you yesterday!"

Now *that* got my attention. I had confided in only one person the night before concerning what had happened, the one person I knew I could trust. If that person had turned on me, then who else had? Were they wearing one of those beepers when I was talking to them? That means they had me on tape confessing I had an ounce of meth the day before. How many people were walking around with these beepers and allowing the police to record their conversations? I started having visions of sitting in a courtroom while recordings of me saying God-only-knows-what were played before a jury.

I looked that cop in the eye and said, "Well, I'm just not going to do Big John. He is my friend, and he will die in there if you send him back. I guess this is just the end for me. Just take me downtown and do whatever you have to do."

He said, "What is wrong with you? With these new laws in effect, people are rolling all over you. We are going to get these guys. The only thing that is going to change is that you will be abandoning your wife, your children, and your parents, and if you don't work with us, I'm going to put the word out on the street that you are a snitch. What do you think your good friend Big John and all of his buddies will think about that?"

All of the sudden, one of the cops on the surveillance equipment leaned over and whispered something in this officer's ear. He said, "You've just been given a 24-hour reprieve. You need to give this conversation some serious thought, and we will see you first thing in the morning." They took their beeper back, shoved me out the door, and sped off. Obviously some great opportunity to bust somebody else must have presented itself.

After going through great extremes to make sure I wasn't being followed, I went straight to Big John to tell him what was going on and get some advice. We met in a tool shed and began to make a plan. First of all, if any serious business was to be discussed, it would be required that all beepers be stored away somewhere while the conversation took place. If anyone protested, that would be an instant red flag.

Also, we could use this situation to gain information and to feed the police false information. For instance, in only one meeting I had learned the identity of someone close to me who was working for the police and about the beepers being used for wires. I knew what their surveillance van looked like and what the undercover agents looked like. It seemed that maybe we could turn this thing around for our benefit to some degree.

For example, we agreed that if I walked up to Big John with a beeper on my side and called him by his real name then he would know this was the time they had chosen to come down on him because I never *ever* called him by name. He would take that opportunity to talk about how he had decided it was time to quit because he had been thinking about how Bobby's car lot had just been raided, and it seemed sure that Bobby would be going back to prison. Big John would say he had decided it just wasn't worth it anymore.

Big John would also get in touch with the guy at the liquor store and inform him that I would be coming wearing a wire so he could use the opportunity to let the police know he had quit as well. Of course, whatever system was in place to bring in the load of marijuana that the police knew about would immediately be changed. And the liquor store guy would search out how the police had gotten the information on him.

Sure enough, the next morning the cops were there, right on time. On the way to the liquor store, I hoped that Big John had been able to contact the guy in time to warn him. When we pulled up, they informed me that an undercover cop was going to walk in with me to make the deal. I knew right away that even if Big John had not been able to contact him, he would never fall for this. It reminded me of the day that Rodney had come to the cleaners with the stranger in the blue Trans Am. He would have to be an idiot to fall for this.

We went in and attempted to make a deal. Sure enough, he told us that he had quit messing around with dope. When we went back to the van, the cops were all nice. They put me in the back and told me not to worry about it, as if I was some friend who had just done my best. I thought, *Are these guys for real? Do they really think I'm falling for this? If I make one mistake, they will throw me in prison without thinking twice about me!*

Then one of them said they knew he was lying when he said he had quit because they could tell from the stress in his voice.

I said, "So you can tell if a person is lying with that recording equipment?"

They all smiled at each other and said, "Oh, yeah!" I couldn't tell if they were for real or just messing with me, but it made me nervous.

That night at home, there was a letter waiting from the FBI. They wanted me to come downtown to some federal building for questioning. I figured it was one of two things. One, it was about a guy Big John and I had purchased some lab equipment from for manufacturing meth. I'd had a bad feeling about him. Or, two, the narcotics squad had informed the FBI they had a new informant who was dealing with Big John, providing an in-road to the circle of men known as the Dixie Mafia? Either way, it was not good.

Surrounded by Idiots and My Life is Over

When I met again with Big John, he said he had not been able to reach the liquor store guy to warn him about the attempted bust. That meant things could have gone terribly wrong if he had fallen for that ridiculous set up. With the FBI involved now, I decided it was too much. I would go on the run. I reminded Big John that the police said if I didn't cooperate, they would put the word on the street that I had turned. That way, when the information started to circulate, they could trace it back to its source, revealing a true snitch.

Roger was not only my main customer, he was also in the business of making false identification. He actually had the equipment to make a Georgia driver's license. Instead of making up a false name or stealing someone's identity, I became John Price, alias "Fat Bear," with his permission. I had legal car insurance, and if I got a ticket, I would pay for it. He lived with his mom, so he had no house, utilities, or anything in his name, so I could safely make use of it. He was self-employed, so if I ever wanted to do contract labor, we would file taxes together and I would pay my share. We had it all figured out, but there was one big problem: I knew deep down that I could not go on that way indefinitely.

Being on the run is very much like doing time. Your life is on hold. There would be no building our dream home. You're living one day at a time, constantly looking over your shoulder. Big John continued dealing with me and never doubted me. I was living in hotels in Buckhead, selling to Roger, and spending my days at the Scientology organization on Ponce de Leon studying everything they threw at me. I was making plenty of money, but I was so lonely. I missed Dani and the kids.

When you have two children in diapers, it seems like you're always going to the baby aisle of the grocery store to buy stuff. I kept finding myself going to grocery stores just to walk up and down the baby aisle and reminisce about better days. Then I would go to great lengths to sneak into our trailer at night to visit Dani and the kids. I wanted to turn myself in, but I was facing so much time that the kids would be grown up by the time I got out. Those were days when I came to realize that no amount of money could make a person happy. If I wanted it, I bought it. If I desired it, I did it. But the emptiness was always there.

There was another drug dealer I still did business with named Donald because his ring of customers was in Bartow County. I stopped by his place to do some paperwork and figure out where I was financially, etc. He wanted to make a purchase the next day so I borrowed a friend's apartment while she was at work. A few minutes after Donald arrived, the police kicked the door down and in walked Officer Relentless. He took one look at Donald and said, "I don't know him, so he can go."

I thought, *Really? You seem to know everything, but you don't know who Donald is? He's one of the biggest meth dealers in both Cobb and Bartow counties, and you've never heard of him? No way!* They didn't even ask him for his I.D., so I knew right then that Donald had turned.

I had only a small amount of meth on me, but I had over a quarter pound in the apartment that Donald was supposed to be picking up. I knew they would find it. While I sat in jail trying to figure out how I was going to beat the case without letting the girl who allowed me to use her apartment take the fall, they brought in someone else who had just been busted and placed him in another cell.

The guy told me what happened to him and said the police had questioned him about me.

I said, "Really? What did they say?"

"They asked if I knew you, and I said yes. Then they asked if I knew you were one of the largest meth dealers in the southeastern United States."

I said, "You have got to be kidding! What did you say?"

"I said, sure, everybody knows that!"

I'll never forget that moment. It was then that the reality of the situation set in. There was no use in even trying to fight back in any way. I was surrounded by idiots, and my life was over. It was a good thing the guy was in another cell or I might have just killed him. I was facing life anyway.

I used my phone call to contact Dani. All I said was, "They got me." Then I lay down and went to sleep. For two weeks.

When I woke up, I thought, *Man, I need my Scientology materials!* I had spent so much time at the Scientology organization, had done different projects for them, and had given them tremendous amounts of money. I just knew I could get them to send me some materials, no problem. They might even bring them up to me. They had come to our home to pick up donations before, so we were close friends, right?

When I called down there and told them I was in jail and wanted to speak to Mike, they put me on hold and never came back. The next time I called, the same thing. Then I started asking for Mark, Joan, etc., etc., etc. I thought, *Man, I wish I could call L. Ron Hubbard, the father of Scientology, and file a complaint.* But I knew I would never be able to get in touch with him! L. Ron Hubbard was dead.

26

"Please, God, Save Me!"

THERE WAS A certain attorney that was famous in the drug world, and I just knew that if I could get him to take my case, there would be hope. It cost $10,000 up front for an initial assessment to see if he would take a potential client. I told Fat Bear where I had my money stashed, and he set things up for me.

About a week later, one of his associates came to see me in jail. They had been looking into my situation, and it did not look good. They would take my case, but he warned me that it could turn out to be a very long, hard road. I knew what that meant—years of filing motions, going to court, and paying them tremendous amounts of money every step of the way. And if I ran out of money, then what?

Facing a Life Sentence: "I've Actually Destroyed My life"

What he said next really got my attention. He said, "Grant, I'm sure you're aware of these new laws, and that this county is the first county to pass down a life sentence for drug charges."

I said, "I know. It's been in all the papers."

He said, "Well, there are several people that the D.A. is going to pursue life sentences against, and you're one of them." He paused. "At this point, the only deal the D.A. is willing to offer you is to plead guilty for 30 years straight up."

I said, "Well, I'll serve the same amount of time! The only difference is that I might get off parole one day!"

He said, "I told them I didn't think you would take it, but I had to ask."

I said, "You can tell them the answer is definitely *no*. And will you please do me one favor? I still have some probation from my last sentence. Will you please get that revoked so at least I'll be getting credit for this time? I really hate serving time and not getting credit for it!"

He said, "No."

I said, "Do what?"

"Before we do that, we need to file a motion of discovery. We need to find out what they really have on you."

I walked back to my cell, asking myself over and over, "Why is it that the whole world is in a hurry until you get locked up? Then everybody wants to beat around the bush!"

I paced back and forth, panic setting in. "This is it! I'm done! Plead guilty for 30 years! This is the best lawyer money can buy? I've actually destroyed my life. I can't believe I'm leaving my children out there again. Oh, man, all I had to do was quit! I knew this day was coming, and all I had to do was quit. Why didn't I just stop?"

God, Either Kill Me or Save Me

I hit the floor right there in cell 454. I said, "God, either kill me or save me. I really don't care which one You do, but something has to give. I've been through six different prisons and this will be my third stretch. I've been through five different drug programs. I've read all these self-help books. I've studied psychology and Scientology. Nothing works! I'm no tough guy like Al Capone. I'm just a weak little wimpy drug addict that can't handle being lonely! Please, God, save me!"

Immediately, I felt the power of God shut me down. In an instant, all panic, all fear, every emotion—just gone. It was as if God scooped me up in those big ole hands and said, "Be calm. I've been waiting for this moment all of your life."

I was down on my knees by my bunk, weeping and in shock. How can a man go from a complete and total state of panic and despair to complete and total peace in a millisecond? I knew I had just been touched by the power of God.

I thought, *Man, I've got to get my Scientology materials.* As that thought went through my mind, I watched my hand go across my bunk to a stack of papers between my mattress and the wall. It was almost as if something was under those papers radiating on and off like a neon light. I pulled a book out, and even though I did not hear any words, the message was clear: I did not need Scientology materials. I needed this book.

It was a simple, worn-out paperback book with a picture of a heart on the front painted like an American flag. It said, *Good News, America. God Loves You.* Under that, it said, *The New Testament.* I thought to myself: *The New Testament. Doesn't that have something to do with the Bible? Yeah, those Bibles in those hotel rooms said that. But this can't be a Bible. It's not pretty enough.*

I opened it and began to read so-and-so begat so-and-so and thought, *Yep, that's it. I remember this from reading the Bible in prison when those guys told me there was a new part and an old part. I guess New Testament is the Bible word for "new part."*

Eventually I would read that these were the ancestors of Jesus, but something happened when I came to verse 6 in Matthew 1: *"And Jesse begat David the king."* Wow! I wondered if that was the same shepherd boy David who killed Goliath. That would mean he was the great, great grandfather of Jesus. How about that? *"David the king begat Solomon."* I wondered if Solomon was the famous rich king you always heard about. He was David's son?

All of the sudden, I was totally engrossed and excited about figuring out who all these people were. I was enjoying reading about who begot whom, and that was supposed to be the worst part? That seemed odd. As I continued to read, it was like reading a children's book. It was so easy to understand. I had heard about those easy-reading Bibles, so I looked on the front again. It said *King James Version.* Yep, that must be one of those easy-reading Bibles. I wondered who King James was? I'd need to find that out, too. Although I didn't realize it, I was experiencing my own "Snuffy" miracle. God was opening His Word to me.

So I kept reading. I came to Matthew 11:28, which said, *"Come unto me, all ye that labor and are heavy laden, and I will give you rest,"* and all the wind seemed to go right out of me. I began to weep. For the first time in my life, I felt "rest." I just lay down and said, "Oh, my God, I am so tired." And I slept.

When I woke up, I picked up the Bible and continued to read. I came to Matthew 12:43 where Jesus said, *"When the unclean spirit is gone out of a man, he walketh through dry places, seeking rest, and findeth none."* I sat there, stunned. How did Jesus know that? Surely it had never happened to Him. That was exactly what happened to me in the drug program when those demons waited all day for us to return. But even though it had happened to me, there was no way I would make that statement as if I knew that is what always happened. If it happened to me twice, I still could not say that's what *always happens.* How could Jesus say that so matter-of-factly?

"Then he says, 'I will return to my house from which I came.' And when he comes, he finds it empty, swept, and put in order. Then he goes and takes with him seven other spirits more wicked than himself, and they enter and dwell there; and the last state of that man is worse than the first. So shall it also be with this wicked generation" (Matthew 12:44-45).

I thought, *That is exactly what the devil was trying to do when he said,* "Bow down and worship me, and you can do that shot." If I had submitted to that demonic spirit, he would have brought with him *"seven other spirits more wicked than himself."* There was only one way Jesus would know this.

Jesus was not just a special man whose mother was made pregnant by God. No, Jesus must have actually come here from God because no one could know that but God. That meant that if this one statement had to come from God alone, then this must be His book. And if God was going to personally write a book, then He was not going to let any man mess with it. That meant that every word in this book was from God!

I closed my eyes and said, "Lord, I have no idea what's going to happen to me, but this I do know: By the time I get through doing this life sentence, I'm going to know this book, and I'll be able to look any man in the eye and tell him beyond a shadow of a doubt whether You are the one God everyone is looking for—or not."

I kept reading through Matthew and Mark. When I came to Luke, I began to pick up on some things. Here was Jesus Christ, the Son of God, walking the face of the earth making the lame walk and the blind see. But there were these other guys, the Pharisees and Sadducees, who didn't like what Jesus was doing. They set Him up and crucified Him. Jesus never complained or tried to snitch on anybody, and the first man He took to Heaven was a convict! How had I been missing this all my life? And why in the world would God let that happen?

I came to Luke 23, and it was like I was there. I could feel the spirit of that mob mentality in the air. In verse 21, when they cried out, *"Crucify Him, crucify Him!"* I could hear their screams and feel their hatred. I took that Bible, slammed it down on my bunk in anger, and said, "Oh, God, I can't believe those people were so wicked back then. I would have killed every one of them!"

Grant Cole, Drug Dealer, a Pharisee?

And *Wham!* It hit me like a ton of bricks! I had heard of Jesus Christ and that He had done all kinds of wonderful things. I had heard He was the Son of God and that He died on the cross. I had even seen it in a vision. Of course, I didn't understand why because I never cared. I just wanted to do what I wanted to do, and I wanted everybody to look at me as though I was some kind of a big shot, just like the Pharisees. As far as I was concerned, you could just crucify Him. All of a sudden, I realized that I was just like the wickedest people I had ever read about!

I had to spend quite a bit of time pacing around in my cell to come to terms with that! That one truth, that one revelation, that one moment in time, had completely turned my world upside down. Now I wanted to go to prison! I deserved to go to prison! They should just come in here and whip the tar out of me right now, and no man would ever stop me from serving God. *No, sir!* I would go to the electric chair before I ever went back to dealing drugs again! It was all turned around. Then it hit me.

The emptiness was gone! That severe loneliness, that terrible void I had been trying to fill all my life was just a big hole where God belonged!

Then the guards turned the lights out! I thought, *Oh, man, what am I going to do? I can't wait until morning to finish this book!* (By the way, I've been studying it for 25 years now, and I'm still not finished.) There was a small, rectangular window about four inches wide, and a small beam of light came through from the searchlights outside. To read, I had to move the Bible back and forth in the beam of light, but I could still read!

I finished Luke, the book of John, and Acts. The book of Romans talked about all kinds of things, and I had no clue what it meant, but one thing was obvious: I was no longer reading stories. This was some deep stuff. So I kept reading. When I came to the part that talks about how we are no longer under the law but under grace, somehow the Spirit revealed to me that I no longer had to worry about the law. Oh, I was to *obey* the law, yes; but it no longer had any power over my life. I was under grace. I had no idea what that meant, except that it was a lot better to be under grace than under the law, and as far as God was concerned, my slate was clean. I was starting a whole new life right there in that prison cell that night. Everything had changed. All of my past was now old and gone, and something new and exciting had now begun.

While the lights were still off, my cell door opened. I heard a voice in the day room yell, "Church call!"

I thought, *Church call? They have church in here? I knew they had church in Stone Mountain, but here in jail? I never knew that. It must be something new.*

For Reflection . . .

If you ask most people in mainline Christianity today what grace is, they will quickly tell you "unmerited favor," which is true. It is a gift (unmerited favor) which Jesus Christ paid for, and there is certainly nothing you could ever do to deserve such a wonderful blessing. But grace is much more than "unmerited favor."

The Strong's Greek Dictionary [5485], which is accepted by all denominations, defines grace [charis] as "the divine influence upon the heart, and its reflection in the life." It is the very presence and work of the Holy Spirit in the believer's life. It is by grace that we are made a new creation in Christ, and it is reflected in the life as old things pass away and behold, all things become new (2 Corinthians 5:17).

Grace [charis] is the word we get "charisma" from, meaning "spiritual gifts." A spiritual gift (charisma) is an endowment of grace [charis] by which the Holy Spirit operates through the believer in the church. And yes, it is the favor of God which one receives without any merit of his own.

Why is this so important to understand? Let's take Romans 5:20, for example. *"Moreover the law entered that the offense might abound. But where sin abounded, grace abounded much more."* When a person only thinks of grace as "unmerited favor," I've seen them interpret this verse to mean that no matter how much they sin, they can expect God's unmerited favor to be poured out on their lives because where sin abounds, grace abounds more.

God's love for you is unconditional but not His blessings—just as I pray that you love your children unconditionally, but hopefully you don't enable them and reinforce their bad behavior by bestowing favor on them when they do wrong.

When you understand that grace is "the divine influence upon the heart which is reflected in the life," then Romans 5:20 takes on quite a different meaning. You understand that no matter how far you have journeyed into the darkness and no matter how bound you are by sin, "grace" abounded much more.

It is by grace, the gift of power, that we have been set free *"from* sin," not set free *"to* sin."

27

"The Gideons Are Here!"

THEY CHAINED US all together in groups of 12 and walked us into a room. The instant I laid eyes on the preacher, I knew he was a cop. I could spot him a mile away. I could understand why cops went undercover and pretended to be drug dealers, but why would a cop go undercover to pretend he was a priest?

Oh, I know! I thought. *They are going to try to get us to go into some confessional booth and use what we say against us in a court of law. Nice try, but if he only knew what happened to me a little while ago, he would know better than to try to set me up. I'm not under the law anymore. I'm under grace . . . whatever that means.*

A lady named Libby Weatherby, who used to be a country singer, came out and sang. It was as though the presence of God came down, and I melted in my seat. Instead of clapping for her, we all rattled our chains. Then up walked the undercover police priest. They called him "Hutch," which was short for Chaplain Hutcheson. He confessed he had once been a cop but now served as a chaplain.

I thought, *Well, praise the Lord! I guess God loves the police, too!*

The Gospel: It had to be True because Man Doesn't Think that Way

Hutch began to explain that we were all a bunch of sinners who deserved to go to Hell and that we would never be able to change our ways and that God knew it, which is why He sent His Son to die on the cross to pay for all of our crimes. It made perfect sense, and I knew that this was God's teaching because man does not think like that. Every self-help book, psychology, Scientology, and every other religion had one thing in common—they were all about man trying to make himself better, and I had already come to the painful conclusion that I could *not* make myself better. That is why they all shunned Christianity. It was the truth!

I thought, *It would be like Jesus' coming into the courtroom and telling the judge that there was no use in sending me back to prison. It wouldn't do any good, so just let Grant go and I'll do his time for him!* But it was far more serious than that. I deserved to die, and Jesus died for me so I could go free!

It got even better. Hutch said that Jesus not only died for me so I could be forgiven but would change me. *"For if any man be in Christ, he is a new creation; old things pass away, and behold, all things become new"* (1 Corinthians 5:17). I thought I hadn't read that one yet, but I already knew it because I had experienced it right there in my cell the night before.

Hutch continued, "And now that you men know that, and if you don't care what Jesus has done for you, then you're no different from the men who drove those nails in His hands!"

I looked straight at the chaplain in amazement and said "Oh Sh--!" When I said it my skin crawled, but all of this was getting to be too much. I knew I shouldn't have cussed in church.

Hutch told us that if we wanted to be forgiven, have our life changed, and spend eternity in Heaven we should say a prayer with him. It went something like this:

"Dear Father in Heaven," and everyone would repeat it.

"I know I'm a sinner and deserve to go to Hell," and everyone would repeat it.

"But I believe Your Son, Jesus Christ, died on the cross so I could be forgiven."

"I ask You now to forgive me of my sins."

"To come into my life and help me to be the man You want me to be"

"In Jesus' name, Amen."

I thought to myself, *That is just too easy and so simple,* but I *knew* that it was true. I knew that I had finally found what I was looking for, and I can honestly say that after 25 years, I have never looked back, let up, slowed down, backed away, or been still since. Oh, I've slipped, but I've never slid. If I make a mistake, I just drop to my knees, ask God to forgive me, and get back up. That's all He's looking for—a relationship—and it is not that hard. One of the most wonderful revelations I've had was when I came to realize it is easier to live right than it is to live wrong. It is actually easier to be blessed than it is to be cursed. *Amazing!*

For Reflection . . .

Now a lot of Christians will argue on that point. Lord knows I've had plenty of them warn me how hard it was going to be to live a Christian life. They would come into the prison and preach whole sermons on how tough it is living for God. Well "tough" and "hard" are relative terms. All I can say is that obviously those people had never really pursued a life of sin, so they really didn't have anything to compare to the Christian life.

I could give you a whole list of experiences that people would consider horrible since I became a Christian—trials, temptations, disappointments, financial challenges, sickness, disease, death of loved ones. With Jesus, it has all been a breeze. It's like going through life running with the wind at your back. You can get tired, but He just blows a little harder. Some folks just don't realize how bad it *could* be, so they can't seem to appreciate how good it really is.

"God is Real, and He is Freaking Me Out"

Anyway, back to the story. When they brought us all back to the cell block, I walked into the day room. Of course, convicts love to let the expletives fly . . . but every cuss word was like an offense to my ears. And when one came out of my mouth, I would cringe. One guy looked at me and asked, "What is wrong with you?"

I said, "Look, I can't explain it, but I stayed up all night long talking to God, reading the Bible. I went to church, said a prayer, and now cuss words sound dirty. Something really weird is going on! God is real, and He's freaking me out!"

About that time, a guard opened the door and yelled, "The Gideons are here!" Immediately, I envisioned that spooky-looking emblem on those Gideon Bibles in all those hotel rooms and thought, *What are those guys doing here?* I pictured them out in the sally port with long white beards and long white hair, in long flowing robes, shining like angels.

All of the sudden, a line of about 15 men formed at the door with books in their hands. I asked one man what was going on. He said, "The Gideons bring us Bible studies every Wednesday."

I said, "So all of you guys are studying the Bible? My goodness, all Heaven is breaking loose in the jail house!"

I could understand how I had missed church call because they announced it at 5:00 a.m. before they woke everyone up for breakfast. It was as if they were trying to hide church call. But this was happening in the middle of the day. How could I have missed this? I fell in line. When you got to the door, you had to lean down and peek through the slot. There was an old man out there. Sure enough, he had white hair and a white beard, but they weren't long. He wasn't wearing a robe, but he was kind of glowing.

I said, "So you're the guys who make the Bibles in the hotel rooms?"

He started laughing and said, "Well, we don't *make* the Bibles; we just put them there."

I said, "Well, how much do your Bible study books cost?"

He said, "They're free, just like Jesus is free!"

I said, "Free? Who pays for them?"

He said, "Jesus pays for them!"

I said, "Wow! He pays for everything, doesn't He?"

The kind old man said, "Yes, son, He sure does."

I thought, *This sure is a lot different from the Scientology guys. I couldn't even pay the Scientologist to sell me their books once I was in jail.* One time I paid them $4,500 to take a course on the word "if." (Don't ask.)

He asked if I had graduated high school, and I said, "Yes, sir, with special emphasis on the word 'high.'" (Just kidding.) He gave me a book called *Journey through the New Testament* from the Emmaus Bible College.

He said, "Now if this one is too hard, we have some other ones that are easier. If you finish this one this week, bring it back to us, and we will give you another one."

Well, I finished it that afternoon and then finally got tired and went to sleep. The next morning, I noticed one of the guys playing cards who had gotten a Bible study the day before. I asked him if he finished his, and he said he hadn't started it yet. I asked if I could borrow it. I made up my own answer sheet because I didn't want to write in his book. When I was done, I gave it back and then did the same thing with another guy, then another, and another.

By the time the Gideons came back, I had a whole stack of answer sheets for them. The guy said that I really wasn't supposed to do them that way because those men were at different levels and it was supposed to be a continuous course. I apologized and said, "Well, I need more books. If money is an issue, I'll get the money."

Once again, he wasn't concerned about money! He said, "Let us grade these and see how you did, and we'll talk next week." He found me a couple of books I hadn't done yet and left.

When they came back the next week, the leader of the ministry, Johnny Ferguson, met me at the door. He said that I had aced everything, and he had brought me some more books that might challenge me a little more. We talked for a while, and I explained that I was going to be in the system a long time.

He said, "Well, Grant, the guys and I have talked it over, and if studying the Word of God is something you're really passionate about, then we want to help you. If you would like to pursue studies, then we have some scholarship money that we award men from time to time. We will follow you as you go through the system, so it won't matter where they send you."

I couldn't believe these old guys! They wanted absolutely nothing from me. They just wanted to give.

He said, "I'm personally Calvinistic in my theology. I've just been raised that way all my life, but the Gideons have members from all denominations, so our chapter provides a scholarship to an interdenominational course so you can compare different theologies and choose for yourself."

Of course, I looked at him like a calf staring at a new gate. I had no idea what the man was talking about. I guess he could tell because he said, "In other words, we want to send you to big boy school if you want to go."

I said, "Yes, sir, I do!"

He said, "Well, finish these for now," and handed me a big pile of Bible study books bound with twine. I could hardly wait to get back in my cell and open my presents. I was more excited than a child on Christmas morning. I couldn't decide which one to open first!

I laid them all out in my cell. One said, *A Study of the Minor Prophets*, and one said, *A Study of the Major Prophets*. I thought, *Why would anybody want to study a 'minor' prophet when you could study a 'major' prophet?* I had the worldly view that the "big" books of the Bible would be more important than the "little" books until I did a verse-by-verse study on the book of James. I thought, *Oh, wow! God's little books are better than His big books!*

I was Now on a Mission, and My Life had Purpose

I was now on a mission, and my life had purpose. I would study until my mind was exhausted and then wake up the next morning excited to take up where I had left off. God would reveal something to me and then confirm it in His Word, just as He had revealed to me that I was forgiven before I understood why.

For example, men would come into my cell to ask a Bible question, and the next thing I'd know, the conversation would turn to drugs and who did what, etc. What my dear friend Greg Moss refers to as "glorying in our shame." The Lord said to me, "Don't talk about those things," so I would just run the men off. Then I turned back to my Bible and read, *"Finally, brethren, whatsoever things are true, whatsoever things are honest, whatsoever things are just, whatsoever things are pure, whatsoever things are lovely, whatsoever things are of good report. If there be any virtue, if there be any praise, think on these things"* (Philippians 4:8).

One day while studying, I looked out of my cell door and saw a new guy sitting off by himself in the day room, looking terrified. God said, "Go give that man a pack of cookies."

I said, "What? You know I can't go give that man a pack of cookies! He'll think I'm funny and making a pass at him, and the other men will think I'm weak!"

God said, "Go give that man a pack of cookies. He's hungry and has no money."

I said, "Okay, Lord, but I'm telling him it's Your fault."

So I walked up to the guy and said, "Now, don't take this wrong. There's nothing funny going on here. God told me to come out here and give you a pack of cookies—so here." As I held out the pack of cookies, he looked at me in disbelief. I said, "Look, all I know is God said you're hungry and you don't have any money."

With that, his eyes lit up and he took the pack of cookies. I went back into my cell to continue my Bible study on the book of John, and it read, *"A new commandment I give to you that you love one another: as I have loved you, that you also love one another. By this, all will know that you are My disciples, if you have love for one another"* (John 13:34-35).

As soon as I read that, the guy walked into my cell and said, "You're for real, aren't you? God really told you that?"

I said, "Absolutely. I would not have done it if He hadn't. You just don't do that kind of thing in here." So we started talking about God. He got saved and started coming to church, and he and I actually formed a Bible study for the men.

That kind of stuff started happening on a continual basis. It was as if the Holy Ghost became my personal tutor, and the Word of God became alive, sharper than any two-edged sword, and became the discerner of my thoughts and the intents of my heart. And you know what? I really wasn't concerned about the law any more.

As I lay on my bunk one day reading the Bible, I came to Galatians 5:22 that says, *"But the fruit of the Spirit is love, joy, peace . . . ."* All of the sudden I had a vision of all the hippies in Piedmont Park with their banners saying, "love" and "peace." That's what we were all looking for in the wrong places. We were looking for God the whole time, but the devil had us believing those things were the fruit of drugs. *Amazing!*

28

"Old Things Pass Away"

A MAN PULLED me to the side one day and said, "I just want to tell you something."

I said, "Okay, what's that?"

He said, "My grandmother has been telling me for years that God could change my life if I would just let Him, but I never believed her until I watched you. You are not the same man who came through those doors four months ago." He prayed to receive Christ and joined our Bible study.

Identifying with the Good Guys

One night, after studying the Bible all day, it really came home to me how much I had changed. My brain felt like it was on fire, so I decided to take a break. I came out into the day room where the men were watching a movie. It was a Steven Seagal movie, and some drug dealer had killed a police officer's wife. When the bad guy finally got what he deserved at the end, I said, "Praise God!" Everyone looked at me as if I was from another planet. I was now identifying with the good guys. I thought, *Man, I don't even belong in here anymore!*

I began to think, *You know, that old pot dealer, Steve Brown, might really be a preacher after all.* So I found the address for Milford Church of God and wrote him a letter. I told him that I was going to be in prison for a long time, but that if he wouldn't mind I would love to come and visit his church when I got out. I told him I would sweep floors and empty ash trays or whatever he would let me do. I figured if Steve Brown had a church, it would be like a giant AA meeting! Except everybody would be happy because they knew Jesus.

I lay in my cell one night telling God how sorry I was for all of the bad things I had done, and I promised Him that I would never do drugs again.

He said, "You don't have any drugs to do, but you smoke cigarettes every day, and you know I don't want you to." The message was clear: It's easy to say you've quit drugs when you don't have any, and talk is cheap.

I thought, *I guess this means they don't have any ash trays in church to empty after all.*

I had been smoking for 22 years, but since that moment of realization, I've never had another puff. It was not easy. God delivered me from drugs, but it seemed that He pretty much let me quit smoking cigarettes by myself. As I was going through it, the Lord taught me that everything we do is our choice—whether it's drugs, cigarettes, getting angry, or eating food. As I began to crucify my flesh, my spirit soared. It was such a liberating experience that I began to look for things to quit.

A Career Criminal Tripping on Jesus!

The time finally came for our motion of discovery. What we found out was not good. They had been building a case against me for quite some time. I had become very elaborate in using codes on beepers. Through a series of numbers, you could tell me who you were, how much meth you wanted, and how much money you had. I could in turn tell you when and where to pick up drugs and drop money, etc. Well, they claimed to have one of my code cards I had made up, so they could decode my messages, and as a result, they were going to charge me as a "career criminal."

We filed a motion to suppress since I was arrested in someone else's apartment, and they found the quarter pound of meth after they removed me from the scene. They denied the motion, and we found out that the warrant stated that they were looking for financial records. That just reinforced our belief that Donald had turned, since I was doing financial records at his house the night before my arrest. I'm sure he is the one who explained the codes, etc. With his testimony, I was a dead duck.

I asked my lawyer to revoke my probation so I could get on with doing my time. He agreed and said that he would keep finding ways to put off my case as long as possible. The police made it very clear that they were angry about how I played games with them. So our thinking was, if we could wait a year or two before going to trial, maybe some other nut would make them mad, and I wouldn't seem so bad anymore.

I hadn't been outside for months and was really looking forward to some fresh air and that ride to Jackson. But when the day came, they chained me like I was Hannibal Lecter, backed up my own personal paddy wagon to the door, and put me in the back of that thing with no windows. When we got to Jackson, they once again backed me up to a door, and I stepped into the prison. They took me straight to the infirmary I had hated years before when they sent me there with Hepatitis.

This time it was because I had been very sick in jail with bleeding ulcers. The doctor figured the acid in my stomach had eaten up the lining. I had gone months without eating food, as I was getting all my nourishment through a needle for a long time, if you know what I mean. The jail had been giving me Tums to eat and Maalox to drink, so I had managed to get by, but now they wanted to see what was going on. They ran some tests that confirmed I had a serious problem and may need to have 30 percent of my stomach removed. They wanted to send me to the prison hospital in Augusta for surgery.

Now *that* did not sound good to me. I mean, the guy they had doing administrative work at Jackson was a notorious convict named Wayne Williams, a serial killer who threw several dead bodies in the Chattahoochee River. If he was working in the infirmary, then who was going to be my surgeon—some doctor convicted of chopping up his wife and kids or something? I guess my anesthesiologist would be Dr. Kevorkian! No, I did not like the sound of this at all, but I couldn't go on the way I was. I would eat that greasy prison food and feel as though I had swallowed molten lava, and for some strange reason they didn't give out Tums or Maalox at Jackson!

They went ahead and sent me to those same old cell blocks, but this time it was so crowded at Jackson that they were putting two men in each cell. That meant one man had to sleep on those nasty floors. My cellmate turned out to be a young Mexican guy who could not speak English. I could tell he was terrified. When they opened the cell door, he immediately put his stuff on the floor as he should because I was obviously the older, more seasoned convict. But I had an overwhelming desire to help that kid. I pulled out my Bible and pointed to it. I said, "Because of this, you sleep on the bunk. I'll sleep on the floor." It took a few minutes, but I got the point across.

I laid my bedding right against the bars, as far away as I could get from the toilet and the urine-soaked concrete around it. Of course, the cell was only nine feet long. As I was lying there reading my Bible I came to the passage of scripture where Jesus was riding into Jerusalem on the back of a donkey and all the people were waving palm branches, crying out, *"Hosanna! Hosanna!"* and the bell rang for yard call.

When I stepped out of those doors, I could not believe how beautiful the sky was. The clouds were so white and the sky so blue. It wasn't just because I hadn't been outside for a long time, either. I once went 11 months without seeing daylight, and when I finally did, the experience was nothing like this. I just couldn't get over how beautiful it was, and I tried to recall other times I had noticed the sky. Could it be that for 33 years I had been looking down?

I walked over to the fence and looked at the pine trees, but they were not just trees, either. They seemed like amazing, powerful creations of God that had burst forth from the earth. I looked at the tree tops swaying in the wind, and it was as if they were crying out, *"Hosanna! Hosanna!"* I thought, *Wow! I'm tripping on Jesus!*

Prison Hadn't Changed—I Had

The men naturally gravitated to the track and began to walk in a counterclockwise direction, just as they always had done. This time, I started walking the other way, against the flow. As a result, I could see the men's faces and was amazed at how many of them I knew. It was as though we were all on some kind of a divine revolving schedule, except that most of them had already been back and were coming through again since the last time I was there!

I would see someone I knew and say, "Man, have you noticed how this place has changed? What is going on?"

They would respond with some dismissive comment like, "Don't pay any attention to Cole. He's sure enough done too many drugs this time." I began to realize that Jackson hadn't changed; I had—to the point that I was seeing the world through new eyes. I had been blind, but now I could see for real.

One man turned around and started walking against the flow with me. He said, "I've been dying to do this!" It turned out that he had gotten saved, too. He said, "Man, have you been to Friday Night Jackson yet?"

I said, "What in the world is Friday Night Jackson?" He explained that it was a church service that everyone was going to.

I said, "You have got to be kidding. They have church here, too?"

He said, "Just wait. It's going to blow your mind."

Friday night came, and sure enough, the men poured out of the cell blocks for the service. We went into a big auditorium with a stage. A huge banner on the wall said *FGBMFI* with a big emblem like a flame. When I asked, "What is 'FGBMFI?'" they said, "Shhh!"

The music started. It was the first time I had ever been in a room with several hundred men standing there praising God with both hands raised in the air. I looked around, and saw that not one man was sitting down and every last one of them was singing at the top of his lungs. The very atmosphere was filled with the power of God.

A man walked out onto the stage and shared a testimony of how God had healed him of bleeding ulcers. He asked if there were any men who were sick and wanted prayer. I raised my hand along with many others around the auditorium. He said, "Now all of you who aren't sick, lay your hands on these men who are," and he began to pray a very simple prayer. I looked around at all of the men being prayed for. I had no doubt that God would heal that man, or this man, but no way was He going to heal me. God would never do that for me!

After the prayer, I bowed my head, stomach burning, and said, "Please, God, forgive me. I just want You to know, that I know, the only reason I'm not healed right now is my lack of faith. I know that You could heal me just like that!" When I said "that," I snapped my fingers. As soon as I did, a coolness started in my throat and flowed down my abdomen, down my legs, and that burning fire from my stomach flowed right out the end of my feet. I knew that I was healed, and I have been ever since. I can roll up jalapeno peppers in greasy pepperoni pizza and not get indigestion.

Eventually, as we left the service, someone told me that FGBMFI stood for Full Gospel Business Men's Fellowship International. These men were not even preachers or pastors by profession. They were a bunch of businessmen on fire for God. I was amazed!

I went back to my cell, lay down on my little pallet on the floor, and suddenly felt myself moving as though I was dizzy, but I wasn't. All of the sudden, I was underground in a courtroom hewn out of rock. There was a platform up high where the judge would be and two tables of stone where the prosecution and defense teams would sit. The tables were not pieces of rock furniture sitting on the floor. Instead, everything was perfectly hewn out of the earth. Off in the distance, I could see a single-file line of men walking toward an area that glowed from heat.

I looked toward the defense table and saw a small book, about the size of a 70-page single subject notebook, and somehow I just knew that the good things I had done since being saved were written in it. Giving the guy the pack of cookies was in there, along with the Bible studies we did and letting the little Mexican guy sleep on the bunk. Then I thought, *I wonder what my little Mexican friend is doing right now?* Had I left my body lying there dead? Had I disappeared? Had God entered our cell and transformed it into this place? I figured whatever God had done, my little Mexican friend was probably scared to death right about now.

I felt a sense of dread come over me. If there was a *little* book with the good things in it sitting on the defense table, then what was the prosecutor's table going to look like? Was it going to be one huge book reaching to the ceiling or were there going to be thousands of smaller books? I knew one thing. This was serious business, and I was in serious trouble. I looked one more time at the line of men walking towards the red glowing heat. I slowly turned to look at the prosecutor's table, but it was absolutely clean! Not one single thing was on that table. Not even a speck of dust! The realization that I had been totally forgiven for everything I had done started to sink in, and I began to weep as that feeling of dread turned to relief.

As I wept, my life began to pass before me. It was like I could see all the details plainly, yet I could tell it was happening in a millisecond. It stopped on those five boys that used to pray at Alto. They were joining hands in the middle of that dormitory, and the boots started flying at them. Kids ran from behind and slapped them as they prayed. This thought came into my mind: "Can you imagine what that service you just experienced would have meant to those five boys?"

Life—Prison was Going to be My Life

I knew what I was going to do. First, I would do my time. Then, when I got out, I would be going back into prisons and holding services, just like Friday Night Jackson. Prison was going to be my life, and that was fine with me.

As I thought about that, I sensed three men standing near talking with one another. I couldn't hear what they were saying, but I knew they were discussing what was happening to me. I could tell they were barefoot and dressed in plain robes as you would imagine men wore in biblical times. I was just there in this underground place soaking up the light. There was no specific source of the light. It was as though the air was light, and it felt good. It was like warmth to my soul.

There was nothing pretty about that place whatsoever, but the presence of God was so wonderful that I started thinking, *You know, God, it really is wonderful being here in this place. I'm not even worried about going to Heaven or back to earth. As a matter of fact, let's not even worry about Dani and the kids, or prisons, or services. I'll just stay right here.*

As soon as I said "here," *Wham!* I was right back in my prison cell. I opened my eyes, and to my surprise, my little Mexican friend was just sitting there reading his Bible as though nothing had happened. I thought, *Man, I should have just kept my mouth shut! If I had just kept my mouth shut, there's no telling how long God would have let me stay there!*

29

"Concerning the Vision"

'VE OFTEN THOUGHT of this vision. The reason I selected the experiences from my past that I have shared in this book is that they are the ones that stood out when my life was passing before my eyes. I've had many experiences in my criminal life that were far more intense than the ones I've shared here, but I figure these must be the ones that are the most important to God.

I have often thought about those men in that vision who were off in the distance walking toward the heat. This is not the lake of fire found in Revelation 20:15, as that day has not come yet. What I saw must have been the place referred to as Death and Hades (Revelation 20:13), which is the temporary abode of the dead until the final judgment. It is a place that is hot.

Whatever Happened to the Fear of the Lord?

In Luke 16:19-31, Jesus tells the story of the poor man, Lazarus, and a rich man who dies, is being tormented in Hades, and begs for a drop of water to cool his tongue. Remember, time is relative. For those in Heaven, I'm sure 1,000 years is like a day, but for those serving time in Hades, waiting to go to court at the Great White Throne of Judgment, a day is like 1,000 years. Then, when that day comes, the true punishment begins.

The point is this: If I had died from that overdose of cocaine, I would have been walking in that line. If you do not know Jesus Christ as your Lord and Savior, you are just one breath away from walking in that line toward eternal punishment and separation from God. No more of God's mercy, no more of God's grace, no more of God's light, no more chances to experience God's plan for your life. It only takes one car to come across that yellow line and hit you head-on, and you're walking in a line, cursing yourself. "Why didn't I just quit?" "Why didn't I just stop?" "I knew this day was coming! Why didn't I just turn to God?" And it will be too late.

People say, "Wouldn't God give you a second chance?" He already has! But not just a second chance. Every breath you take is another chance to accept Christ, but one day your breath will cease, and with it, so will your chances. Then you will find yourself in a situation with *"no place for repentance."*

For those of you who know Jesus Christ as Lord and Savior, let me remind you that we also have a date with Deity. In 2 Corinthians 5:9-10, the Apostle Paul writes, *"Therefore we make it our aim, whether present or absent, to be well pleasing to Him. For we must all appear before the judgment seat of Christ, that each one may receive the things done in the body, according to what he has done, whether good or bad."* And how will we be judged for what we have done?

That's what the little book on the defense table was about. After 25 years of serving the Lord, I pray my book is much larger by now. I believe that particular book is the same book that Malachi 3:16 refers to as the Book of Remembrance. *"Then those who feared the Lord spoke to one another, and the Lord listened and heard them. So a book of remembrance was written before Him for those who fear the Lord and who meditate on His name."*

For the most part the *"fear of the Lord"* seems to have been lost in the church today. I believe this is a crying shame. The *"fear of the Lord"* is one aspect of my relationship to God that I value above all others, just as Jesus did. Listen to the words of Isaiah as he prophesied concerning the soon-to-come Son of the living God; the Alpha, the Omega, the Bright and Morning Star; the King of Kings and Lord of Lords; the very Word of God who became flesh *"as the only begotten of the Father, full of grace and truth."*

Isaiah 11:1-3 says, *"There shall come forth a Rod from the stem of Jesse. And a branch shall grow out of His roots. The Spirit of the Lord shall rest upon Him, the Spirit of wisdom and understanding, the Spirit of counsel and might, the Spirit of knowledge and the fear of the Lord. His delight is in the fear of the Lord."*

I believe these are the same seven Spirits of God referred to in Revelation 4:5 burning before the throne, and again in Revelation 5:6 revealing the many expressions of the Holy Spirit's working. And of these magnificent expressions that rested upon the Messiah, *"His delight is in the fear of the Lord."* Not the Spirit of might, knowledge, counsel, or wisdom, but the *"fear of the Lord."*

So what is the fear of the Lord? Israel was introduced to it in Exodus 19 when the Lord told Moses, *"Go to the people and consecrate them today and tomorrow, and let them wash their clothes. And let them be ready for the third day. For on the third day the Lord will come down upon Mt. Sinai in the sight of all the people"* (Exodus 19:10-11).

Then the Lord told Moses to set bounds around the mountain to keep the people at bay *"lest they break through to gaze at the Lord, and many of them perish"* (Exodus 19:21).

It is obvious that the people had an idea of God that was far from the reality of Who He truly is. They had what I call a "rock star mentality." If they announced that Justin Bieber was going to be at the mall, the first thing they would do is set up boundaries so all the fan-girls couldn't rush Justin Bieber. Well, apparently, the Israelites had in their minds a made-up image of God whom they could just come running to any way they chose, but the reality was that *"whoever touches the mountain shall surely be put to death"* (Exodus 20:18-19).

Of course, they didn't need the boundaries for long because when God came down, *"the people witnessed the thunderings, the lightning flashes, the sound of the trumpet, and the mountain smoking, and when the people saw it, they trembled and stood afar off."* Then they said to Moses, *"You speak with us and we will hear, but let not God speak with us, lest we die"* (Exodus 20:18-19).

The experience of who God really is was quite different from what they imagined Him to be. So why did God reveal Himself in this way? It was to prepare them to live a new life and be a *"special treasure to God above all people"* (Exodus 19:5).

Moses explains in the next verse, *"Do not **fear**, for God has come to test you, and that His **fear** may be before you, so that you may not sin"* (Exodus 20:20, emphasis added).

So Moses says, *"Do not fear,"* and declares that God has *"set His fear before you."* So are we to fear or not to fear? Well, let's look at the purpose of fearing God. What purpose does God-fearing serve. *"His fear may be before you, so that you may not sin."* So the fear of the Lord is what keeps us from sin, so then *"do not fear."*

You could say it like this: Do not fear or be afraid, for God has come to test you; that His fear may be before you so that you may not sin, and as a result, you will have nothing to fear.

A Comfortable God

You see, the fear of the Lord is what keeps us from sin, and the love of God is what inspires us to serve Him. The fear of the Lord, for the most part, has been lost in the church. That explains why we have . . . people shouting *hallelujah!* while they're as high as a kite; worship leaders going to bars after the service; pastors' committing adultery; people walking around with Christian t-shirts on cussing and huffing on cigarettes. And then we wonder why the world looks at us as a bunch of hypocrites.

For the most part, I blame modern-day preachers and teachers for this. We have done the same thing the Israelites did. We have made up an image of God that we can be comfortable with. He's our big easygoing friend. .

While Moses was up on the mountain receiving commandments from God and specific instructions on how to build the tabernacle, the people decided to make up their own image of God. *"And he received the gold from their hand, and he fashioned it with an engraving tool, and made a molded calf.*

Then they said, 'This is your god, O Israel, that brought you out of the land of Egypt!' So when Aaron saw it, he built an altar before it. And Aaron made a proclamation and said, 'Tomorrow is a feast to the Lord'" (Exodus 32:4-5). That word *"Lord"* is the Hebrew word *Yahweh*, which is the most holy name of God!

I see people make up their own image of God in their minds today so they can be comfortable with Him based on their own terms. We are all tempted to do this for the same reason the Israelites did. In Exodus 32:1, they said, *"Come, make us gods that shall go before us."* This is appealing because when we make up our own image of God, we can decide where it leads us and how we should approach it and worship it in our preferred way. When we create our god in our own image, that god usually turns out to approve of us just the way we are and never calls us to anything higher or better.

The reality is that there is a *"Truth"* and a *"Way,"* and we don't get to make it up as we go along. We cannot relate to God any way we choose any more than we would allow people to have a relationship with us any way they choose. Would you be in a relationship with someone who ignored you, was inconsiderate of your feelings, and spoke *of* you and *to* you any way they chose, while at the same time asking you to grant their every wish? I think not.

Proverbs 1:7 says, *"The fear of the Lord is the beginning of knowledge."* This passage is referring to the knowledge of who God is. If a person does not fear the Lord, then he has not even "begun" to know who He is. For the fear of the Lord is the very key that opens the door to the knowledge of God, just as Proverbs 9:10 says: *"The fear of the Lord is the beginning of wisdom,"* or you could say the "key" to God's wisdom. It is wonderful to think of Baby Jesus a holy infant so "tender and mild" sleeping in heavenly peace in a manger . . . . But, if you can ever get your mind around the fact that the fire on the mountain who came in thunderings and lightnings, the sound of whose voice caused men to fear for their very lives, is the same magnificent, terrifying, all-powerful, holy God who loves you so much that He came in a manger to give His life for you, *then* you begin to have wisdom, knowledge, and 20/20 vision of who He is, just as Israel began to see in Exodus 20:20.

God is Not Our "Daddy café latte buddy"

A lot of preachers today would do well to remember that one of the things that make the good news so wonderful is that the bad news is so terrible. I'm convinced this is why in the vision I first saw the men walking in a line toward Hades where I deserved to go. It was that reality that made the experience of seeing that table, which should have been filled with books recording my sins, standing there empty so awe-inspiring! How could I ever thank God enough?

Here is the beauty of the fear of the Lord. It is that fear that keeps us from sin and that opens the door to the knowledge and wisdom of who God is. It is that relationship that opens the door to God's blessings so that fear becomes rooted and grounded in our love and reverence of God.

That's how it was with Job, who was a man who *"feared God and shunned evil"* (Job 1:1). That's what the fear of the Lord does—causes us to shun evil so that we may not sin. Because of that, Job was *"the greatest of all the people of the East"* (Job 1:3).

Satan said that he couldn't get to Job from any side and so he asked God the question, *"Does Job fear God for nothing? Have you not made a hedge around him, around his household, and around all that he has on every side? You have blessed the work of his hands, and his possessions have increased in the land"* (Job 1:9-10).

In other words, Job feared God and shunned evil, and as a result God blessed Job. So even Satan realized that Job feared God because he didn't want anything to interfere with the hedge of protection God had placed around him, and the way the work of his hands were being blessed as a result of his fear of the Lord.

Here is my definition of the fear of the Lord: The fear of the Lord is when we love and revere God so much that we have a tremendous fear of doing anything that would interfere with our relationship with God in any shape, form, or fashion.

People say, "Well, God doesn't want you walking around afraid of Him." Let me just tell you that the reason I'm not *afraid* of God is that I have the *"fear of the Lord."* Because I fear the Lord I am not going anywhere I would need to be afraid of God. I'm not messing with anything that would interfere with the flow of what God is doing in my life. It's just too good to take any chances.

It's like this. At our church, the stage is about four feet above floor-level. Around the platform is a cap wall that rises about a foot higher. I get to preaching and the anointing comes upon me, and I start thinking, *It would be awesome to step up on that cap wall and start walking along while preaching the Gospel!* But I don't. Why? My fear of gravity.

When I'm in the center of the platform, I'm not walking around afraid of gravity. There's no reason to be afraid of gravity in the center of the stage, so that's where I stay. Even if I fell off the wall, it wouldn't kill me, but it sure would mess up the flow of the anointing. It would be embarrassing, and I'd feel like a fool for doing it, so I just don't do it. So it is with God.

The fear of the Lord brings you to a place where you don't concern yourself with whether you can get by with doing something. You just stay in the center of God's will so you don't have to worry about messing up what you have going on with God. You would have to be a fool to risk it.

Sometimes I'll get busy and be running around doing ministry when, all of the sudden, I'll think, "Man, I need to get home!" You know why? My fear of Dani! Oh, I don't fear that she will quit loving me. It's just that our relationship is so important to me that I fear allowing anything to interfere with our marriage so I run to her. Not away from her.

That's why Jesus delighted in the fear of the Lord. He certainly wasn't *afraid* of God. He *is* God. The fear of the Lord is what kept Him in the center of God's will. That's why in John 8:29 He could say, *"I only do those things that please Him."* Jesus found great delight in walking the earth as a man in the fear of the Lord and experiencing all of the blessings that came with it. My prayer is that you will do the same.

I'm afraid that many people have made up a false image of God they can be comfortable with. When the day comes that they have to meet with Him, they may find out that He is quite different from the "Daddy café latte buddy" they have imagined Him to be.

30

"I'm Going to Jackson"

BLESSING MY FOOD and thanking God for my meals took on a whole new meaning after my healing. I signed all the papers refusing any medical treatment, and before I knew it I was through with diagnostics and ready to be shipped out.

God and I had become very close by this time. I had come to realize that studying the Bible was not about learning a subject, but about getting to know Him—just as if a man sees a beautiful woman and thinks, "Wow! I'd really like to know her!" Well, that's why the Lord has given us His Word—so that we can get to know Him. And with that comes knowledge of His ways, His love, His will, His kingdom, and His plan for our lives.

After 33 Years a Slave of Satan . . . I'm Free at Last!

I was convinced that Jesus had a special prison picked out just for me—a place where the Lord sends all those who love Him; a place where "Friday Night Jackson" happens every day. My cell door opened.

"Cole, pack your stuff. You're going to Jackson."

"I'm already in Jackson!"

"Not *that* Jackson, you're not!"

They sent me to Jackson County Prison in Jefferson, Georgia. It's a work camp that has four dorms with about 100 men in each dorm. When I stepped into Dorm 2, the heat was stifling. It had to be well over 100 degrees, but what really got my attention was the overwhelming smell of reefer smoke. And not just any reefer smoke. I'm talking about high quality, piney-tasting, Christmas-tree-smelling, sensimilla reefer smoke. I stopped right there with all my belongings in my hands, closed my eyes, and said, "Oh, my God, that reefer smoke smells wonderful! But Your Word says in James 4:7, *'Therefore submit to God. Resist the devil and he will flee from you.'* So that is what I am doing right now. I love You, I want to serve You, and I'm not going back!"

Then I opened my eyes and said, "Satan, I resist you in the name of Jesus. I have served you for 33 years, and this is where it has gotten me—in this stinking dorm with sweat pouring off of me. You are a thief and a liar, and I will never serve you again!"

I found my bunk, threw my mattress up on there, climbed up, lay down, and opened my Bible. My eyes fell on the 23rd Psalm. Now, when I was a child, there was still prayer in the public schools. I had to memorize the 23rd Psalm to graduate kindergarten, so I was familiar with verse one but had never thought about what it meant. When I read those words, *"The Lord is my shepherd. I shall not want,"* all of the sudden I did not *"want"* anything. I didn't want to smoke pot, or get out of prison, or anything else. I had never been that satisfied and content in my whole life. I had just made the Lord my Shepherd, and I did not want.

I laid there amazed and tried to think of a scenario that would make me happier. I imagined being on a beach in the Caribbean, sipping a cool drink with an ocean breeze blowing, with all the money in the world, with Dani and the kids, and it just made no difference. There was no place in the world that I would rather be at that moment than laying right there on my bunk in Jackson Prison.

When the realization hit me, I panicked. I sat straight up and said, "Oh, no, I've been institutionalized!" I'd seen men institutionalized before.

I saw one man get his parole papers, and without saying a word, walk over and punch a guard in the face so he could catch another case and stay in prison. Ever since I saw that happen, I had a fear in the back of my mind of becoming just like that.

Then I realized that of course I'd rather be home, but it no longer made any difference. My environment had become totally powerless over me. I was a free man for the first time in my life. I understood what the Apostle Paul meant when he said, *"For I have learned in whatever state I am, to be content"* (Philippians 4:11). When the Son makes you free, you shall be free indeed. Whether you're in prison or not is irrelevant.

Then all the men started coming in from detail, so I met the man who had the bunk under me. He was a Muslim and the main drug supplier for the entire prison. Now, I mean really! What are the odds? So I spent my first months at Jackson County studying the Bible (as the Gideons continued sending my studies), with a continuous poker game going on under me, and a cloud of marijuana smoke surrounding me, in total peace, wanting for nothing.

Lo and behold, they did have a Christian warden there named J.J. Dalton. So Jackson had a chaplain on staff, church services four nights a week, and Sunday School every Sunday, taught by Warden Dalton himself. His class was my favorite.

The first service I went to was held by the chaplain, Robert Akin. It was obvious that he genuinely loved God and loved the men. Out of over 400 men in the prison, only about 10 would come to service.

The next night, a man came in to preach, but no one wanted to attend because they said he was boring. I arrived at the service to find that I was the only one there. Up walked this little old man who looked mean, but you could tell he was sweet. He reminded me of Snuffy. He stood behind the podium, and instead of looking at me, he stared at the floor over in the corner of the room.

He opened his Bible and began to preach. *Hum, hum, hum, da dum, dum, dum. Hum da dum dum, dum. Hum! Da dum, dum, dum, dum, dum. Jesus! Hum, mum, mum, da, da, dum, da, dum dum dum . . . .* After a while, he closed his Bible, turned, and hurriedly walked out the door. I felt so sorry for him that I never missed one of his services. I kept thinking that one day I would learn to understand what he was saying, but I never did.

The next night was quite different. When I walked through the door, I noticed that our congregation had almost doubled in size to about 18. So had the visitors. There was a group of about four or five men and three or four women. They let us choose the songs the chaplain had taught us— *Victory in Jesus, I'll Fly Away, Amazing Grace*, etc. They brought in guitars and tambourines, and we had a great time praising God.

When the man got up to preach, he was on fire. You could tell that he not only knew the Word but believed every word of it, and was downright excited about it. He had no doubt that God was real. God was here. God loved us and had a magnificent plan for our lives. And through faith in Jesus Christ alone, we could be saved, healed, and delivered.

After the preaching, they invited us all to come up and join hands in a circle to pray. They all got in the middle, and as we prayed, they walked in the circle laying hands on us and praying for us individually. When that preacher laid his hands on me, I felt the power of God as if a wind was blowing through me. When I walked out of those doors that night I knew that I was different, but I couldn't put my finger on exactly what had happened.

The next night, an ex-con came in to preach. The men were still excited about the night before and it was obvious when we began to sing. As we sang *Victory in Jesus*, some of the guys started clapping their hands, and the ex-con preacher freaked out and stopped the worship. He said, "I'm an independent, separated, fundamentalist Baptist from the top of my head to the tip of my toes, and what you men are doing is wrong! Now, let's try again." Then he started the song over very calmly, and, frankly, it was quite boring. For the first time, I experienced what it was like to actually feel the Holy Spirit leave a place.

Later in my studies, I came to understand that the man had (unintentionally, I'm sure) quenched the Holy Spirit (1 Thessalonians 5:19). All I thought at that time was that Christians sure were some confused people, but then I began to understand what the warden was doing. He was a Baptist Sunday School teacher, yet he was allowing us to experience the different denominations so we could choose for ourselves. That way when we walked out of Jackson we would have some direction as we hopefully searched for our own church home.

It was the same thing the Gideons were doing for me concerning my education. The courses they sent shared different points of view—usually three. One was kind of out there, and I would wonder why anyone would believe that. Then one view would be reasonable. You could see how someone would come to that conclusion. But then there would be one view that would ring true. At this point, they did not specify where the different views came from, just that they existed.

Little did I know that I was becoming doctrinally sound in my theology, and I was lining up with the group whom the inmates referred to as the "Wild Ones." They were from a holiness church.

For Reflection . . .

I've noticed over the years that doctrine has little to do with why most people choose a church. Someone invites them to church, they get saved (hopefully), they join the church, and they accept whatever they are taught. Many people join a church because they like the music or because they like the children's program, or because it's a big pretty church, or whatever, and then just accept whatever the preacher says.

Please don't just blindly follow whatever you hear preached, because if the preacher happens to be blind, you are both going to fall in the ditch (Matthew 15:14). Read the Word of God for what it says. Do not stop until you have the Word of God in your hand and it becomes the experience in your life. Then no one can take that from you.

People still debate whether Jesus Christ is the Way, the Truth, and the Life, and that no one comes to the Father except through Him (John 14:6). But when you become a new creation in Christ, and behold, old things pass away, and behold, all things become new (2

Corinthians 5:17), then the debate is over! First John 2:3 says, *"Now by this we **know** that we **know** Him, if we keep His commandments"* (emphasis added). He is not talking about religiously trying to obey some rules. He's talking about a changed heart that loves to obey the commandments of God.

If you have prayed to accept Christ as your Lord and Savior and have no experience of being born again, and the old things are not passing away, and behold, all things are not becoming new, and if you have no joy in obeying the commandments, then get back down on your knees and pray again. Then when the Word of God in your hand becomes the experience in your life you will be ready to move on to the next issue you need to settle in your walk with God.

And for goodness sake, if someone tells you that you do not need to obey the commandments of God, then get out of there because the next verses in 1 John 2:4-5 say, *"He who says, 'I know Him,' and does not keep His commandments is a liar and the truth is not in him. But whoever keeps His Word, truly the love of God is perfected in him. By this we know that we are in Him."*

If someone is contradicting scripture, then I don't care how good the music is, or how big the church is, or how famous the preacher is. Get out of there. In 2 Timothy 4:3, it says, *"For the time will come when they will not endure sound doctrine, but according to their own desires, because they have itching ears, they will heap up for themselves teachers."*

Did you catch that? *"They will heap up for themselves teachers"* who will tell them what they want to hear because of their *"own desires."* If people are going to *"heap up"* these teachers in the last days, that tells us they will not be in short supply.

31

"Look at the Birds of the Air"

Jackson County was a work farm, of that there was no doubt. I was placed on the carpentry detail, which really just meant that if there was any carpentry to be done, we did it, but those jobs were few and far between. For the most part, it was just good old-fashioned Georgia chain gang labor.

I spent a lot of time having long talks with God while picking green beans in the blazing Georgia sun. I never realized that green beans grew along the ground. We would bend over and pick beans as long as we could, until our backs hurt so badly we would have to drop to our knees and crawl. Then, when our knees would begin to bleed and we couldn't take that anymore, we would stand up again for a while.

I told the Lord that I didn't mean to be critical, but it seemed to me that if He had created green beans to hang from trees, the world would have been a much nicer place.

Many days we would just cut bushes along the side of the road, slinging a bush ax for miles on end. On one such day, I knew the Lord was up to something because the conversation among the men just wasn't normal. All they could do was talk about what they were going to do when they got out, which is something that never happens.

Lord, Miracle Me Out of this Place

As I said before it's kind of like Christians when they talk about Heaven. We all want to go but never give much thought about what we will do once we get there. We think of Heaven as a wonderful place that is so far away. Since we have no idea when we will go, we never make plans for what we're going to do when the time comes. We just know we want to go.

So it is with getting out of prison. It's a wonderful thought, but it is so far away and you have no idea when that day will finally come, so you don't really make any plans. You just want out. On this day on the chain gang, however, it was all the men could talk about—how they got out last time, the mistakes they made, and how they would do it differently this time. It reminded me of all the times I had tried to come up with some new plan, but my plans always led me back to the same place, and this stretch was going to be for a very, very long time.

There was one comforting thought that I had learned to hold onto during my years of doing time: "time does pass." No one can stop it. Oh, it may seem to stand still, but God created this universe and set it in motion, thus creating time, and its very nature is to move. The experience of time is relevant based on our circumstances, but the fact is that nothing can slow it down.

If you are going through some kind of trial or tribulation that seems as though it will never end, just know that *this too shall pass*. You may be suffering from some sickness, or be in a drug program, or maybe you're in prison right now. The one thing I can promise you is that it will end. The question is not "if" that moment will come. The question is, "What is going to happen when it does?"

This was my dilemma. What was I going to do? I had done nothing but deal drugs all my life and work at the family dry cleaning business while on parole. My parents were in their sixties. That business wouldn't be there by the time I did a life sentence. And doing all this time wasn't going to help anybody. It didn't even make sense. Jesus paid for my sins, and I know they call doing time paying your debt to society, but you're not paying them anything. You're just costing good people more money every day.

So I began to think. I'm not that person anymore. My only desire is to live for God and to sincerely make amends for all the pain I had caused people, and swinging this bush ax wasn't helping anybody. Besides that, I had an all-powerful Father in Heaven who loves me, and no father would want to see his son do a life sentence!

It hit me. All God needed to do was just miracle me out of that place! So I prayed and asked Him. I said, "Lord, You have the power to miracle me right out of here. You could just snap Your fingers, and *poof!* I could just be home and no one would notice. I could just be home right now doing good, and I wouldn't tell anybody what You did. It could be our secret. Yeah, Lord! That's what You need to do. Just miracle me out of this place and let everyone just forget about me!"

Then God began to make that thought real to me. To make a long story short, God showed me that as much as He would like to do that, I wasn't ready to go home and face what I would have to face. See, a father's love is like that. No father wants to see his son suffer, but he will allow it if it is for his son's own good, and that is where I was. I was not ready to face all those people with money wanting drugs, and all those people with drugs wanting money. The devil had me believing a lie. I could not imagine how anyone could live on a normal, menial paycheck. I thought that unless you made $1,000 a day, you couldn't pay your light bill. The truth is, when you're a criminal, you do have to make $1,000 a day to pay your light bill because that money is cursed.

Facing the Facts: I Had Destroyed My Life

I had no understanding that money can be cursed or blessed. All I knew is that when I went into a grocery store, I could spend $400 and come out with nothing to eat, so obviously I could not support my family on a minimum wage paycheck. And I couldn't see how serving another 10 years in prison was going to help! A dark cloud of despair began to set in on me as I came to realize that I had destroyed my life. It was just that simple.

By this point, we had worked our way up to a bridge that went over the Oconee River. The detail officer decided that would be a good place to stop and eat lunch. One of the inmates said, "Hey, Boss. How about letting us walk down by the river?"

To our amazement he said, "Go ahead."

Now, just in case you don't know, that never should have happened. The inmate who asked was making a joke. Guards just don't let 16 convicts loose in the woods unsupervised to walk by any river for lunch! All they would have to do is jump in and start swimming, and even the dogs wouldn't be able to track them.

So we all went down to the river and found a fishing line extending from a bush it was tied to. The men pulled it in. Lo and behold, it had a hook on the end. One man said, "Hallelujah, let's go fishing!" That's certainly not something men serving time get to do.

All we needed was bait. We all started looking for a worm. Now, I'm not a fisherman and had never taken time to go fishing, so I had no idea where to find worms. But we had some country boys out there who had been digging worms all their lives. They were yelling, "Roll that log over!" "Look under that mulberry bush!" or whatever. They searched to no avail and then began to panic. Time was running out. All 16 men ran to the detail truck, got shovels, and started digging. I'm telling you, we plowed up an area for a good-size garden along the Oconee River that day and never found a single worm.

After the day was over and we were headed back to the prison, we stopped by an old building that the county was going to refurbish for use as a 911 emergency call center. (That's right. We were so far out in the boondocks that they didn't even have 911 service in 1991.) Our detail was going to do the carpentry work on rainy days, so the detail officer went in to see what they wanted us to do. We all hung out around the van.

I stood there thinking about how I would never make it in the free world ever again. I could hear some birds chirping and looked around. I spotted a hole in the cornice board of the overhang. Apparently a bird had made a nest up in there, and it sounded like she had four or five baby birds just a-crying.

About that time, she flew out of that hole, went right by my head, landed in the grass, picked up a worm, and flew right back into the hole. Then she flew right back out of the hole, went right by my head, landed in the grass, picked up a worm, and flew right back into that hole. As far as I knew, she may have been doing that all day long.

I have never in my life been walking along on a bright, sunny day and looked down in the grass and seen worms crawling around on it. Not to mention that we had already concluded they didn't grow worms in that county anyway because we had already looked! There was only one explanation: God Himself was giving that bird those worms.

After we came in from detail, I opened my Bible to study as always. I had left off at Matthew 6:24, which says, *"No one can serve two masters, for either he will hate the one and love the other, or else he will be loyal to the one and despise the other. You cannot serve God and mammon."* The word mammon simply means wealth or riches, and the message was clear: I was going to have to choose whom and what I was going to trust in.

But when I got to Matthew 6:26, I sat there stunned. It said, *"Look at the birds of the air, for they neither sow nor reap nor gather into barns, yet your heavenly Father feeds them. Are you not of more value than they?"* As I sat there staring at the verse, I realized that was what that pastor, Charles Sineath, was preaching on many years before when I had walked into that Methodist church and Satan had sent those profane images into my mind so I could not hear it.

Facing the Truth: God Provides and Redeems

I began to weep as I realized just how much God loves us and how far ahead of time He had been planning that day for me. Sixteen men swinging a bush ax the perfect number of times to end up by a river that God created long ago. He touched a guard's heart to trust a bunch of convicts to go down by the river where He had some fisherman leave a line tied to a bush. God hid His worms from a group of men, and had a mother bird and her babies in the perfect place at a perfect time just to teach a broken-down convict with no hope a lesson in life.

And what was that lesson? That I was worried about the wrong thing! I thought that my life was too complicated to ever straighten out, that I could never really make it on the outside, when all I had to do was, *"Look at the birds of the air, for they neither sow nor reap nor gather into barns."* They have no harvest stored up. No food in a pantry. No money in a savings account. Their very existence depends on the mercy of God day by day. And I have never seen or heard of a bird starving to death, for our heavenly Father is faithful to feed them, and we are of more value than they.

Then Matthew 6:27 says, *"Which one of you by worrying can add one cubit to his stature?"* My whole life I wished I had been taller, but there was no use worrying about that. I was worried because I had paid those lawyers all that money and couldn't get them to answer my calls. I was worried about Dani and the kids, but there was not one thing I could do for them while I was locked in a cage. I was worried about going to court, but I had no power over the system, jury, or judge. I was worried about my parents and the family business, but I was undeserving of both.

All I had was time, and I was wasting it worrying about things that I could not change.

Matthew 6:28-29 say, *"So why do you worry about clothing? Consider the lilies of the field, how they grow. They neither toil nor spin, and yet I say to you that even Solomon in all of his glory was not arrayed like one of these."*

Think about that. Solomon, the richest man who ever lived, had thousands of servants to make him clothes, but his royal purple robe was never as purple as the lilies or as red as a rose that God would simply grow. All of Solomon's efforts to toil and spin beauty did not compare to what God simply grows all around us every day.

Matthew 6:30 says, *"Now, if God clothes the grass of the field, which today is and tomorrow is thrown into the oven, will He not much more clothe you, o you of little faith."*

Well, there was the problem, and I knew it. At that point in my life, I just didn't have the faith to walk out of those doors and start a whole new life in the midst of what I had to face. I had so much to overcome that I wouldn't even know where to start.

Matthew 6:31 says, *"Therefore do not worry, saying, 'What shall we eat?' or 'What shall we drink?' or 'What shall we wear?'"*

Even on my worst days I would make sure that my family had food to eat and clothes to wear before myself. So now God was telling me that I didn't even have to worry about them. How could this be?

Matthew 6:32 says, *"For after all these things the Gentiles seek. For your heavenly Father knows that you need all these things."*

Yes, I was definitely a Gentile who had spent his life seeking after stuff. It made me tired just thinking about how hard I had run my life, making things so complicated, when all along I could have simply turned to God who knows exactly what we need and has absolutely no problem providing for us. I had been such a fool, and now it was too late!

Then Matthew 6:33 starts with *"But."* But *what?* You mean there's a "but" to this situation? *"But seek first the kingdom of God and His righteousness and all these things shall be added to you."*

I knew right then that God had just given me the key—the key to open prison doors. The key to taking care of my family. The key to a whole new life on the outside, for God would add all of those things to me if I would *"but seek first the kingdom of God and His righteousness."* There it was. Life made simple.

I didn't need to worry about lawyers, courts, judges, juries, wives, kids, family, business, or the other multitude of things I could not change. All I needed to do was focus on one thing—seeking His kingdom and His righteousness, and He would take responsibility for everything else.

As soon as I was ready, God would open those doors, and when I flew out of this nest, the worm would be there. He would have everything in place. I like to interpret Matthew 6:33 like this: "Truly make God the most important thing in your life, and leave the rest of the mess you've made to Jesus." He's the only One who can straighten it out anyway.

32

"Seeking the Kingdom"

THE KINGDOM OF God operates much differently from the kingdom of the world, so it takes a whole paradigm shift in the way we think to understand it. For example, in the world's kingdom, the rulers are the greatest and the servants are considered inferior. Then, on the very bottom rung of the ladder, are slaves. A slave is so low that his position is considered to be worse than that of a convict. But not so in the kingdom of God.

Matthew 20:25-28 says, *"But Jesus called them to Himself and said, 'You know that the rulers of the Gentiles lord it over them, and those who are great exercise authority over them. Yet it shall not be so among you; but whoever desires to become great among you, let him be your servant. And whoever desires to be first among you, let him be your slave—just as the Son of Man did not come to be served, but to serve, and to give His life a ransom for many.'"*

In the kingdom of the world, if you want to be rich, you hoard all you can. Not so in the kingdom of God. If you want to prosper in the kingdom of God, you give away just as a farmer sows (gives away) seed to reap a much larger crop.

The Law of the Harvest—A Law You Cannot Break

2 Corinthians 9:6 says, *"But this I say: He who sows sparingly will also reap sparingly, and he who sows bountifully will also reap bountifully."* The Apostle

Paul is speaking of money here. He says if you only give a little, then you are only going to have a little. But if you will give away a lot, then you are going to have much. In the kingdom of the world, this does not add up.

Yet, we see this principle of sowing and reaping in all of God's creation. In the world's kingdom they think it applies only to literal seed, but when you begin to understand kingdom principles, the law of sowing and reaping applies to all things.

Galatians 6:7-8 says, *"Do not be deceived, God is not mocked; for whatever a man sows, that he will also reap. For he who sows to his flesh will of the flesh reap corruption, but he who sows to the Spirit will of the Spirit reap everlasting life."* Simply put, if you do something bad, you're going to get something bad. You can't commit sins and expect a fruitful life any more than you can plant a grain of corn and get an apple tree.

God created all things to *"yield fruit after its own kind"* (Genesis 1:11), and this is a principle that we simply cannot violate. It does not matter how smart you are, or how well you plan. It doesn't even matter if you *know* this to be true or *believe* it to be true. You are not going to take something bad and make it into something good. God knows I tried, and if you are trying to do the same, then I'm sorry to tell you that you are wasting your time. It's just not going to happen.

Most of the men that I've met in prison are actually in there for this very reason. Oh, they were in for many different crimes, but in every case it was the law of reaping what you sow. Very few of these men really meant harm. Most of us were just like Adam and Eve. We believed the lie that we could disobey God and have a better life, but it just isn't so. When we try to sow something bad and get something good, we are attempting to violate the very nature of creation and overcome the very God who created everything, including us. You're not going to beat Him, so you might as well join Him. Then you'll have peace, love, and joy.

One thing you must understand is that sowing and reaping is not instantaneous. When you sow a seed, it takes time to germinate before it sprouts, grows, and brings forth fruit. When God blessed Dani and me with our first home, I went to Home Depot and bought some tulip bulbs. I followed the directions and placed them under the dirt and watered them.

I would check on them from time to time. If leaves fell on that area, I would clear them off. After a while, I thought, *Those things aren't going to grow. Home Depot has ripped me off!*

Then one day, I walked by my kitchen window, and what do you think I saw? That's right: Tulips. Big ones! I never even noticed they had sprouted. So it is with sin. We do something wrong, and there are no immediate consequences. We think we have gotten away with it, but *"God is not mocked."* The seed has been planted and is now germinating. You may see it sprout up and suffer some small consequences before the fruit manifests. Or you may be blind to it and be caught by surprise like I was with the tulips. One day, the doorbell may ring and there will stand a man with a badge. Or you may come home and find that your wife has left you. But know this: *Whatever a man sows, that shall he also reap.*

People like me are often asked to give our testimonies, but in our eyes the greatest testimony is a person who has lived his or her whole life for God. Pastor Keith tells of times when as a young boy he would wake up in the middle of the night to find his mother lying across the bed at his feet pleading with God to protect him. Now *that* is a great story!

I can't count the times people suffering some consequence from sin, such as being caught, will actually try to tell me it is the first time they ever did it. I'm quick to tell them, "Not only do I know better, but that's not even biblical!" When you sow something, it takes a little time to come back. Now, I'm not trying to put God in a box. He is the only One who can and does from time to time overcome the nature of His creation. It is what we refer to as miracles—such as when He walks on water, divides the Red Sea, raises the dead, heals the leper, or busts somebody the first time they do something wrong!

But here's what we really have to understand: Once we get the process of sowing and reaping going in one direction or the other, it takes quite a bit of energy, effort, and time to get it turned around. For example, if you have a parcel of land filled with big trees and thorn bushes, etc., it will take a lot of work to clear out the old so you can plant a new, productive, fruitful crop. So it is with our lives.

I've seen men go to jail, repent, and get saved. They know they are a new creation in Christ so they fully expect God to just let them out (just as I wished God to miracle me out and make it like nothing happened), but then they go to court and get their time. Then the enemy comes along and begins to whisper in their ear things like, "See, changing your life makes no difference. God doesn't care. You have just imagined the whole thing!" And they turn their back on God again. The only problem is that they are still reaping the old things they have sown. If they would just continue sowing righteousness, that too would come back as the old crop passed away.

If you have been living a life of sin and are reaping what you have sown, ask God to forgive you, repent of your sins, and start sowing to the Spirit. Read your Bible, do good to those who are persecuting you, consider God in all your ways. Though it may take a little time to germinate, it will sprout and bring forth fruit. Here is the good news: Nobody can stop the good things from coming back to you. The police can't stop it. People who hate you can't stop it. The devil can't stop it. All the powers of hell cannot stop the process of your reaping what you sow. Whether what you reap is good or bad is up to you.

Seeking First the Kingdom and His Righteousness

Now of course, learning the principles of God's kingdom is a lifelong journey for all of us, but you don't have to know everything for the wonderful promise to *"seek first the kingdom of God and His righteousness, and all these things shall be added to you"* to become a reality in your life. This promise is not based on "knowing" the kingdom of God but rather on "seeking" it. I'm not saying this because I think it. I know it, for I have the Word of God in my hand and the experience in my life to prove it.

I'm going to give it to you in a nutshell. Trust me when I say that it will be enough to straighten out your life any time it needs an adjustment.

The word "kingdom" comes from two words: "king" and "dominion." A king has complete and total dominion and authority in his "kingdom."

Jesus said, *"The kingdom of God is within you"* (Luke 17:21). As I have said, there is much more to the kingdom of God, but for Matthew 6:33 to become a reality in your life, this is where you start—with seeking the kingdom of God that is within you.

That means simply give Jesus Christ, the King of Kings and Lord of Lords, complete and total dominion in your life. It's not always easy, but it's definitely not complicated. Would Jesus rather you lie in the bed or go to church? Would He rather you hold a grudge or forgive? Would Jesus rather you spend your time and money on this or that? If you honestly don't know, just ask Him. He will tell you.

Jesus loves you more than you could ever love Him. He wants you in His will more than you want to be there! He wants to save your soul more than you want to live, and He wants to bless you more than you want to be blessed.

Then when you give Him complete dominion in your life and are plugged into His kingdom, you have all kinds of *"great and precious promises, that through these you may be partakers of the divine nature, having escaped the corruption that is in the world through lust"* (2 Peter 1:4). To be a partaker of the divine nature means that you participate in the supernatural life of God. The very divine nature of Jesus Christ has become part of who you are, *"far above all principality, power, might and dominion, and every name that is named, not only in this age, but also in that which is to come"* (Ephesians 1:21).

God Opens Doors: From Helpless Convict to Partaker of the Divine Nature

I made up my mind that unless it had to do with Jesus Christ I wasn't going to read it, watch it, talk about it, or even think about it. It wasn't long before I realized that I was no longer a helpless convict. I was a partaker of the divine nature, and I did not need a telephone to "reach out and touch someone" or be concerned if God could "hear me now."

Men began to turn to me for prayer and advice. At times I would be concerned about someone who didn't make it to church that night or whatever and feel I needed to check on him. One of the most serious offenses in the prison was to break security protocol by going into another prison dorm where you did not belong, but the men I ministered to were scattered all over the prison.

I could walk up to a dormitory door and say, "Lord, will You please open this door so I can go pray for Henry?" and I would hear a big *click*. I'd open the door and walk right in. The men would look in terror because they knew the guards would put the whole place on lockdown if a prisoner was not where he was supposed to be, but I knew there was nothing to fear because God had opened the door. I'd go over, pray with Henry, then walk up to that door without ringing a buzzer or calling a guard and say, "Thank you, Lord. Will You please open this door so I can get back to my dorm?" and *click*. I'd just walk right out, go to my dorm door, pray, *click*, walk right in. If I felt I needed to go into a dorm, but the Lord didn't open the door when I prayed, it never bothered me. I figured if God didn't want me in there enough to open the door, I certainly didn't want to be in there either. This is a principle I still apply to this day, metaphorically speaking, of course.

There is a park on the Oconee River in Jackson County called Hurricane Shoals. The Indians considered this area holy ground, and it was easy to see why. The beauty of that place truly reflects the nature of God. One day our carpentry detail went there to repair a pavilion, and I spotted a huge rock down by the river. I said, "Lord, I sure would love to go down and sit on that big rock and pray someday."

The next day, the detail officer said, "They need one man to work at Hurricane Shoals, so I'm sending you." I worked that morning, and I asked the park guard if it would be okay if I went down to sit on that rock to eat lunch and pray. He looked at me as though I was up to something, so I explained the whole story of how I had prayed the day before.

He said, "Well, in that case, I guess you better go on down there!"

I had an intimate time with God that day that I will never forget. When I got back to the guard house, all that man wanted to do was ask questions about God. He prayed to receive Christ, and from that day forward, if he ever needed an inmate to work, I was the man. I had many wonderful days with the Lord in that place.

No Longer the Daddy with Long Hair and Brown Boots

I had not seen Dani and the kids for several months. It was a long drive, and since Shane was only 3 and Chelsi 18 months, they didn't really understand what was going on anyway. Besides, Dani had already waited for me through one prison term. I had no illusion that our relationship would survive a life sentence, so I never pushed the issue of bringing the kids to see me. But I started to really miss them, so I prayed. And, of course, there they were, just like everything else I prayed about.

I loved on Chelsi for a while and noticed that Shane kept looking around as if he was looking for someone. I got down on the visitation room floor to roll toy cars and play with him. About the time visitation was over, Shane stood up, walked over to me, looked me right in the eye, and said sternly, "I came here to see my daddy with the long hair and the brown boots."

I said, "I am your daddy with the long hair and the brown boots."

He started screaming, "No, you're not! I want to see my daddy with the long hair and the brown boots!" He turned to Dani, "You promised me I could see my daddy!"

He clung to my leg, looking up at me with those big baby eyes, begging me to get his daddy. Visitation ended, and the guards literally had to pull Shane off of my leg, screaming and crying for his daddy! It was one of the worst moments of my life.

As I stood against the wall in the search position for the guard to make sure I wasn't attempting to smuggle in any contraband, I could see Dani's car going down the prison drive. Then it hit me. Shane was right. I was not his daddy with the long hair and the brown boots anymore. That man was dead and needed to be, but it did not change the fact that this little boy loved that daddy, no matter how messed up he was.

This went way beyond the fact that my hair was now short, I had gained 50 pounds, and I was dressed in a white prison uniform with blue stripes and no boots. No, this was a spiritual thing. And the only hope I had of touching that little boy's heart was by partaking of the divine nature. As I stood in the spread-eagle position being searched with my hands up against the wall, I noticed that my watch said 2:30.

I began to pray and ask God to touch Shane—to relieve his pain, give him peace, and so on. I could hardly wait to get to a phone that night to check up on him. When I called the house, Dani said that while they were driving down the road going home, Shane was still crying. She looked at the clock on the car dashboard: 2:30. Shane stopped crying, looked at Dani with bright, clear eyes and a smile on his face, and said, "Now I know that was my daddy!" and just happily played the rest of the way home.

She put Shane on the phone, and before I could ask anything he said, "I know you're my daddy."

I said, "You do?"

He said, "Uh huh. And it's going to be okay."

When he said, "It's going to be okay," it was as if God Himself was speaking to me. I knew right then that I was not going to lose my family. I couldn't imagine how, but I knew that as I was *seeking the kingdom of God* my family was going to *"be added to"* me.

33

"And His Righteousness"

BY THE SUMMER of 1991, I was sold out to God, and we were having a great time. I was praying, and He was answering. I was studying, and He was teaching. We actually organized our own church in the prison that still exists today—"The New Alpha Church." We had a choir and the chaplain would take us to local churches on Sunday mornings to sing. My whole detail got saved, and I became their spiritual leader and teacher.

Grieving the Holy Spirit

One beautiful day we were building a pole barn to store the prison equipment under. We were talking about the church service the night before, and as usual they were all asking me Bible questions. Then it happened. I dropped my guard. I allowed the conversation to turn from God to ourselves. Now we were all talking about the old life, and began to "glory in our shame."

As we began to talk about who'd had the most dope or who'd pulled off the wildest heist, I felt the quenching of the Holy Spirit (1 Thessalonians 5:19), but I just kept flowing with it. Then it happened. I told a lie to make myself look better than I really was to one of the men. Now I felt the grieving of the Holy Spirit (Ephesians 4:30). I knew right then I should just repent and confess to that man right on the spot, but I couldn't bring myself to do it. I just let it go, and with it went my love, joy, and peace.

When we got back to the dorm, I opened my Bible studies but could not concentrate because all I could think about was telling that lie and how I should have confessed it to that man. I went to church and could not concentrate in worship or stay focused on the message. When I got down on my knees that night by my bunk to pray, it was as though God was pushing my prayers back into my mind.

I kept thinking it would pass, but it didn't. It was this continuous conviction, so I started trying to justify it.

"Lord, why are You so upset? All I did was exaggerate. I didn't hurt anybody. You know I can't confess to that man. That would be a sign of weakness, and if he told other men, it could be dangerous. Besides, it will mess up my testimony. And look at all these other guys and all the stuff they do. You never get on to them, and I make one little mistake, and You won't let me slide!"

Well, that was a mistake, because for quite a while, God just brought one offense after another to my mind—things I had said, things I had done, and things I had thought. By the time God began to lay bare the motives of my heart, my self-righteousness had turned to dust.

That night when I went to church, the message was on the self-righteous Pharisee and the repentant tax collector from Luke 18:9-14! Before the altar call was over, I had confessed sins that I had already confessed, just to make sure they were really confessed. I started confessing sins for the whole world. I don't know who you are, but I probably confessed some sins for you! I thought for sure this had been the whole point of this very painful lesson. Yet the burden to confess that particular lie, to that particular man, was still there.

For Reflection . . .

Applying God's Word "Rightly"

To be a *"partaker of the divine nature"* through His *"great and precious promises"* (as 2 Peter 1:4 says) you must apply God's Word exactly as it is written, or *"rightly"* as it is written. Never ignore any part of a verse or take something out of context. Righteousness is living right based on God's Word.

In seeking the kingdom, you are submitting your will to God's will—learning to do things His way and applying His principles. You are giving Him dominion in your life, but then we must learn how to live that out in righteousness. Listen to the words of Dr. Jack Hayford:

"Putting God's kingdom first is the first step on the pathway of God's miracles, and you cannot walk on this pathway unless determining His will, purpose, and glory is your first priority as you pursue His call on your life."

In other words, as we give the King dominion in our life and ask our King whether we should do this or that, we come to the place where we learn to do this or that the "right way." There is only one right way, and that is God's way. It's not up for debate or subject to a vote. God is not running a democracy. He is running a monarchy. A kingdom in which He is the King and we are his subjects.

In Revelation 3:14, the last-day church is described as *"the church of the Laodiceans,"* which means "people rule" or "people's rights." It describes an atmosphere of being neither cold nor hot, which makes God sick. It's an attitude that we *"have need of nothing"*—that somehow God's Word is old and outdated. For example, that mindset says it is unreasonable for God to expect a woman and a man to accept responsibility for their actions and have a baby that might be inconvenient. They should have the "right" to choose. That's a democracy.

When you speak of pursuing God's righteousness, some people will accuse you of being legalistic. The truth is that obedience is not legalism or a legalistic attitude. Lawyers do not study the law to obey it. Lawyers look for loopholes—how they can question it, debate it, and use it to their advantage.

And what were the first words out of Satan's mouth in the Garden of Eden? *"Has God indeed said?"* (Genesis 3:1). When you pursue righteousness, you go from *"Has God indeed said?"* to simply "What does God say?" Then once you find out "what God says" you do it. It's not complicated, but it can be very hard sometimes because we are very unrighteous people. God's righteousness goes against the grain, so to speak, to the point that we feel as though we have been scourged.

Hebrews 12:6 says, *"For whom the Lord loves He chastens, and scourges every son He receives."* This chastening has everything to do with righteousness. As a matter of fact, Hebrews 12:11 says, *"Now no chastening seems to be joyful for the present, but painful; nevertheless, afterward it yields the peaceable **fruit of righteousness** to those who have been trained by it"* (emphasis added).

The reason we have to be *"trained by it"* is that righteousness does not come natural to our sinful nature. What comes natural to us is to justify our actions—to brush off sin as though it is no big deal because, after all, no one got hurt, and we are under grace.

The truth is that those seemingly small offenses and the acts of obedience God requires that follow are actually training us for greater things. Very often it is the small, seemingly insignificant things or events that ultimately determine our destiny. What I'm about to share with you is probably the greatest lesson that God ever taught me concerning our walk with Him.

Crossing the Bridge to Go Farther with God

Then I got the bright idea to start debating scripture with God, knowing good and well the Pharisees had tried that one, too. I said, "Lord, Your Word says in 1 John 1:9 that if we confess our sins to You, You are faithful and just to forgive us our sins, so that should be the end of it!"

God said, "Read the rest of the verse."

"I don't want to read the rest of the verse!"

Just in case you don't know, the rest of the verse starts, *"And . . . ."* Don't you hate that word sometimes?

"And to cleanse us from all unrighteousness." I knew then exactly what was going on. I was being "cleansed," scrubbed, and scourged. I had been a bottom dweller of the muck and mire of sin for so long that unrighteousness

had grown on me like barnacles on the bottom of a riverboat. Pouring water over me wasn't going to cleanse me. I needed a good scrubbing.

I gave it one last try. I got down on my knees by my bunk and said, "Lord I get it. I understand. I won't forget this lesson. Please take this cup from me!" And of course, the rest of the verse, *"but not my will, but Yours be done,"* came to mind. I also understood that this act of obedience was no comparison to what Jesus went through for me, but by this point I realized there was no comparison between the two of us anyway.

In helplessness I said, "Lord, don't You love me?" And immediately I felt all pressure and conviction leave me. I thought I had found my loophole because somehow I knew that God was never going to pressure me to confess my lie to that man ever again.

But then these words came into my mind: "Yes, I love you, and we can stop right here."

I knew exactly what God meant. If that was as far as I wanted to go with God, then that was my choice. I could just keep on studying the Bible, and praying on my rock at Hurricane Shoals, and singing in that hideous-sounding prison choir, and God would just love me and we could do that life sentence together. But if I wanted to go farther with God, if I really wanted to know what God had in store for me, then I had to cross this bridge.

I said, "Of course I don't want to stop here. I don't ever want to look back, let up, slow down, back away, or be still. Consider it done." I didn't know what going farther with God was going to look like, but I was finished with the old life. The ball was in my court.

I crawled into bed to get some rest, for I knew the next day would be long and hard. As soon as I confessed my weakness and the news spread across that dormitory, there was no telling how many fights I would be in by this time the next night. Maybe God would have mercy and transfer me soon. But it was also just the humiliation and embarrassment of the whole thing—to look a man in the eye and confess that I had told him a lie to make myself look better than I was. I mean, there was no pressure to lie. No one even asked me a question. I just lied because I was a liar!

As I lay there, I came to realize there was not one righteous ounce of blood in my body. Apart from God, I was nothing but dirt, and *dirty* dirt at that. The new life I had found in Him was also completely and totally dependent on Him. God had not made me a new person so that I could go live a new life any more than you charge up a battery so it can run your phone forever. My new life flowed from Him. Unplug us and before long we are nothing but a dead battery.

"Now I get it, Lord! You are the vine and I am the branch. Apart from You I can do nothing but rot. Oh, I can stay green for a little while but not for long, so why take the chance? If I had not allowed myself to drift down that old path of self-exaltation, then I never would have told that lie! Oh, that liar is still in there. We just need to make sure he doesn't get loose any more. If we don't give him any air, maybe he will just die. Until then, I'm hanging on to You, Lord, because apart from Your righteousness, I have none! I get it, and if we live through tomorrow, I'm going to cling to You like white on rice, like a peel on a banana, like a . . . ."

All of the sudden, at about 3:00 a.m., I sat straight up in my bed, wide awake. I had no doubt God had just awakened me, and to my surprise as I looked around the dorm, every man was sound asleep. There is never a time when all 100-plus men are asleep in a dorm. It just doesn't happen. You could hear a pin drop in that place. I looked over at the bunk of the man I was to confess to, and he sat straight up, wide awake, looking around trying to figure out what had just happened to him.

I said, "Okay, Lord, here we go."

I walked over to the man's bunk and just kept it simple and to the point. I said something like, "You know I'm a Christian and trying to live for God, and I told you a lie the other day. I was just trying to be something I'm not, and I'm done with that. I don't know why it is so important to God that I confess this to you, but God is more important to me than any fallout from showing my weakness."

He climbed down off his bunk with tears in his eyes and just started shaking my hand, saying, "Thank you, man! Thank you so much! You just can't know what that means to me! Thank you, brother!" and just walked off.

I said, "Well, Lord, that certainly went a lot better than I thought it was going to!" As far as I know, that man never told another soul.

When God Says "We Can Stop Right Here"

I'll never forget the Lord's words: "Yes, I love you, and we can stop right here." What a defining moment in a person's life! To know that there are moments in life when we have a choice to make that will completely and totally change our destiny—and very often we think of those choices as being small or insignificant. Here's the truth: *If God is in it, then it is significant.*

I was talking to a man not long ago and mentioned that God had said something to me. He said, "God used to speak to me, but He hasn't in a long time. I guess He has me in a holding pattern, just waiting on Him."

I said, "Really? What was the last thing He said?"

He just stared at me. So I asked him again, "What was the last thing God said to you?"

He said, "That He wanted me to quit smoking these cigarettes."

"Well, how long ago was that?"

He hung his head down. "Years."

I said, "Well, the good news is that all you have to do is quit smoking cigarettes, and He will start talking to you again. You're not waiting on the Lord, my friend. He is waiting on you."

So what happened to my friend? Well, he came up on an uncomfortable situation with the Lord and decided to "stop right here." I'm sure that he never imagined that one act of disobedience would have such an impact on his life, but I'm sure it has. I mean, if he had just crossed that bridge and continued to be led by the Holy Spirit, listening to that still, small voice, what would his life look like now?

If I had just gotten off my bunk in Stone Mountain prison as a teenager and gone to that church service knowing that God was going to do something in my life, what would my life look like now? Joshua 24:15 says, *"Choose this day whom you will serve,"* and every time we choose our will over His, there are going to be consequences. The sad part is that most of the time we don't have a clue what blessings we have missed.

I've seen this played out many times in people's lives. I'm over the benevolence ministry at our church, and I can't count the times I've had people come to me and say that the Lord has touched their heart to help someone who is changing their life. They may want to buy a new believer a car, or give some ex-con a job, or help a single mom buy a house, etc. So we start putting the plans in motion, and the next thing you know, the person they wanted to help disappears.

The ex-con is going to receive a job offer at church on Sunday morning but doesn't show up because he was arrested for shoplifting the day before. Everyone is excited to present the new believer with the car on Sunday morning, but she doesn't show up because she's back in the dope house. We have the money to help the single mom get a place to live, but then we have to track her down, only to find out that she has decided to shack up with some loser who can't take care of himself much less her and the baby. Before, she had a child to take care of, but now she has a grown man to take care of on top of it all, and just missed the blessing that was on its way.

Coincidence? I think not. So it's not a case of God beating you over the head when you fall short, for God loves you and is patient and kind. The question is: *What did you just miss?*

34

"Tell Those People That
I Set You Free"

A FTER I CONFESSED that embarrassing lie to that man, God took me to obedience school. Romans 8:14 says, *"For as many as are led by the Spirit of God, these are the sons of God."* We're talking about spiritual maturity here. Going past the point of childish behavior where the Holy Spirit has to convict us to obey. Coming to a place where we are *"led"* by the Spirit of God. Learning to be faithful in the little things so that God can trust us with the big things (Luke 16:10).

Using a Turtle to Save a Criminal

Things started happening. For example, one day we would be out on detail and the Lord would say, "Pick up that piece of paper."

I'd think, "Where did that thought come from?"

Then gently the Lord would say, "Pick up that piece of paper."

"Yes, Sir."

I've been a Christian for over 25 years now, and from time to time God still tells me to pick up paper.

One day we were out on detail and the Lord said, "Rescue that turtle."

I said, "What turtle?"

The Lord didn't say anything, so I began to look for a turtle. We were all swinging bush axes, so I figured we were going to hit one. I told the guys, "Hey, be careful. The Lord just told me to rescue a turtle. Watch out for him."

One new guy looked at me like I was out of my mind and said, "Are you for real?"

About that time, he yelled, "There he is!" Sure enough, about 50 feet behind us there was a turtle walking right out into the highway. I guess we had disturbed his habitat.

The guard told the new guy, "Well, go down there and get him, and put him back in the woods."

So we all stood there watching him rescue the turtle and talking about how much God cares about even the little things. We joked about how Jesus often used birds as examples, but could anybody think of a scripture where God used turtles?

About that time, the Lord said, "Take the turtle up beyond the fence," as there was a fence running parallel to the highway farther back in the woods. I told them what the Lord said, so we all walked back down there. Sure enough, that crazy turtle was headed right back to the highway. Of course, I did what the Lord said and climbed through the fence with that turtle. I'm sure he was fine after that.

The new guy said, "I wish God would speak to me like that."

To make a long story short, he prayed to receive Christ right there by that busy highway. One good thing about a bunch of convicts' laying their hands on a man to pray while surrounded by guards armed with shotguns is that no one ever tries to interrupt you!

In 2 Samuel 12:1-7, God used the story of a lamb to change the heart of a king. On this day, He used a turtle to change the heart of a criminal.

I had been locked up about a year, so I knew my court date would be coming soon. I started getting nervous because I knew that I would be tempted to take matters into my own hands. I had made up my mind that if I was put in a position in which I was faced with telling the truth or telling a lie, then I was going to tell the truth, even if it would condemn me for life. I knew that if I was going to walk through a trial in truth, it would only be by the grace of God. (The divine influence upon the heart that is reflected in the life)

As I mentioned before, we had a prison choir. The chaplain would take us out to local churches, and one of us would share a brief, two-minute testimony between the songs. We were terrible, but God must have anointed Chaplain Akin's ears because he thought we were great. He would be leading us with the biggest smile on his face while the congregation behind him would look at us with horrified expressions. Sometimes they would hold up their hands and give us the stop signal, and I remember one man doing the cut signal across his throat as if to say, "Please cut it off!"

Then Chaplain Akin would turn around to the congregation and take a bow as though he had just led the Atlanta Symphony Orchestra. I was one of the better singers, and people at my church have told me that I have a supernatural voice. It raises the dead and kills the living.

At one such service, my time to speak came. I told the congregation that my only goal in life was to seek ye first the kingdom of God and His righteousness and leave the rest of the mess I'd made to Jesus. I told them that I should be going to trial soon, so I had a prayer request. It was not to get out, but that God's will be done. If I was going to have to do a life sentence, then I just needed to know that Satan had no place in that courtroom. As long as I knew when I walked out of that courtroom that my Father's will had been done, then I would be at peace. And I meant that from the bottom of my heart.

Just One Shot . . . What's the Harm?

Not too long after that, the guard from Hurricane Shoals pulled me off my regular detail to come and work out at the park. It was early on a beautiful summer morning and people were just starting to show up. I noticed this one guy sitting at a picnic table by himself. I knew immediately that there was something going on with that man, and it was not good.

As I trimmed with a weed eater and worked my way closer to the guy, I discerned in my spirit that he had a demon. He was pure evil. I prayed and asked God, "Why is he here?"

The Lord was not speaking to me in words, but I had no doubt that man was there to do harm. I began to think that maybe he had come to snatch a child out of the park, or maybe rape one of the many little girls who would be in the park that day.

About that time, he waved me over. As I walked up to him, he showed me a syringe already full and ready to shoot. The moment my eyes hit it, I tasted ether in the back of my throat and my body began to tremble. You can put a lot of drugs in a syringe, but I had no doubt this was my drug of choice—methamphetamine.

Sure enough, he said, "Hey, man, let me make your day. This is the best meth you have ever done in your life."

My mind kicked into high gear. *Well, it's just one shot.*

I've been helping drug addicts for 24 years, and I wish I had a dollar for every time I've heard that. "It's just one shot." "It's just two beers." "I only took one hit."

Anyway, I was thinking, *It's just one shot. It wouldn't hurt anybody. I could have a great day today. I'd even get more work done speeding my brains out. God would forgive me. I'm under grace and not the law. For God knows . . . .*

Right there, I snapped back into reality. I've read those words before, which were spoken in the Garden: *"For God knows."* I've heard so many people use that phrase. "God understands how much we want to be together." "God knows what I'm going to do anyway." "For God knows that I love Him." "For God knows that I'm not perfect." Or my all-time favorite. "For God knows my heart."

Yes, God knows. That's why Jesus Christ died a horrible death on the cross, and it certainly wasn't to give you an excuse to sin. It was to set you free from it. It was to show His love in spite of the fact that He knows you. While you were yet a sinner, Christ died for you, and your reasonable response should be to present your body a living sacrifice, holy and acceptable to God (Romans 12:1).

The fact that "God knows" scares the daylights out of me, and to know that He still loves me! Well, I'm certainly not going to hurt God's feelings just because I know He will forgive me. To take God's love for granted for one shot of this, or one night of that is just despicable. I certainly wasn't going to shove aside the God who loves me so I could get high with this sorry dope fiend.

I said, "First of all, I doubt seriously if that is anywhere close to the best meth I've ever done because I've done the best. And you'd better not drop that syringe out here in this park where a kid could find it. What are you doing out here anyway?"

He said, "I'm about to meet somebody."

I said, "You have got to be kidding me! Of all the places in the world to do a drug deal, you choose a family park with guards walking around. What are you, some kind of an idiot? Why don't you just go on down and check yourself into the jail right now!"

All of the sudden, something broke in the spiritual realm. His whole countenance changed from a sinister drug dealer to a scared rabbit.

I said, "You don't have to live like this. God loves you and has a plan for you." With that, he took off walking toward the parking lot.

As I followed behind him, trying to witness to him, the guard came out of the guard house and yelled, "What's going on?"

I said, "Just telling this dope fiend about Jesus, and he's running from me."

The guard yelled, "You want some help catching him?"

By then, the guy was literally running and jumped into his car. When he looked back at me through the windshield, he was struck with absolute terror. I started running along beside the car, yelling, "If you ever want to change your life, come back out here!"

At the same time, guards were running, yelling, "Get his tag number!" It was quite a scene.

After he was gone, we all walked everywhere we thought he may have been to make sure he didn't drop or hide any drugs or paraphernalia in the park. We had a great time talking about the power in the name of Jesus and so forth, but deep down inside I just knew that something special was going on in the spiritual realm.

That night, the pastor of the church where I asked for prayer concerning court came in to preach at the prison. As the service was beginning, I had the urge to pray. I sat there silently and closed my eyes, but when I started to pray my mind just shut down. Off in the distance, I heard the pastor say, "On August 11, we're having a homecoming at our church, and we want you men to join us."

Then these words came into my mind: "I want you to go to that church and tell those people that I set you free." I opened my eyes and looked at my watch, and the date was July 11, 1991.

I said, "Hmm. August 11 is exactly one month from today. What a coincidence."

I sat there thinking that would be impossible. I knew court would be soon, but I hadn't even gotten a date yet. Even if I did, I still had to be transferred back to jail. As I sat there thinking of reason after reason why it would be impossible for me to go to that church one month from that day and tell those people that God set me free, a joy was also welling up in me like fountains of living water.

During the altar call, I went up and told the pastor what had happened. He said, "Well, we need to pray." His prayer went something like this: "Lord, at least this man has the faith to believe You could do something like this."

I interrupted him and said, "But I don't have the faith. It's impossible. There is no way it can happen, but I do know that is what the Lord said, and right now I've got a joy welling up in me that's undeniable."

The pastor was very kind and patient, but he said that while God can do all things, his experience over the years was that when people started calling out dates and times it often led to disappointment.

I said, "But I didn't call out dates and times. I don't even believe the dates and times."

So we prayed that God would help me to understand what He meant and that I would not set myself up for a disappointment. The truth was that I had picked up enough paper, and rescued enough turtles, that I knew exactly what God said and exactly what He meant. The only problem was that it was impossible.

Now I just want to ask you a question. Do you think that I had the free will to choose to get high that day? Do you think that if I had done that shot I would have even come to church that night to hear about that homecoming service? Do you think that God would have still spoken to me or that I could have even heard Him while my mind was racing on methamphetamine? Do you think that one shot was a big deal or not?

Well, I'm convinced it was, and all I can say is that I'm so thankful that I will never know what would have happened if I had done that shot. I would much rather live my life never knowing what would have been the consequences of disobedience, rather than wondering if it really would have made a difference if I had just given up that one . . . .

35

"From Prison to the Pulpit"

AFTER THAT NIGHT, I tried to stay calm, but those words "I want you to go to that church and tell those people that I set you free" would run through my mind. That joy would well up in me, and then it would happen. I would tell someone what God said and then they would proceed to give me all of the explanations for what God may have meant.

"Grant, you always say you're more free now than you have ever been. Maybe God just wants you to share that when we go to that homecoming."

"Well, Joe, the only problem with that is we were not invited to come back and do our program. No one ever invites us back to sing twice, nor will they ever. They're just being nice to us because they love us. No one will be sharing testimonies."

"Maybe God just wants you to walk around during the dinner on the grounds and tell people that God set you free from drugs."

"Well, maybe." But deep down I knew what God meant. Either I had heard God or I hadn't, and I had come to know His voice. It was all very puzzling.

From Prison to the Pulpit without Passing Go

Then some strange things started happening. All of the sudden, I started getting letters from all of my old drug buddies. The first time you go to prison, a lot of letter writing takes place, but when you get older and you're going to prison for the third time, all that kind of stuff dies. Prison just becomes part of life. Someone in your circle is always going in or coming out of prison.

I had been in almost a year and hadn't heard from anybody, and now in one week I'd gotten seven letters. I knew exactly what was happening. God was giving me the opportunity to witness to these guys, but also to let them know where I stood, so they would know what to expect when I got out.

I never told any of them what God had said about August 11. I just told them of my conversion experience, how they too could be saved, and that my only goal in life was to *"seek ye first the kingdom of God and His righteousness."*

I only received one letter back, from a guy named Tim, who said something to the effect of, "Well, Grant, I'm glad to hear that you found a crutch to lean on while you're in there, but hurry up and come home. We haven't had anything good since you left." Apparently he didn't get it.

I had just finished reading the Bible from front to back and was on the verge of finishing my education as far as I could go in the correspondence courses offered. I sent off the last lessons the first week of August.

Dani's car had overheated when she brought the kids to see me, so Fat Bear had a new motor put in it and had been using my money to pay the mortgage, lot rent, and lawyers for a year. The last mortgage payment was sent the first of August. All the dirty money was gone.

It got all the way down to Friday, August 9, and I had not heard a word from my lawyers concerning any court date or anything. It is absolutely, positively impossible for a man to get out of prison on a Sunday if he hasn't heard anything by Friday. Even when the parole board decides to let a man go, it takes four months to complete all the necessary paperwork.

Even if a man is proven innocent and has been falsely imprisoned for years, he doesn't just walk out the door in less than 48 hours. Plus, they don't even let men out of prison on weekends because the prison system is a business like any other. Their offices are closed on weekends, so they schedule men to be released Monday through Friday.

Before a man is released, every county in the state must be notified, and every state in the nation, to make sure that you don't have any holds on you for other charges. I knew I had a hold because I had not even been to court yet.

Before a man is released, clothes are actually made for him because they take your clothes away at Jackson and burn them. Transportation has to be set up because prisoners don't have cars in the lot. No, there is no way a man is getting out of prison on a weekend if he hasn't heard anything by Friday, so I spent the day working and apologizing to God.

"Lord, I'm sorry that I told men that You were going to let me out of prison. First, I was a bad witness when I lied, and now this. Please, Lord, help these men to understand that I'm just messed up and this is no reflection on You. I can live in prison, but please don't let my insanity be a stumbling block to these men!"

Then I would try to encourage myself with things like, "Well, Lord, I guess we have something else to work on. I just get too excited sometimes. I definitely talk too much. I'll back off from ministering to these men, and You just let me know if You ever want me to do anything. Until then, I'll just be still."

After we came in from detail, I heard a guard yell, "Cole, to the captain's office!"

When I got to the door, the captain was sitting at his desk staring at a little slip of paper, bewildered. He said, "Cole, you're going home Sunday morning."

"I am?"

He said, "We don't even have a bus ticket for you."

I said, "That's okay. I'll get a ride."

He said, "We don't even have any clothes for you to wear."

I said, "That's okay. I'll figure something out."

He said, "Well, you're free to leave at midnight Sunday morning."

I thought about it for a second and said, "No, sir, God told me to go to a church and tell those people He set me free. I'd just as soon stay here until it is time to go to church. I don't want to mess this up. I want to do exactly what He said."

The captain replied, "Well, Cole, I guess that would be okay, but I'll have to check with the warden. I'm not even sure if that's legal. You may have to wait outside."

As I walked away from the office, I was just dumbfounded. One minute I was never getting out of prison, and the next minute I can't get them to let me stay a little longer! I thought, *Wow, God! You are amazing! You can turn things around in a heartbeat. One minute it seems like You're not there, and the next minute I can't keep up with You! I don't know if I'm coming, going, up, down, happy, or sad!*

So I went down to Henry's dorm, walked up to the door, prayed, *click*, and I went in.

"Hey, Henry. It's really going to happen!" and I told him the whole story.

Henry said, "Aww, Grant. I'm sorry to have to tell you this, but the reason they don't have a bus ticket and clothes is because the police are coming to pick you up for court. They're coming on Sunday because the court calendar call starts on Monday mornings. It happens all the time. It's just that there has been a breakdown in communication, but the captain will figure it out soon."

For just a moment I had a twinge of doubt, but I said, "Come on, Henry. So God tells me to go to a church and tell those people He set me free, and it just so happens that on that particular day they decide to come and get me for court? Besides, the captain said I'm free to leave at midnight."

Henry perked up then. He said, "Well, there's your way out. Tell Dani to be here right at midnight with some clothes, and maybe you can slip out before the police show up. Then go to North Carolina and see my friend, who can make you some new identification, and then start your own church, and when I get out I'll come and help you!"

I said, "Henry, that's not going to work. I can't be a pastor while I'm on the run from the police!"

Henry said, "Well, I know exactly what God would be telling me if they let me out by mistake. God would be saying, 'Run, Henry, run! Run as fast as you can!'"

I thought, *Well, I guess that's why God isn't letting Henry out. He's got the same problem I had—a lack of faith and no fruit of righteousness.*

Time should have just stood still for the next 40 hours, but I had a peace that surpassed understanding. I had a great time witnessing to the men and saying goodbye and even went to sleep Saturday night. I got up Sunday morning a free man, went to breakfast with all the men, and then went to the warden's Sunday School class. I wanted to ask the warden what he thought about the whole thing, but I thought maybe I should just leave everything well enough alone.

Dani and the kids came to pick me up at about 9:30 a.m., and I took them all to Hurricane Shoals to show them what I now considered to be my "holy ground." I showed them my praying rock and the picnic table where I was tempted by the demonized dope fiend. Chelsi, at 18 months old, walked over to the river and jumped right into the white water rapids. I barely caught her by the hand just as she was being swept away. Yes, it was good to have my crazy family back.

We went to that church, and I told the pastor what had happened and introduced him to my family. He said, "Well, I guess you need to get in the pulpit and tell these people that God set you free." As I walked to the pulpit, the back door opened, and in came Chaplain Akin and all the men in the choir from Jackson.

It hit me that someone in that church had been praying for me after I asked them to on my last visit, so I asked and three little ladies sitting together raised their hands. I thanked them and shared a little, and when I looked over at the pastor, he just waved his hand in a circle like he wanted me to keep going. So I did.

I started out sharing my bird story, and before I knew it, I was preaching on *"seek first the kingdom of God and His righteousness, and all these things shall be added unto you."*

36

"You Shall Be Free Indeed"

Aᴏᴏ FTER I ɢoᴛ home, I began to think, "How can this be?" I was not on bond, parole, or even under arrest. I kept expecting the police to kick the door down at any moment. I mean, there was a big bag of dope in some evidence room somewhere with my name on it.

Remember that Prayer ... "Lord, Just Miracle Me Out of Here"?

I felt as though I was drifting away from God. I knew there was a church out there for me somewhere so I decided to go visit Steve's church first, as he was the only straight human being I knew on planet earth other than my parents. And, of course, that was only because we had been in the marijuana business together.

During the altar call, I went down front and prayed that God would put me back in prison if that's what it would take to keep me close. As I prayed, I felt the hand of a man on my shoulder. He said, "God has raised you up for a time such as this." Then he just moved on to pray for someone else. With that came comfort from the Lord.

Then I realized what was going on. I was going to have to learn to hear that still, small voice with my children crying, my wife talking, bill collectors knocking, and bosses yelling. Prison life is not easy, but it is simple and routine. Out here in the free world, there seemed to be thousands of voices coming from all directions. In prison it was as though I had God on the phone and could hear Him clearly, and now hundreds of people had entered the room and it was all I could do to hear what He was saying.

I had been trying to get in touch with my lawyer that first week, but he was on a big drug case in Virginia. Finally the phone rang, and my lawyer was whispering as though he was afraid someone was listening.

He whispered, "How did you get out?"

I whispered back, "Jesus let me out."

He whispered, "That's impossible."

I whispered, "I know."

He whispered, "Someone had to put the key in the door and turn it."

I said, "Jesus must have put the key in the door and turned it."

He whispered, "Let me see if I can find out what's going on."

I said, "Okay."

He called back a few hours later and said, "Well, Grant, I don't know what is going on, but the best I can tell is they seem to have forgotten all about you."

I said, "Have you ever known them to forget about someone? And how do you process a man out of prison if you have forgotten about him?"

He said, "I can't answer that, but do you really want me to go down to the courthouse and start a bunch of trouble over it?"

I said, "No, that's okay!"

When I hung up the phone, that prayer came to mind. "Lord, why don't You just miracle me out of here and let everyone just forget about me?" I stood there and wept. Then I thought, *I guess I'd better get a job and get busy living.*

The Blessing of Clean Money

My dad had his doubts about my transformation, and I didn't blame him. He gave me a job at the cleaners for $6.50 an hour. The man who had laid his hand on my shoulder during prayer turned out to be a man named Paul, an elder and teacher in the church. He would pick me up and take me home on Wednesday nights. On one such night, I was telling him that I just couldn't see how I was going to pay my bills on $6.50 an hour.

Paul was big on tithing. I remembered studying about it in prison, but he brought up something that I didn't realize. There is only one time in the Bible where God says to test Him, or prove Him, or you could say "challenge" Him, and that was concerning the tithe. He had my interest because I knew God could curse money when you made it the wrong way, so it just made sense that God could also bless it.

So I took the challenge. It wasn't very long before I knew a power bill was coming, and there was absolutely no way that I would be able to pay it. I went to church and just threw all I had in the collection plate. I knew there was no way we were going to pay our bills anyway, so I might as well give it all to God.

The Georgia Power bill came. I opened it up and it said "$293.00." At the bottom, it said, "Balance.....$0.00. Do not pay." There was some explanation on the bill about how years ago I had been overcharged so the balance had been wiped clean. The verse of scripture came to mind where it says that God stores up the wealth of the wicked for the righteous. In this case, I had played both roles.

I fell to my knees and asked God to forgive me for ever doubting Him. If He could open prison doors, then why in the world was I fearful concerning money? It didn't even make sense. It's been 24 years, and I've never had a dollar come into my hands that I didn't give God His tithe and usually more. I could write a book on times when I know for a fact that God performed this miracle or that, and over 90 percent would be financial.

The news of what had happened began to spread among the churches in Jackson County, so almost every Sunday for months we were traveling back up there to share my testimony. Chaplain Hutcheson invited me into the county jail to share. They would bring the inmates out all chained up, just as I had been, and I would preach six services in a row.

The first time I shared my testimony of how there was no explanation for why I was out, other than God, I noticed a guard in the back whose eyes got really big. He went straight into an office and got on a phone, looking right at me while I was talking. I thought, *Oh, boy! I've done it now!* Yet, I walked right back out of those doors.

Of course, Chaplain Akin invited me to come back to Jackson County Prison to share my testimony. I got some musicians from the church to go with me, and we were really excited. As soon as we got there, Warden Dalton asked, "So, Cole, how did you get out?"

I said, "I was hoping you would tell me."

He said, "The only thing I can figure is you must have made a reprieve."

I told him that I'd heard of reprieves, but I had never known anybody to get one. He said he hadn't either.

I said, "So can a man get a reprieve without knowing it or asking for one?"

He said he didn't know, but my case was still open-ended so he couldn't let me in.

I couldn't believe it. I was going into jails and prisons all over the place, and I couldn't even get in my own! He was my Sunday School teacher, for crying out loud! Man, was I mad!

Then the warden pulled up a Lowboy trailer used to carry heavy equipment to serve as a stage, and we ran power for the equipment over to the jail, which was right next door. Then he had yard call. So instead of going into the chapel and ministering to 20 men, as I had hoped for, we had over 400 men on the yard. There is no telling how many men in the jail also heard the Gospel that day.

Only about 40 gathered at the fence like they wanted to hear it, but they all heard it. And when God's Word is breathed by His Spirit, it never comes back void. When you're led by the Spirit, don't ever become disappointed because things don't go *your* way. *God's* way is much more fruitful.

Of course, Johnny Ferguson and all the Gideons were excited about what happened, so I became a Gideon and went into the jail with them. Now I was the one handing books through the slot in the door. The only difference was that I knew a lot of the men, so I often slowed down the process preaching through the slot.

Ministry: Setting the Captives Free

I told Pastor Steve I had only come to visit his church, and wanted to find a good holiness church somewhere. He said, "Well, you found it, because that's who we are." He put me in a training program called the "Timothy Plan" through the Church of God and started sending me to prison ministry conferences and things like that. Before long, we had a prison ministry started called "Free Indeed." We had about 20 counselors, four preachers, and 14 bands, and we were in four to nine prisons every week.

Sometimes we traveled with the Bill Glass Prison Ministry, and there we were with all the men I had read about in the books by Chaplain Ray while I was locked up. Murph the Surf, who pulled off the largest jewel heist in American history. Bob Cole, who was the con man they made the movie *The Sting* about starring Paul Newman. I organized an eight-day crusade for Bill Glass, and to bless me they flew me to California and let me preach in San Quentin.

Sowing and Reaping a Ride

One day, I got a letter in the mail to come and pick up my car from impound. I couldn't believe it. The police always confiscated my cars. I had never gotten anything back and had not tried to get my car back. So I went down there with the letter, and they gave me the keys and told me to go get my car. It was all covered with dust because it had been sitting there for almost two years. I figured there was no way the battery would be any good. Tires and hoses should be dry-rotted.

I opened the door and saw the car was all torn apart. The back seat was detached, and the console was lying in the front seat, with the dashboard dropped down. They had pretty much dismantled the car looking for drugs. It was an Acura, and the hatchback was filled with hundreds of Scientology books. Just looking at them gave me the heebie-jeebies.

I sat down in the car and was just kind of looking around. I opened the change drawer, and there was about an eight ball (3½ grams) of meth. I thought, *I'm being set up here*. I mean, how did they miss that? That would be like the police searching a car and never opening the glove box. It made no sense, but I had come to understand that God can conceal and reveal whenever He decides.

I turned the key, and the engine started right up. I figured there were cameras on the lot, so I just held that dope in my hand so I could throw it and make a run for it if I was being set up. On the way back to the cleaners I started thinking: *I wonder if this dope is still good? Maybe it's like wine and it's even better, as it was wrapped in aluminum foil*. Of course, I knew it wasn't true, and I knew the source of the temptation.

As soon as I got to work, I walked straight into the bathroom, opened the lid on the toilet, and said, "This is for You, Lord." I sent that meth where it belonged—right into the sewer.

I started looking at the Scientology materials and figured there was about $10,000 worth. I thought about going down to the Scientology organization and trying to sell them, but I knew where that temptation was coming from. I didn't want to throw them in the dumpster because somebody might find them. So I went to an apartment complex that had one of those huge trash compactors and sent that garbage where it belonged, too.

I cleaned that car up and put it all back together, and it was like brand new. I bought some new tires, put in a new clutch, and drove it for a little while. Then one day I was walking through the cleaners, and God said, "Give that car to Ronnie and his family."

Ronnie and his family were one of those Church of God families who sang and ministered together. Granny played the tambourine, Ronnie was on the guitar, the wife sang, and the 10-year-old boy played the drums. We ministered together every month in a prison in Alpharetta.

I was standing right by my dad when God spoke to me, and I told him what the Lord said.

He asked, "Are you sure?"

I said, "God just spoke to me so clear that I have a choice to make. Either stop right here, disobey God, and drive my car, which means I might as well quit the ministry; or give it to Ronnie and not have a ride to work again." I chose obedience.

It has been 23 years since that day, and I have yet to buy a car. I've never told anyone that I needed a car, nor have I ever prayed and asked God for a car. Yet, I have been given one Ford Taurus, one Chrysler Concorde, one Mercury Marquis, one Nissan Titan pick-up truck, and two gorgeous Cadillacs. I sowed one car, and so far I've reaped six.

To Win the World, Don't Act Like the World

I went to witness to Big John, whom the police were never able to get without my help after all. I learned an important lesson that day. I tried to act like my old self in an attempt to connect with him. After I left, Big John told his wife, "If Grant was really walking with God, he wouldn't talk like that." He dropped dead from a massive heart attack a few days later. His funeral was the first I ever preached.

The second funeral I preached was another man from that same circle of criminals. If I had reached Big John, maybe I could have reached him, too. I made up my mind that I would never try to act like the world to reach the world again. I see many ministers do that. Maybe it works for them, and the Apostle Paul alluded to the idea that he had to some degree, but I can tell you that when I fell to my knees and cried out to God, I didn't get up looking to anything familiar for answers. I was looking for something different and Godly, just as Big John was looking for from me.

I had been out about eight months and had just bought my airline ticket to go to Polk City, Florida, with Bill Glass to do prison ministry on May 7-10. I got a letter in the mail from the Superior Court saying that my trial had been set for May 7, 1992. When I read that letter, I heard these words: "It's just all been a mistake. Go and do a shot of dope." Actually, I left out the cuss words. I was stunned. I knew whose voice I had just heard, and it certainly wasn't God's.

I told Pastor Steve, and he said that he wanted to go with me to court. When my name was called, the District Attorney stood up and said, "Your Honor, we need to set back this court date until we can have this man brought back from prison to face these charges."

My attorney stood up and said, "Your Honor, he is not incarcerated, as he is sitting right here."

The District Attorney looked at me, and his mouth just dropped. It was obvious that he was embarrassed.

The judge said, "So do you know where your man is or not?"

The District Attorney said, "Your Honor, we will get it straightened out."

As we were leaving, my lawyer said, "They are going to be coming to get you. Go ahead and get your property deeds ready, and maybe I'll be able to get you out on bond."

I said, "I've got a plane to catch at 2:00 to visit a prison with Bill Glass, so it will have to wait.

When I came back, no one ever came to get me. The court said that I needed to report for calendar call in June, so I did. I kept wondering if I really had to. I wasn't on any bond or probation, nor was I even under arrest. It just made no sense. I reported again in July. The crowd was getting smaller, so I knew my trial would be soon.

I had just scheduled to take a group of people from "Free Indeed" to join Bill Glass and go into several prisons in Mt. Meigs, Alabama, on September 10. I showed up for calendar call in August, and then Monday, September 7. The judge said they were going to begin my trial on Thursday, September 10. I knew right then something was about to happen. I knew I was going to prison on September 10, but not for man. I was going for God.

The District Attorney stood up and said, "Your Honor, due to the death of an informant, we will never be ready to try this case, so we are dropping the charges."

Peddling the Good Stuff, the Pure Stuff, the Right Stuff

I knew that Donald had died. He was high on cocaine, running from the police, and his heart exploded. Not too long after that court date, one of Donald's old girlfriends came up to the cleaners, approached my car, and said, "You got anything good?"

I said, "I sure do. Hop in."

I took off driving so she couldn't jump out and started telling her about the good stuff, the pure stuff, the right stuff, the holy stuff of God. Once she calmed down, I pulled into a parking lot, and when I got to the part of my testimony where on July 11, 1991, God told me that He was going to set me free, she turned white as a ghost. She jumped out of the car and took off. After several steps, she turned back around with tears in her eyes and asked, "Do you know what day Donald died?"

I said, "No."

She said, "July 11, 1991," and walked off. I sat there amazed at the God we serve—a God who has the right to require one man's soul and set another man free. All of a sudden, I had a heart of compassion for Donald.

I said, "Lord, I would have gladly done that life sentence if it meant Donald could have come to know You as I have." I meant it, and God knew it.

Well, I got the bright idea to call up Officer Relentless and ask for an old mug shot picture that my ex-wife had once given me of when I was arrested as a teenager. She managed to get it while she worked in the solicitor's office. She gave it to me as a reminder of how messed up you can be on drugs and not realize it. I had no idea how a person could look in the mirror and not know something terrible was wrong. I was 18 years old, and my hair was falling out, my eyes were sinking into my head, and I was obviously in serious pain.

I figured they had found the photo in my car when they searched it and had kept it. I thought it would be great to have when I shared my testimony at the youth detention centers, so I called Officer Relentless. I was surprised by his reaction.

He said, "What is going on with your case?"

I said, "They dropped the charges because Donald had died."

He said, "Oh, no, we're not. I don't need his testimony. We don't drop charges on large quantities of meth. How did you pull that off?"

I said, "Sir, I have turned my life over to the Lord!"

He said, "Save it for the judge.

I Hated to Go, and the Cops Were Glad to See Me Leave . . . Jail

A couple of days later, Dani called me at the cleaners and said, "The police just kicked the door in and they're searching our home. They are on their way to get you." While I was still on the phone, I looked out the front window of the cleaners, and in pulled four police cars. They poured out of those cars like they were expecting trouble.

I said, "Whoa! Whoa! Whoa! In the old days, I would have already been out the back door. I'll come willingly."

On the ride to the jail, I began thinking, *Maybe there is somebody God wants me to witness to in there.* I'm telling you, I've never been so excited to be in jail. I felt like a fox that had been let loose in a hen house. I was telling everybody about Jesus.

They had about 20 of us crammed in a big cell, and next to us there was one man in a cell just as big as the one we were in. Obviously, he must have done something really bad, and he looked really sad so I thought maybe he was the one God sent me in there for. I asked the guards to put me in there with him. When they refused, I said, "I demand my rights as a criminal to be locked up in that cell."

They said, "Shut up! You don't have any rights as a criminal!"

It turned out that the officer fingerprinting us was a believer. He said the best preacher he had ever heard was an ex-con who wrote the book *Twice Pardoned.* We were having such a good time laughing and talking that the colonel came to the door and said, "What is going on in here?"

The officer looked down as he rolled my fingers in the ink and said, "Just fingerprinting convicts and talking about Jesus, boss."

The colonel smiled and said, "Well, hold it down in here."

By the time my dad came to bail me out, they had pretty much separated me from the rest of the prisoners. I think they were afraid that all my preaching was going to start trouble. I hated to go, and the police were glad to see me leave. My, how God can turn things around.

There was an older man at our church named Bob Smiler who took me under his wing and became my spiritual father. He encouraged me and worked right alongside me. As I think back, I'm surprised he didn't fall over dead from exhaustion. He reminded me of a scripture, *"When your ways are pleasing to the Lord, no weapon formed against you shall prosper"* (Isaiah 54:17). We stood on that promise, and of course God held true to His Word. A court date would come up and my lawyer would be on another case, or the District Attorney couldn't be there on that date, or some officer would have some issue, so it would be put off.

Jesus is Just Showing Off Now

When the trial day finally came and I walked into that courtroom, everything had changed. Judge White, whom I had always gone before, had retired. The usual District Attorney had run for some office and won. Even Officer Relentless had gone on to bigger and better things, as he should have. He was one passionate police officer.

Pastor Steve was there once again and said that he felt the presence of God so strong that he was afraid they were going to let the dangerous criminals go free right along with me. We were talking about all the times the authorities said they were going to put me in prison, and God would have me set to go to prison for Him on the same date. Except this time.

At that moment, my lawyer walked up to me with a sheet of paper and asked if I could explain it. His office had received a fax that morning from the sheriff of Buchanan, Georgia, asking if I would come and preach in the jail.

I said, "Well, Jesus is just showing off now."

My lawyer said, "Well, I can't imagine how some sheriff in the little town of Buchanan would even know that our office was defending you, so I'm going to tell you the truth, Grant. I'm a Jew, and all this Jesus stuff is starting to make me pretty nervous!"

He showed the fax to the new District Attorney and said something to the effect that this case had gone on long enough and there was no use sending me to jail, as that seemed to be my favorite place to be anyway. The District Attorney waved me over, and he had that fax in his hand.

He said, "Do you have any idea how many men I've seen cry, 'Lord, Lord' from the courthouse to the jail?"

For some reason, that made me mad and I said, "Well, I can't speak for them, but I can tell you this: You can send me to jail if you want to, but I guarantee you that I'll have a Bible study going by nightfall."

He looked up at me and said, "I have never done anything like this before, and I had better not ever see your face back in a courtroom again."

With that he took my three-to-four-inch-thick file and dropped it in a trash can.

About a month or two later, I was going to preach at the County Youth Detention Center. A new guy was standing there with my volunteers. I knew he was a cop as soon as I shook his hand. He said, "Fast Frank said that I could just show up and come in with you one time to see if I like it."

I said, "Oh, yeah. They have given us special security clearance to bring in people one time to check it out, but if you want to become a part of the ministry, we will have to do a background check."

We went in and I preached, and he ministered to the kids afterward right along with the rest of us. When we got back to the parking lot, he said, "I have a confession to make. I'm on the force with Officer Relentless, and he knows that I'm a believer. He asked me to come down here and see if you are for real. I'm going back to tell him that you have found your calling and that he needs to let it go."

I have never heard another word since.

One evening, I was about to go preach at a prison in Alpharetta and the phone rang.

"Homey Jack!"

I said, "Hey, Randy! What's going on with you?"

He said, "Just drinking a few beers and shooting a little pool."

I couldn't believe it. That is exactly what he said the first time I met him in the ninth grade.

"So you're out?"

"Yes, I'm living on Highway 92 with my brother."

I said, "That's okay. I'm about to drive right down Highway 92, and I'm coming to pick you up!" I thought: *This is it! This is why I ended up in the bunk next to Randy, and then he calls just as I'm going to preach, and I just so happen to be going right past his house. Incredible! Randy is about to get saved!*

I picked him up and started driving before I let him know that we were going to prison to have church and that I was the preacher! When we pulled up in the parking lot he got sick to his stomach, but he eventually came in with me.

We had a glorious service, and the anointing was strong. I just knew that Randy was going to respond with the other men during the altar call, but he did not. When I took him home, he said, "Grant, what you're doing is a good thing." He got out of the car and I never heard from him again. Not too long afterward, his parole was revoked, and as of 2015, he is still in prison.

Randy was at a crossroad and made the wrong choice, and now he has been in prison for 38 of the 58 years of his life. And how did it all start?

With me, I just wanted to "joke a little, smoke a little, and have a good time."

With Randy, he just wanted to "drink a few beers and shoot a little pool." But you know what? As long as Randy is still breathing there is always hope. There can still be a great life for Randy if he will just "seek ye first the kingdom of God and His righteousness." It's never over until Jesus says it's over.

I remembered how much it meant to me when Fat Bear brought my kids Christmas presents while I was in prison, and I heard about a ministry of Prison Fellowship called Angel Tree. Churches all over America buy

Christmas gifts for families of inmates, so we began that, and then God gave us a burden for all single parents—not just the ones who have someone incarcerated. A ministry was birthed out of that called Parents With A Purpose. We still do the Christmas project faithfully every year and have given birth to other great ministries such as the "Give A Kid A Chance" Back-to-School Outreach which has spread to 18 states and 3 nations, the Good Samaritan Health Center of Cobb, and the Good News Counseling Center. I would tell you about all the wonderful ministries God has allowed us to be a part of, but it would take too long.

In January of 2001 the phone rang, and it was Congressman Bob Barr's office. Bob Barr was appointed by President Reagan in 1986 as the United States prosecuting attorney for the northern district of Georgia and served until I was arrested in 1990. He now served in the House of Representatives so I knew exactly who he was, and I knew that whatever had come up from my past could not be good.

The female voice said the White House was hosting a "Faith-Based Community Initiative" in March of 2001. Each congressman had been asked to choose one person to represent the faith-based community of their particular district. Congressman Barr had chosen me. Where would I like the invitation sent?

I sat there stunned. All I could do was think of all the mega-churches and high-profile pastors in the 7th Congressional District of Georgia. At that moment, I could barely remember my name, much less my address, so I took out my driver's license and had to read it so I could tell her where I lived.

I immediately asked to bring Pastor Steve with me because without him I would not have been able to do all the things we were accomplishing in the community anyway. Soon, we were seated with Bishop T.D. Jakes on one side and Paula White from Church Without Walls on the other. I still have no idea how The Lord pulled that one off, but that is just the God we serve. He is no respecter of persons and loves to use the foolish things of the world to confound the wise.

On a Personal Note . . .

Remember my young teenage wife? She went to night school and ended up with a very successful career which is the reason we have left her name out of this. Some of the companies she works with may not understand the redemptive work of God in a person's life. By the time I came home and first saw our son Joshua, he was a teenager. He had on a t-shirt that said "I'm not prejudiced. I hate everyone just alike." He was playing in a punk rock band called *The Stool Sample* in a bar called the "Somber Reptile." To make a long story short, he got saved in the bathroom at the cleaners.

I said, "Son, don't ever think that God does not have a sense of humor. Here you are playing in a band called the Stool Sample, and you just got saved in the bathroom."

Today, he has a lovely wife Monique and four beautiful children. He is a full-time missionary with an organization called E-3 Partners. I can hardly keep up with what nation he's ministering in from month to month.

My son Shane is a gifted musician and has 10 times the pastor's heart that I do. He is a worship leader and just married one named E.B., who has a voice like an angel. I can't keep up with what state the two of them are apt to be ministering in.

Chelsi, who the doctors said would probably have a learning disability because she was born 12 weeks premature at 2 pounds 10 ounces, graduated *magna cum laude* and is now a teacher for the Christian school at our church. She is married to a fine young man, Matt, and Chelsi just gave birth to their first child, Jack. Only God knows the impact Chelsi is making and will make in the lives of those children..

Dani and I have been together for 33 years, and are more in love now than we have ever been. She, too, works at our Christian school and has ministered right beside me, whether in prisons, churches, hospitals, or wherever God calls us at that time.

Dani has one son named Jason from when she was a teenager. He is a very intelligent and hardworking man and we pray for him continuously.

The point is this: I don't know what you may be going through, but I want to challenge you to take your eyes off the mess and *"seek ye first the kingdom of God and His righteousness,"* and you will stand amazed at the life He will add unto you.

God bless!
-End-

"But you are a chosen generation, a royal priesthood, a holy nation, His own special people, that you may proclaim the praises of Him who called you out of darkness into His marvelous light."
(1 Peter 2:9)

Pastor Steve, Congressman Bob Barr, and Pastor Grant at the 2001 National Faith-Based Leadership Summit in Washington, D.C.

The Bible Pastor Grant found in his jail cell.

Dani back in the day. I told you she had beautiful hair

Dani ministering in a prison yard in North Carolina.

Joshua with his lovely wife, Monique, and their four children.
Natalia is the oldest, then Gabriella, Ryan, and little Serena

(Left to Right) Pastor Grant, Dani, Joshua, Shane and
his wife EB, and Chelsi and her husband, Matt.

Made in the USA
San Bernardino, CA
22 November 2019